Wash. D.C.
June 10th
1945

Dear Fred
    I hope you will enjoy
reading this book = something
in it you will remember I was
saying in 1944
            Cliff.

REVOLUTION

SPECIAL EDITION
printed for and distributed by
COMMITTEE FOR CONSTITUTIONAL GOVERNMENT, INC.

$2.50 per copy
postpaid anywhere
SPECIAL PRICES FOR QUANTITY SALE

Orders for this book should be sent to:

COMMITTEE FOR CONSTITUTIONAL GOVERNMENT, INC.
205 East 42nd Street   New York 17, N. Y.

REVOLUTION
WHY, HOW, WHEN?

By ROBERT HUNTER

Published by the
COMMITTEE FOR CONSTITUTIONAL GOVERNMENT, INC.
205 East 42nd Street   New York 17, N. Y.

Dedicated in loving gratitude
to my industrious and intelligent children,
ROBERT, PHELPS *and* CAROLINE
who have not had to be taught that
in our American Democracy
the world is not made for us
but is what we make it.

CONTENTS

PREFACE

Revolution is not the work of a casual student but the essence of over forty years of study and of several years of association with socialist and communist groups. It is a survey of the conditions which breed profound social disturbances and give force, impetus and opportunity to those who are determined to carry through abrupt and comprehensive transformations in political or economic institutions. One chapter is devoted to the technique of revolutionary leaders who have been successful in effecting fundamental changes in the structure of nations. Last of all the reader will find here a hasty tracing of the cycles of revolution and a commentary upon the class formations produced in the course of their rotation.

Revolution is a term so frequently used by all of us that it would seem superfluous to define it. We are in an era of revolution. Momentous changes are occurring all about us and yet a moment's reflection will convince most of us that we do not know what we mean when we speak of revolution. Although a fundamental change in the political organization of a nation has been accepted for many generations as a satisfactory definition, it is quite obvious that in our day it has come to mean more than that. Since the Bolshevists came to power in Russia we have been forced to think of revolution as a fundamental change not only in the political but also in the economic organization of society. Political revolutions are sudden, violent and often of short duration; but those which destroy an old economic machine and install a new one exhaust the energies of many generations.

It will be necessary to bear in mind that revolution, as the term is used here, is a forced transfer of power within a nation from one class, group or individual to another—a transfer sufficiently permanent to enable those who have obtained possession of the State to make basic changes in the social, military and economic position of the several classes. History presents to us no more startling dramas than these tempestuous and often portentous periods when power is being transferred.

Revolution breeds revolution. The worst of revolutions is a restoration, remarked Charles James Fox, and nearly everyone will agree when they recall the reigns of Louis XVIII in France and of Charles II and James II of England. Once the violent shifting of power

begins, it usually goes on for decades and sometimes
for centuries. These movements may be called revolutionary cycles. In the revolutionary cycle in England
in the seventeenth century which fortunately ended in
the transfer of power from king to Parliament, there
were five movements. The cycle of a revolution begins
with the downfall of the Old Regime and continues to
the point of equilibrium in the New. When the curtain
falls upon the last scene of the great drama, the nation
is exhausted and either the Old Regime with its privileges and institutions has returned or a new group has
become the ruling power. In many cases these new
groups have been supported in their conquests by
bodies of armed men, such as the Legions of Caesar,
the Ironsides of Cromwell, the Grenadiers of Napoleon, the Red Army of Lenin, the Black Shirts of Mussolini, or the Storm Troopers of Hitler.

It was not uncommon before the Christian era for
clear-headed and competent revolutionists at the head
of armed forces to seize the State and to remodel radi-
cally the essential institutions of a nation. The time has
arrived again when such conquests are becoming more
and more frequent, since revolution manifests itself
today in one of two ways, either by the victory of the
communist militants among the populace and their
control of the State and the entire economic system by
means of a dictatorship, or by the overthrowing of an

unstable but more or less democratic form of government and the rise to power of an individual at the head of a well-disciplined group capable of controlling the military forces and dominating the political and economic institutions of a nation. Between these two types of revolution, it is difficult to discern any material difference unless it should lie in the hidden and variable objectives of the dictators. However, if we wish to grant that there is a distinction, we may say that in Russia, Mexico and sections of China we find the first, while in twenty or more other countries—including Japan, where the army leaders are now dominant—we find the second.

We are concerned here mainly with those abrupt changes which may be either temporary disturbances in a long-term trend or the beginning of a new epoch in the life of a nation. While for purposes of illustration or discussion it may be convenient to be less precise at times, revolution, as a term, will be used here only when speaking of those movements which have suddenly overthrown and materially altered previously existing institutions, and to those counter-revolutions which have restored in some measure the old structures or built new ones whose value, purpose and permanence the future alone reveals. The most fundamental transformations are long-drawn-out movements in which wealth is gradually redistributed, social relations are materially altered and new groups acquire a dominant position in matters of State. In some periods such movements travel for centuries in one direction toward, let us say, an increase in liberty, a wider diffusion of wealth, a closer approach to equality and a kindlier feeling among classes. In other centuries these movements proceed in an opposite direction toward the suppression of liberty, a greater concentration of wealth, and an aggravation of class distinctions and rigidities. Of less importance are the revolutions which temporarily accelerate or reverse these long-term trends.

By defining strictly our field, the task undertaken is rendered less formidable than if an attempt were made to discuss the irritations which have caused so many insurrections, social upheavals, class struggles, radical shifts in political control and violent racial conflicts— all of which sometimes have been called revolutions. It will be clear also why we must exclude most of the rebellions which are so often called revolutions, such as the American Revolution, the successful revolts of the Spanish colonies and the winning of independence in Holland, Poland, Ireland and elsewhere; in other words, many, if not all, of those conflicts by which one territory, tribe or nationality becomes independent of another. In these wars of independence there have been transfers of power from one people to another, but rarely any basic changes in the position of the several classes.

As a result of a revolution a democracy becomes an oligarchy, or an oligarchy a democracy, or either of these a dictatorship. Other shifts may occur which alter the relative position of the classes in a nation, but the ones mentioned are the most important. When the Barons won Magna Carta from King John, the landed gentry emerged as a powerful influence not only in the State but also in the economic affairs of the nation. The English Revolution of 1688-1689 transferred power from king to Parliament. Later when the industrialists forced the landed gentry to yield to them a dominant position in the State, there was a transfer of power which may properly be called a revolution. The French Revolution of 1789-1799 was a rapidly moving, all-inclusive cycle of revolution as it transferred powers and privileges frequently from one group to another. At the end of the shuffling an imperialist stood in the place of the monarch, the Church had returned rather emaciated and impoverished and the Bourgeoisie had largely displaced the Nobility.

A reader unacquainted with the writings of the revolutionists may be surprised that their views upon the conditions which provoke popular upheavals are so often quoted. This has been done because as a rule intelligent men who want something desperately are

the ones best qualified to tell us how to get it. Some
of them spent years in libraries, often in exile, poring
over books of history and economics in order to learn,
if possible, how and why revolutions occur. They
eagerly grasped at every fragment of information
which might be useful in forwarding their designs.
Their prejudices and ambitions often misled them but
a few were keen students whose observations are most
instructive. In any case some of them knew far more
about the particular subject which interested them
than many less ardent and industrious historians,
economists and sociologists. This was admitted by
such distinguished historians as Theodor Mommsen
and Hans Delbrück.

To support some thesis of the revolutionists or for
purposes of illustration or comparison, certain uniformities have been selected from various periods of
history which have preceded or accompanied revolutions. In one chapter special emphasis is laid upon the
striking similarity between the fiscal policies of France
in the last decade of the eighteenth century and those
of the United States in recent years. Because some of
these remarkable analogies are recalled, the reader
should not conclude that we must inevitably travel to
the bitter end the paths indicated by these similitudes.
They are maps of dangerous roads where others have
wrecked themselves and their nations. Their lessons

will not be lost if they persuade us to move cautiously, stop, turn back or seek another road.

When we see in our own day appalling disasters overwhelm nations and find that they often result from the same mistakes being made in the present as were made in the past, the comment of Hegel seems justified: "Peoples and governments never have learned anything from history nor acted upon the principles deduced from it." Our knowledge of history can never be adequate. Moreover, our interpretations of its meaning will always clash—most of them certainly with those of Hegel—and yet we must admit that if no use is made of the experiences of the past, life is far too short to permit us to acquire wisdom.

FOREWORD TO NEW EDITION

I am deeply grateful to
George L. Treadwell and many others
for their militant faith in its message,
and to the
Committee for Constitutional Government, Inc. —
"noble warriors" in the cause of Democracy — whose
high purpose and endeavor won them the esteem
and commendation of my late husband, the author.

CAROLINE HUNTER

CHAPTER I

MEMORIES OF SOME REVOLUTIONISTS

There are some persons who think that the first object of government should be to regulate well everything relating to private property. . . . Upon the whole, those who aim at equality are the cause of seditions.

—ARISTOTLE

IN ALL revolutions, there appears a miraculous conjunction of forces—provocations, ideas, organizations and leaders. Let us begin with a cursory view of some of the leaders of the upheavals of recent years. Most of them were affiliated with the International Socialist Movement and at a conference at Stuttgart in 1907, during a dull session one afternoon, I began to meditate upon what could be expected of the men and women gathered there should they become the rulers of the world. It was a huge gathering of delegates who had been sent there to represent the socialist and labor movements of nearly every country in the civilized world.

1

At first sight four distinct classes appeared. One group embraced the Utopians, the makers of programs and of creeds, enchanted with their visions of a perfect world planned by idealists. In another group were the orators who thrilled not only the delegates but huge masses of the populace. Some of them were clever politicians who had become famous in the political activities of their countries. In both the above-mentioned groups there were rich men, scholars, journalists, lawyers and labor leaders. The great mass of delegates, a third group, were representatives of trade-unions and cooperative societies. They made few speeches and abhorred acrimonious debates, revolutionary heroics and dogmas. As executives in the powerful labor movements of Finland, Norway, Sweden, Denmark, Holland, Belgium, Germany and Great Britain, they were interested first of all in the progressive improvement of the working class. Most of them were able, industrious, quiet, honest and sincere. In a revolution the safest place to put one's purse would be in their hands. In the history of later years, it was proved again and again that they had no desire to confiscate the property of others.

In the fourth group were the conspirators. Though few in number they later proved to be the most influential when the post-war revolutions got under way. Each minute step in the revolutions of the past was studied by them as each minute step in a great battle is studied by a student at West Point. They had schooled themselves in the strategy and tactics of revolutionary movements and while they signed their names to the programs of the Utopians they cared little about them. They were interested solely in obtaining power. Revolution was the means and the end. The world would be a satisfactory place to live in if only their armies were victorious. Though calling themselves socialists, a few of the leaders of the conspirators were incorrigible individualists—megalomaniacs of a sort. They believed that they alone could be trusted to lead a revolution and that they alone were fitted to undertake the task of reconstruction. These men were neither prominent nor influential in the International Movement of pre-war days.[1]

At Stuttgart, Copenhagen and other places where I attended national and international labor and socialist conferences, a clairvoyant could have pointed out men who were destined a few years later to become presidents, prime ministers or absolute rulers in nearly every country in Europe, Russia and the United Kingdom. Nothing like such a widespread transfer of power from one group to another had ever before been seen in the world as that which occurred in the years from

[1] As this book was completed before the Germans entered Poland in September, 1939, the author had in mind when using "pre-war," "the Great War," "the World War," etc., the conflict which began in 1914.

1917, when Lenin came to power in Russia, to 1924, when MacDonald became Prime Minister in Great Britain. When the first revolution in Russia cast out the Romanoffs, it became clear to the student of revolutions that anyone who ventured to defend or protect the rulers of the old regimes was doomed. With astonishing rapidity the monarchs, who had led their people into the disastrous war, were displaced by republicans, democrats and socialists. That was to be expected but who could have believed in 1914 that Lenin would become in a few years the czar in fact though not in name of all Russia, that shortly afterwards a working saddle maker, Friedrich Ebert, would become the first President of Germany, that a socialist journalist, Renner, would displace the Hapsburgs and that Mussolini, the son of a blacksmith, would conquer Italy?

No one would have been surprised to hear that August Bebel of Germany, Jean Jaurès of France, Émile Vandervelde of Belgium, Victor Adler of Austria, Ramsay MacDonald of Great Britain and Karl Branting of Sweden would become the dominant political leaders in their various countries. These socialists possessed qualities of mind and character which made them outstanding not only in the conferences of laboring men but also in the political and parliamentary activities of their nations. They were the leaders of the millions affiliated with the International before the outbreak of the war and while the ones who lived played important roles in post-war history, they were not the ones to cast into new forms some of the greatest nations of Europe.

The socialists who had risen from poverty and the lowest ranks of labor to become influential political leaders in their nations could not fail to make a profound impression upon an American. Some of them had never had a day of schooling and yet a hundred names could be mentioned of working-class leaders whose brains would have "furnished forth a dozen noblemen . . . in a fashion that would make them shine among their peers." That was the comment made by Theodor Mommsen upon August Bebel, a German workingman, who distinguished himself as an able historian, an orator who held thousands spellbound and a parliamentarian who again and again goaded to the point of madness not only the Kaiser but the Iron Chancellor, Prince Bismarck. What man in any rank of public life could fail to envy the qualities of greatness possessed by John Burns, Tom Mann and Keir Hardie of England, of Gustave Delory of France and of Edouard Anseele of Belgium? In America men of their character and ability would have risen to the highest positions in industry. Men of inferior quality had in fact done so. In every conference of socialists

in pre-war days there were many able men who had
been frustrated by the caste formations in society and
who were leading into dangerous paths the classes
from which they sprang. In most of the countries of
Europe there had been a stoppage in what Pareto calls
the circulation of the *élites*.

When I was in residence at Hull House in Chicago,
at Toynbee Hall in London, and at the University Set-
tlement in New York, I was drawn by some bond of
sympathy into close association with the labor and socialist leaders of the three great cities. For many years,
at home and abroad, I passed from one group to another in a world little known at that time—a world
almost exclusively occupied with social problems and
their solutions. The groups in America were small and
without influence but in Europe the leaders were in
Parliament and lines were forming in preparation for
the class conflicts which followed the World War.
From Ireland to Russia and from Sweden to Italy, I
found in all the larger centers many groups engaged
in agitation and organization. In those days the leading socialists, syndicalists and anarchists were ardent
missionaries—all of them tirelessly planting upon good
soil and bad the seeds of revolution. Any youth would
have been received by them, as I was, with open arms.
Although busy men, and many of them poor, they
astonished a visitor by the warmth of their hospitality

and the lavish expenditure of their time in pursuit of a possible convert.

Only a cold-blooded cynic could have resisted the charms of the Utopians and only a cool, keen mind could have refuted the arguments of the brilliant men and women who were then active in undermining the old faiths and loyalties. Karl Kautsky, Eduard Bernstein, Paul Lafargue, Jules Guesde and George Plekhanoff were dangerous men for a weak mind to battle with. They were the outstanding masters of Marxian dogma and the many days I spent with them and with their books were, so it seemed then, the most illuminating hours of my life. The aims, scholarship and mental equipment of these theoreticians of the socialist movement acted like a magnet to one seeking, as I was, a sovereign remedy for poverty.

As orators there were no men in the other parties equal to Bebel, Jaurès and Briand. Among the women, Rosa Luxemburg, Clara Zetkin and Angelica Balabanoff were pre-eminent. Great orators grow in power and stature when they are speaking to huge masses of sympathetic listeners and after their work is done they shrink to less than normal proportions. This was true of those I have just mentioned and it was often disappointing to discuss with them in private what they had set forth as eternal verities under the spell of their audiences. They were nourished emotionally,

spiritually and intellectually by the masses who sat in
wonder at their feet.

I am at a loss to know how to classify some of the
groups of social revolutionists which were to be met
with in Paris and other centers of Europe in pre-war
days. They were random wantons out of tune with
their time but there is something symptomatic of disorders to come in the gathering of the elegants "of
fragrant ringlets, of fashionable mustachios and ruf-
fles . . . of no mean descent and unusual abilities,
who only waited the signal to fall like a gang of robbers upon civil society . . ." Thus Mommsen describes
a variety of revolutionists in Rome on the eve of Cataline's insurrection. The Comte de Segur has left us a
picture of the same class in Paris before the French
Revolution: ". . . without regret for the past, without misgiving for the future, we trod gaily on a carpet
of flowers which hid the abyss beneath us . . . All
that was antique seemed to us tiresome and ridiculous
. . . There is a pleasure in descending so long as one
is certain of being able to rise again whenever one
wants to do so . . . we enjoyed at one and the same
time the advantages of a patrician status and the
amenities of a plebeian philosophy."

Some of the Parisian varieties of these exquisites in
the early days of this century seemed to me *enfants
perdus*, possessed by a suicide complex—a passion

which, though estimable in such cases, could not hold their attention long enough to accomplish so desirable an end. Failing that, they were attempting to get "in touch with proletarian reality," not by going to work but by trying to translate into elaborate philosophical terms some of the rude slogans of the more militant leaders. Violence and yet more violence became their theme. In every key the tune was played, in a manner rivaled only by Beethoven.

On the few occasions in Paris when I went to the *salons* of these advocates of ferocious physical vigor, primitive brute force and bloody mass upheavals, it was surprising to find assembled about the high priests, Lagardelle and Sorel, a gentle and cultured group of ladies and gentlemen, fashionably dressed and luxury-loving, but obviously overcome by fatigue, inertia or ennui. Their conversation was lively, the wine and food excellent, but they were so weary of the tedium of life that I was always startled when, at the mention of some "myth," *diablerie* or slogan of violence, their boredom was transmuted into uncontrollable exaltation. Only Freud could have diagnosed the hidden maladies afflicting the neurotics who were assembled on these sumptuous evenings to herald the coming of the proletarian revolution. Hamlet's explanation may be sufficient: "conceit in weakest bodies strongest works." Most of those who attended these assemblies were not strictly speaking intellectuals. They could hardly be called rational, or competent of being useful in any of the constructive activities of life.

In a different class should be placed the poets, essayists, preachers and scholars, who, in all ages, have combated with all their power the inhumanity of their times; but the effect they have had upon the trend of events has usually been exaggerated. No one has studied with more care than Georg Brandes the writings of the rebels of recent centuries. One evening in Copenhagen, he made to me this interesting comment upon his years of research: "My heroes in literature were loved and understood only after they were dead and only after the reforms some of them had fought for had been accomplished. In no revolution have they ever been the *provocateurs*." Brandes was thinking of men of letters; surely not of such gifted propagandists as Caesar, Cromwell, Lenin, Mussolini and Hitler. It is true that Bernard Shaw, the Webbs, Anatole France, Lagardelle, Sorel and most of the other socialist writers have not been actively at the head of revolutionary movements but their books, plays and pamphlets pollinated the minds of hundreds of *provocateurs*. Almost without exception the men who actually led the revolutions of recent years were students of Marx and of the socialists who had popularized his doctrines.

Most of these writers were glowing and fervid, enchanted with the roles they were playing in the labor movement. When one thinks of the varied characteristics and talents of these famous writers and their absolute confidence in their own infallibility, it seems incredible that they should have been able to work together for so many years in harmony. Bernard Shaw rejoices in being an irritant. I suppose he still likes to stand before his fireplace in his house in Adelphi Terrace lecturing his visitors with the cocksureness of an omniscient schoolmaster. But he is not conceited, mark you, nor discourteous. He is merely asserting his intellectual superiority. His vanity, complacence and egotism are the tools of his profession and they have served him well as a source of handsome profits. As a socialist, his zeal is, as it always has been, delirious. During his years of poverty, after he had completed his days of hard work as a journalist, he went regularly two or three times a week into the street to address crowds of workingmen. Moreover, in higher circles Shaw has been for more than fifty years the bellwether for a flock of socialist intellectuals. As an orator, essayist, economist, playwright, musical critic, novelist and tub-thumping propagandist, he was doing the work of ten men when in 1898 he fell, ill and exhausted, "a wreck on crutches," into the motherly arms of a lady of wealth and was married to her wearing a ragged Jaeger jacket.

Fame soon followed upon the heels of wealth and more of each came rushing after, but no matter what came, nothing could divert the great iconoclast. With unabated zeal, he continued to assail the basic principles and the prevailing customs and activities of the capitalist system. Nothing connected with it escaped his attacks—medicine, diet, marital relations, morals, religious creeds, education, government, the courts, finance, industry and social arrangements were denounced as parts of a consciously designed system for the sweating and slave-driving of the multitude. One who attacks everything can believe in nothing, I driveled, when Miss Gertrude Toynbee insisted in Haslemere in 1899 that I had to be introduced to Shaw. Having read most of his writings and heard some of his lectures, I expected to be irritated and I was not disappointed. Like Mr. Squeers of Dotheboys Hall, when he was preparing to beat little Smike, Shaw instantly whisked up my "drapery in a most dexterous manner" and lost no time in administering his lashes to certain tender spots on my anatomy. As a resident of Toynbee Hall, I was accused of administering opiates to the workers to keep them from rebellion.

However, unlike Squeers, Shaw delivered his floggings with gaiety and good humor. His laughter is hilarious when he smashes the sacred images of his time and breathlessly belabors the worshipers. Eternal rebel against this "sorry Scheme of Things entire," the great nihilist would "shatter it to bits" but how he would remold it, he had little to say, and who was to be the Potter remained a mystery until Lenin came to power in Russia. Not quite a mystery. In one of his early essays he had revealed his devotion to Hegel's "conception of the perfect State." Later through Mad Keegan, Shaw again released the same vision: ". . . it is a country where the State is the Church and the Church the people;" but men must have an anthropo-morphic god and Shaw created consternation when he said, in 1929, "I am a Bolshevist." Like that famous son of a potter, Agathocles, who became king of Syra-cuse, Lenin was destined to mold the new social order out of the shattered fragments of the old. Nothing re-mained for Shaw to tell us. We already knew the Pot he would shatter; we had some conception of the Pot he would mold and, after Shaw went to Russia, we knew the Potter.

While Shaw was at work breaking images, Sidney and Beatrice Webb were absorbed in making plans and blueprints of the new State, the completed figures and specifications of which they passed over to the en-gineers and craftsmen. The Fabian Society was in the first decade of this century a busy workshop for social-ist artisans, and many young intellectuals were being attracted. When H. G. Wells joined the Society, it was a day of great rejoicing; but he soon found himself at odds with his new associates. Wells has a mind too searching to become a fanatic and too skeptical to accept confinement within the narrow limits of Marxian dogmas and socialist creeds. Fancies, personalities, science, mechanics, politics, events of the past and the present as well as visions of the future set his mind into action. I often suspected him of having committed to memory a page or two from one of his books when he delivered as he often did an improvised and inspired monologue.

Two meetings of the Fabian Society remain vivid in my mind: the one at which Shaw demolished Sidney Webb, who had ventured to suggest that there might be some merit in a protective tariff; and the other when Shaw flayed Wells, who had been impertinent enough to criticize the political tactics of the Fabians. Without one word of answer, Wells fled back to his country place at Sandgate, leaving me, his guest, stranded in London without a nightshirt. I doubt if Wells ever attended another meeting of the Society.

On the Continent also some of the foremost writers were sympathetic to the socialist movement. Anatole France is perhaps the best known. Diffident as Shaw was pretentious, inquisitive as a child, he would have been the last of all men to think that he possessed the wisdom of the ages and the only key to the future.

Throughout his gentle, timid flow of words, humor and tragedy played like lights and shadows. Late in life he followed Tolstoy and Kropotkin in quest of justice. Again and again they hoped they had found the way to it. At each stage in their intellectual and spiritual progress they had been bold to say what they believed but when they found themselves on the wrong road, they were the first to admit it. Never before, perhaps, had so many able men been so closely united in their views. Private property was the object of their attack but their assaults were unavailing until the war and the subsequent inflations and deflations had wrecked the economic machinery of the defeated nations. That should be emphasized.

The Russians faced many problems which did not exist in the Western world. The masses were illiterate and poor, industrial development was backward, the peasants remained serfs in spirit, and dominant over all was the autocracy with its bureaucracy, Okhrana (secret police) and armed forces. A social, economic and political system of that type can exist only by suppressing immediately all men and groups showing the slightest inclination toward rebellion. Thousands of the ablest minds of Russia were revolutionists and many of them had fled or had been driven into exile. One can say without unpardonable exaggeration that almost an entire generation of humanitarians had found their way abroad. Some of these men without a country were charming and cultivated, richly endowed with the high qualities which would have made them outstanding in the democratic countries. The Friends of Russian Freedom brought to America a number of revolutionists. Those who created a profound impression here were Tchaikovsky and Breshkovskaya—the first lovingly called the father and the second the mother of the Russian Revolutionary Movement. Gorky's visit was disastrous and, when he fled into hiding, H. G. Wells and I spent a good part of a night trying to find him. Wells was furious over the treatment given Gorky by our newspapers. Almost all Russian rebels in those days called themselves socialists but actually their chief aim was to overthrow the Czarist regime.

Tolstoy was not associated with any revolutionary group but his writings had a tremendous influence. A continuous stream of Utopians, rebels and cranks passed in and out of his doors. When I was a guest at Yasnaya Polyana, his country estate, I was shocked by the depth of his despondency, and after he had forecast, with a foresight given only to genius, the bloody upheavals to come, I left his presence deeply regretting that age, moral distress and spiritual loneliness rendered him incapable of looking joyfully forward to what many believed would be the birth of a great and enduring democratic Russian Republic.

At Hull House first and later at his cottage at Bromley in Kent, I had many long talks with Kropotkin about the coming tyranny of the State. Years before, in Switzerland, he had left the ranks of the socialists because of his fear of a politico-economic despotism. There was no doubt in his mind that the logical and inevitable outcome of Marxian dogmas would be not a democracy of proletarians but a dictatorship of the all-powerful State. He lived long enough to witness in Russia what he feared above all things. The last note I received from him arrived after the papers had brought me the news of his death.

The downright conspirators differed in almost every way from the Utopians, politicians, writers and labor leaders. They were few in number and their activities were confined almost entirely to Russia, Poland and Ireland. There was no necessity in any nation of Western Europe for the socialist and labor leaders to do their work underground. Where the object of the movement was to overthrow a government by force, it was necessary to form nuclei of conspirators. When I presented letters of introduction to Arthur Griffith, the leader of the Sinn Feiners in Ireland, and to the revolutionists in Poland and Russia, I had my first opportunity to study the psychology of conspirators. Nat-

urally no observer however trustworthy was permitted
to learn anything of importance about their activities;
but their spirit indicated clearly enough the extreme
dangers which confronted them and their determination to carry through their projects at whatever cost.

Very few Westerners took the Russian exiles seriously. There were hundreds of them in Paris, Brussels,
London and Switzerland. Some of them were brilliant
men, but their entire time seemed to be spent in quarreling over the most trivial questions. It was unbelievable that they should accomplish anything of importance. In their shabby rooms and in cheap cafés around
untidy little tables, they debated with bitterness upon
every subject under the heavens. The implicit confidence which the conspirators had in themselves and
in their imaginary armies of revolutionists was fantastic. One often forgot that rebellious Russians at
home and abroad were forced to live in a world of
thought, denied any opportunity to employ themselves
in practical activity. Many friends of the Russians
believed that Czardom was doomed but it is doubtful
if a single socialist in the West dreamed that Russia
would be the first country in the world to fall into the
hands of the communists.

Of the Russian exiles, Lenin is the last I should have
picked as a man of destiny. Balabanoff says that she
cannot remember where she first met Lenin and that

even when she became conscious of his existence he made no impression upon her. Many others could say the same, but I remember vividly my first meeting with him. It was at dinner in a small Greek restaurant in Soho, not far from the house which bears the tablet commemorating the fact that Karl Marx once lived there. I met him again at Stuttgart, in 1907. In the meantime he had acquired the reputation of being a brilliant student of Marxian economics, a dangerous antagonist in all intra-party controversies and a master of revolutionary tactics and sectarian conspiracies. At the conference he was usually surrounded by a small group of whispering disciples. He was always in opposition to the popular Russian leaders and attacked them savagely both in public and private. Although comparatively isolated in the larger international gatherings, where few of the leading socialists of his own or other countries were ever seen with him, he was nevertheless feared for reasons which became clear only after the Bolshevists conquered Russia.

In recalling one's impressions of an old acquaintance, it is often difficult to remember whether or not they had their origin in personal contact or in the judgment of others. Some of Lenin's enemies believed that he was a paid emissary of the Russian police. His tactics and the dissensions which he promoted among the Russian socialists aroused suspicion. He was a fanatic, a disorganizer, a sectarian, who gave no indication in pre-war days of having the qualities of a national leader. He won his battles but they were always directed against his comrades. His conflicts within the party aroused distrust but if the Okhrana were employing him, they were financing the one agent who was foreordained to destroy them. It was generally believed that Lenin would use any means available to accomplish his aims; but that is true also of nearly all the "master-minds" who have conquered nations.

It is inherent in the nature of a man with fixed ideas, believing only in himself, to thrust aside everyone who opposes his views or gives any promise of becoming a rival. As a rule he must choose as his aids only those whose lives are at his mercy. This is the reason, I believe, why Lenin chose so many Russian Jews as his chief agents. When seeking power in Russia, he relied mainly upon Trotsky, Kamenev and Zinoviev. Later Radek and others were placed in key positions. Undoubtedly they were assistants of great ability and energy but it happened also to be true that not one of them could ever become his rival. Lenin could destroy any one or all of them at any time he cared to do so. This is a strategic position for one aspiring to dictatorship and when the great days of October arrived, Lenin was left almost alone in the first rank of gentile leaders to ride the whirlwind and direct the storm.

Had Trotsky not been a Jew he would have become the ruler of Russia after the October insurrection. He was a genius and, as a man of action, far superior to Lenin; but as a Bolshevist he was a new recruit and the Revolutionary Committee, not to speak of the Russian rank and file, did not trust him. Besides there were other reasons why, despite his exhaustless energy and brilliant talents, he could never have united the forces required to carry on the revolution after the *coup d'état*. Lenin was the man for that task and it is obvious now that his qualities eminently fitted him to survive in the acute crises which followed one another so rapidly in the first years of Bolshevist domination. Nevertheless, it is doubtful if anyone ten years earlier would have believed Lenin capable of leading and holding together the jealous and ambitious men of action who served under him during the period of chaos which existed in that country from 1917 to the day of his death in 1924.

Success often changes what most observers believe to be the characteristics of their acquaintances. Their qualities seem to alter, or at any rate they appear in quite a new light, once they become dominant in their field of action. And so it was with Lenin. He developed surprising tolerance and moderation in his effort to hold together the factious elements which had placed him in power. To come suddenly out of a storm cellar,

to be able to avenge the slaying of a brother, to find all
the forces of the earth obedient to your will and to rise
from poverty and exile to the throne of the Czars must
have some effect upon the character of any man. Cohesion among his followers was, however, not so much
due to Lenin as to the enemies of the revolution inside
and outside of Russia. It was imperative for the Bolshevists to hang together or to hang separately.

Another socialist not suspected of latent greatness
was Mussolini. He was not one of the notable or influential leaders. If he had been born thirty years earlier,
he would have become at the most a second-rate tragi-
comedian like Ferdinand Lassalle. He was always a
dynamic personality, vain, arrogant and willful. He
was all this even in his days of poverty when I first met
him. He was then playing a minor role in the socialist
movement of Italy but he was Caesarean in mind,
character and attitude, as he is today. One could see
that he was determined to rule or ruin. His vitality
seemed exhaustless; his nervous movements made him
conspicuous; his sharp, clear sentences came from him
like jagged flashes of lightning; his gestures, facial con-
tortions and protruding eyes indicated the presence of
inner forces which mere words could not express.
Obviously nothing but absolute, undisputed mastery
would satisfy him. That was written in clear, large
letters on forehead and jaw. Like Lenin, he accused

all antagonists of being traitors. A man with his intolerance could never have become a national leader in a democratic political movement. The qualities which later made him Il Duce appeared extremely obnoxious in the old days. The egocentrics, who were irresistible after the war, could not have won in earlier days the loyalty of any considerable following of capable men.

Of course at that time no one was thinking of dictatorship. Indeed all the tendencies seemed to point the other way. The Italian Socialist party was becoming more and more moderate, and Mussolini—then an advocate of uncompromising class war—denounced the older leaders as bureaucrats and mercenaries. The revolutionary era of the party, which began in Milan in 1898 as a result, it is interesting to note, of a sudden increase in the price of bread, was ended, and the socialists were following meekly Turati and other moderates who advocated labor legislation and municipal ownership. As a revolt against these forms of Statism, Syndicalism was attracting the younger revolutionists in France and Italy. Arturo Labriola had for years been harassing the "Reformists," State Socialists and "Parliamentarians," and Mussolini came in later with his dramatic fury to support the more revolutionary policies. For a year or so he edited *La Lotta di Classe* which made his name famous throughout Italy.

While making studies of the revolutionary movement, I was aided for a time by Angelica Balabanoff. This restless, diminutive Russian knew almost everyone engaged in socialist and communist activities. Aflame with the spirit of revolt, she spared no effort to infect others with her hatred for the capitalist regime. She was very useful as she not only brought me in contact with everyone I wished to meet, but she also spoke fluently many of the European languages. She would often sit beside me at conferences and in restaurants, translating into my ear, in a soft and to others almost inaudible voice, everything of interest said by the various speakers, no matter from what country they came. She was afterward one of Mussolini's chief aids and became his assistant editor when he took control of *Avanti*. In 1917 she went back to Russia with Lenin and other communists in the train provided by the German government, which expected them to augment the chaos already paralyzing its enemies on the East.

Revolutionists talk fast and are often well educated. In some groups at dinner three or four languages would be spoken and, of course, at all the socialist and labor conferences delegates from many countries delivered their addresses in their native tongues. These different languages were laboriously translated by official interpreters. It was unnecessary to follow these dreary repetitions when Balabanoff sat beside me. She was often the official interpreter at the larger gatherings and her translations were never questioned—although she often excelled the orator in eloquence when he was expressing some of her cherished and more violently revolutionary views. Although she was a valued aid to both Mussolini and Lenin—I believe she brought them together at one time—and the most impassioned revolutionist I have ever met, she left Russia in 1921, ill and thoroughly disillusioned by the Reign of Terror.

The socialists I have mentioned were of high rank among the forces mobilizing for the troubled days to come; but many other able warriors were earnestly working in the trenches, few if any of them, except possibly the Russians, ever dreaming they would see the series of cataclysms which was so soon to open to a few of them the gates of heaven and to condemn most of them to hell and damnation. Certainly very few had any foreboding of the impending catastrophes —the war, the revolutions and counter-revolutions. When some of them discussed revolution one might readily have believed that it could be made with rosewater and that the new society would appear as certainly and beneficently as the finished product of a great engineer. Even some of the Russians seemed to believe that a socialist republic or even communism could be established after a brief period of disorder, very much on the lines set forth in their brochures.

It is curious how in certain periods of history all forces seem to work toward one end. The chief aim of the socialists was and is to capture the machinery of government. From Marx and Engels to those of the present day, they have desired above all things to persuade or force the people to place their lives under the control and their productive property into the ownership of the State. Although most of the socialists labored under the delusion that when this was accomplished classes would disappear and the State, as a compulsory institution, would (to use the words of Engels) "die out," what they actually wanted was to compel humanity to live and work in a way which they believed would bring to it a more abundant life. As we know, this trend toward State ownership of property has become the most striking phenomenon of our time. Since the first days of the World War the rapidity with which governments have increased their powers and functions has rarely been equaled. Although this has been almost entirely a result of the war, it is nevertheless what most of the revolutionists have been working for ever since 1848.

It is doubtful if the socialists had any conception of the political and economic institutions which would be most likely to develop as a result of their program of action. Calling themselves "scientific socialists" they ridiculed as Utopian the systems of Fourier, Saint-

Simon, Robert Owen and others, and severely rebuked those who attempted to make plans for the world to come. Marx, of course, had his idea of the machinery required to bring into being the new society. The proletarians had only to take possession of the instruments of production and, by means of a dictatorship, to make them function for the sole profit of the workers. Once this was done, they would, naturally and inevitably, create for themselves a socialist commonwealth. Many years ago I heard Bernard Shaw suggest to a large meeting of socialists that he was probably the only one present who had taken the trouble to read Marx. Very likely he was also the only one present who had read Hegel and knew the terminus toward which the doctrines of both led. Hegel's "divine idea" of the all-powerful State was eagerly grasped by Marx as the instrument which his proletarians could use to make the forces of production obedient to their will.

Marx departed from Hegel (and also from Hobbes) in his program for placing the control of the mighty engine of the State—the Great Leviathan—in the hands of a proletarian dictatorship, a myth of his own. Mythical conceptions when they become flesh, blood and bone, as they sometimes do, and move about upon this earth usually confound those who called them out of a world of dreams, and so we find that the "divine idea" has been personified in Mussolini and Hitler. They have become the Great Leviathans.

While I hope to make it clear that the social systems which have sprung into life out of the ruins of the old are the logical outcome of the doctrines of the Marxists and the methods they employed to destroy their opponents, many of the older socialists have been appalled by the dreadful retribution which these monsters have already exacted from their creators. Like Frankenstein, "the scientific socialists" have been destroyed by their own works. Many socialists have become apostates in the last quarter of a century. Some of these have rebelled against terrorism, the return of autocracy and the crushing of democracy. Bernard Shaw is one of those who have not been horrified. "I don't really want to see a Hitler in this country," he said recently, "but I am not sure it would be a bad thing. The point is, do we want to get things done or not?" Is Hitler getting the things done which this lifelong socialist, who happens also to be an admirer of Stalin and Mussolini, wants done?

Those who have obtained and held control of the State have been able to get done the things they wanted to do; but it is quite clear that they are not the things which the masses expected them to do. The Leviathans have been absorbed in remodeling the structure of society on the lines best fitted in their opinion to maintain themselves in power. With this as their program they have been amazingly successful within their national boundaries. Moreover they have thrown into confusion and disorder the economy of other nations. Fundamentally revolutionary readjustments have been made in the economic, monetary, juridical, social and political institutions and customs of the democracies in order to enable them to continue to function vis-à-vis in the same world with the new economic and political systems. Difficult adaptations to a new environment are being forced upon the productive classes, power is being transferred and fundamental transformations hastily introduced which are rocking the foundations of modern civilization.

Since the days when I was seeing much of the socialists, some of whom became the heroes in the great dramas of recent years, we have been living for a quarter of a century amidst wars and revolutions. During a similar period, Thucydides, the historian of the Peloponnesian War, wrote his annals for "those who desire an exact knowledge of the past as a key to the future, which will in all probability repeat or resemble the past." He knew of the convulsions in Persia after her defeat by the Greeks, witnessed the cost of living mounting and the war of the classes being intensified in Athens.[2]   He wrote first-hand vivid accounts

[2] In the fifth century prices increased five-fold and continued to rise until the Greeks were overpowered by Alexander.

the plagues which devastated his city and the revolutions which followed in the wake of war. He lived to tell most of the story of the World War of his time, twenty-one of the twenty-seven years of it, and to describe some of the seismic disturbances which it set in motion. Many pages of his illuminating narrative read as if they were the history of the past quarter of a century.

There have been many wars since the days of Thucydides, but not one perhaps which has shaken so profoundly the entire world as that which began in August, 1914. Mighty and uncontrollable forces, comparable to subterranean disturbances, have ever since been activating world-shaking upheavals which have thrust into new formations the structure of many nations. It is possible, when the period of strains and stresses is passed, we shall find that, like the pangs of childbirth, they were the necessary painful prelude to the creation of a new and better social order. There are many who hold this view. Most of them believe that revolution is a metamorphosis in which the structure of society is invariably changed for the better and that when the acute disturbances of the present transitional period of adjustment are past, mankind will find itself upon a higher level of civilization. This assumption is deeply rooted in the modern mind because most of the revolutions of recent centuries have brought many benefits to the masses. Such a conception of revolution would not have been justified in the time of Thucydides or of Cicero and may not be today.

My memories of the revolutionists of recent years could be extended into a book, but in this volume they have only one value. Is it possible to believe that men such as those I have mentioned were the forces, or were capable of setting in motion the forces, which have convulsed a large part of the world for the last twenty years? There is but one reasonable answer to that question. Powers infinitely greater than any at their command were whipping up the wind and the waves, and as master mariners, with perfect control over their little craft, they used the tempest to their own advantage. Indeed they displayed incredible skill not only in capturing the wrecks of the old regimes but also in becoming the skippers of many seaworthy vessels in the troubled waters of democracy.

There is, indeed, a tide in the affairs of men; and when conditions are ripe for revolution, leaders, organizations and sympathetic multitudes appear upon the stage as if by magic. When conditions are not favorable, revolutionists live and die, as Marx, Engels, Wilhelm Liebknecht, Bebel, Jaurès and scores of others lived and died, without having had an opportunity to accomplish their aims or to satisfy completely their ambitions. When the tide is with them the luck of the revolutionists is amazing. Even their opponents are helpful. The warring factions in the Roman Senate, in the Council of Five Hundred, in the Russian Cabinet, in the Italian Parliament and in the German Reichstag were occupied in slaughtering each other when Caesar, Napoleon, Lenin, Mussolini and Hitler arrived to deliver either the *coup de grâce* or the *coup de pied*. How notoriously inept, arrogant, mad, or imbecile were King John, Charles I, James II, Louis XVI, Nicholas II, and Wilhelm II. What counter-revolutionist could desire a more incompetent opponent than Kerensky, Giolitti, Salandra or Bruening? The revolutionists of quality who arrived at the right time have been irresistible. Those who arrived at the wrong time, no matter how able, have been failures and forgotten. How many of us remember any more than the names of Spartacus, Cataline, John Ball, Wat Tyler, Pougatchoff, Stenka Razin, Hans Mueller, Blanqui, Bakunin and Nechayeff? But when is the right time? Mussolini has said that "Revolution is not a surprise-packet which can be opened at will." To find out when this packet can be opened is the first object of our inquiry.

CHAPTER II

WHEN MEN REVOLT

The war-mood brought with it many and terrible symptoms such as have occurred and always will occur, so long as human nature remains what it is.

—THUCYDIDES

---

1. *Revolutions Which Follow War*

MARX, Engels, Liebknecht, Bebel and Lenin were convinced that at the conclusion of a general European war the revolutionists would have their innings. Amidst the boisterous clatter and furious interruptions of the militarists I once heard Bebel warn his opponents in the Reichstag of the catastrophic consequences to the German ruling class of a defeat in war. He presented a formidable list of revolutions and serious popular uprisings which had immediately followed defeat in war. Refusing to vote for any funds to be used for the support of the army and navy, Bebel warned the Kaiser and the war lords of Germany that a general European war would wreck modern civilization. A great war would further the socialist cause more, he declared, than years of agitation. He exhorted the war lords to beware of a conflict that would "tear up the very roots" of their existence. When they scoffed at him, he retorted that if they were undisturbed at the prospect, he could only say, "Go ahead; we are your heirs."

Speaking of the coming European war in which "fifteen or twenty million armed men will slaughter one another," Friedrich Engels assured his comrades that this "war must either bring the immediate victory of socialism, or it must upset the old order of things from head to foot and leave such heaps of ruins behind that the old capitalist society will be more impossible than ever, and the socialist revolution, though put off ten or fifteen years, will surely conquer after that time all the more rapidly and thoroughly." Many revolutionists agreed with Bebel and Engels and some of them actually hoped that war would break out in Europe. At the international conference at Stuttgart, a majority of the delegates supported a resolution of Lenin and Rosa Luxemburg which declared that a European war would bring with it the opportunity to overthrow the capitalist class.

If Engels' prophecy concerning the aftermath of war seems remarkable, not less notable was his accurate timing of the periods of post-war deflation, of the inter-

vening inflation and of the secondary deflation. His
analysis of the post-war trade cycles led him to expect
a world-wide collapse of the economic structure in ten
to fifteen years after the Great War; that is, sometime
between 1928 and 1933. Engels was often a false
prophet but this time how right he was! The "Social
Democrats" have not conquered the world—indeed
the democratic and labor forces have been overpowered in many places by a violent reaction—but the
Bolshevists now rule Russia while Fascism, Nazism,
New Deals and Planned Economy are gaining ground
on all fronts. State Socialism or State Capitalism,
whichever one may prefer to call it, is having its day.

Before the Armistice, Russia had collapsed and after
the republicans and moderate socialists had had their
brief innings the Bolshevists came into power. Immediately following the war, revolutions in all defeated
countries placed socialists and communists over 300,-
000,000 people in Russia and Europe. In the victorious
states the active heads of nearly every government
were or had been socialists. So much for Bebel as a
prophet. As for Engels the fifteen years he mentions
are past, and even in rich and remote America the old
order of things is upset from head to foot. These revolutionists had evidently learned something from history.

When defeat in war initiates the cycle of revolution

we find a nation unable to extricate itself from what Lenin has called "an imminently revolutionary situation" and our inquiry must be first directed to that. In all times and places we find the conditions almost identical. The governments are discredited, terrified and bankrupt; their obligations are in default; their money is becoming worthless; the taxpayers and public officials are rebellious; the demobilized forces are armed and unemployed; the cost of living is rising while industrial operations are decreasing or stagnant; the economic basis of life is shifting uncertainly because of rapidly changing prices, and inflation and deflation play alternate roles in torturing the people. The living conditions of the entire populace are so confused and chaotic that revolution itself with all its horrors seems to all but a few the sole chance of relief from the agonies of the moment.

In all post-war periods, as we see, there is plenty of revolutionary dynamite lying about and groups intent upon doing so often find in the defeated countries no force able to prevent them from lighting the fuses. We all know that fear, hatred and uncertainty lead to suspicion, intolerance, cruelty and especially the determination to survive. Out of these come violence, rebellion and sometimes revolution. No one who has watched attentively the upheavals of mind, body and estate which followed the Great War will need to have painted for him pictures of that tragic period and no one familiar with history will believe that what occurred at that time was unique. Here are some brief notes upon a few of the more critical periods in the last seven centuries when defeat in war and a collapse of government have preceded, or a comprehensive upward spiral of prices has coincided with, revolutionary upheavals:

1204-1268. The theme of later post-war upheavals is fully developed in the thirteenth century. English army crushed by the French. The King discredited and in financial distress. Heavy increase in taxation. Tenants and nobles in rebellion against the King. The uprising forces the King to grant the Great Charter— the first pledges of English liberty. Certain taxes are abolished, usury of the Jews outlawed and a new principle of freedom emerges: no taxation is to be levied without the consent of the Great Council of the Realm. The rights won by the Barons were to be assured to every Englishman: the tenants, sub-tenants, craftsmen and merchants. To enforce the King's pledges a civil war followed; indeed there were battles between the Crown and the people for four hundred years.

1344-1381. The Hundred Years' War. Many crises in the finances of both England and France. First the crushing defeat of the French and later the equally crushing defeats of the English left both governments discredited and in distress. The Black Death rages throughout Europe. Massacres of the Jews, accused of poisoning wells. The French peasants rise, burning and pillaging large areas in France. Attempt made in England to enslave the workers by the Statute of Laborers. The coinage debased in 1344, 1346 and again in 1353. Rents of the landlords diminishing; prices of commodities rising; merchant princes profiting. The impoverished and hated government driven to levy the graduated poll tax. Agrarian communist uprising under the leadership of John Ball, Jack Straw and Wat Tyler.

1450-1487. Humiliating defeat of the English armies in France. Government in distress seeks new sources of taxation. Debasement of the coinage in 1464. Civil war. The revolt of Jack Cade (John Amend-All). Rising prices. The Court of the Star-Chamber instituted.

1540-1660. Over a century of unrest in England. Debasement of the coinage in 1549 and in 1551. Cost of living soaring from 1542 to 1564. Government in financial distress. Incessant quarrels between King and Parliament over taxation. Widespread rebellions. Many communists among the Levellers and Diggers. Religious and civil wars. Revolution. Regicide. The Commonwealth. Cromwell. The only time in England which could be described as the Reign of Terror.

1520-1600. Rapidly increasing supplies of gold and silver arriving in Spain from the Americas. Uprising of

the *Comuneros* and *Germania* in Valencia. Rebellion
of the Moorish serfs. For a century a gigantic inflation
ensued. The many revolts of the peasants and workers
were brutally suppressed. Government always in need
of money. Heavy taxation. Foreign wars; bloody persecution of all protestants; rebellions in Holland and
elsewhere exhausted the vitality and immense resources of the Spanish people and, by about 1598,
Spain began to descend from her exalted position as
the mightiest of European powers along that downward path which so many nations have been forced to
take after uncontrolled inflation has run its course.

1789-1796. French government had not balanced
its budget for many decades. Oppressive taxation.
Rebellions against collections. Defaults in government
obligations. Gigantic inflation. The cost of bread rose
to fifty francs a pound. Regicide, the Terror, Massacres, Communism and complete bankruptcy follow
each other in due order, as if by logic.[1]

[1] A rapid and vigorous upturn of prices and industrial activity often
causes violent conflicts between employers and workers. After years of
severe deflation in England a brisk recovery, beginning about 1834,
found itself confronting a revolutionary labor revolt. Robert Owen
planned to establish his New Moral World, a socialist commonwealth
based upon unions of workingmen. Many serious strikes occurred in
America toward the end of the long deflation following the Civil War.
The rapid rise in prices and industrial activity, beginning in 1879, was
attended by extremely violent riots and insurrections. Militant socialists,
anarchists and communists, advocating the use of incendiarism and dynamite, fomented widespread and violent disorders which continued into
another depression which began in 1883.

1814-1848. A post-war period with many abortive upheavals, including the so-called revolutions of 1830 and 1848. A dark cloud of reaction settled over all Europe. Deflation permitted to run its course.

1871. Defeat of France by Germany. Government discredited; army in revolt; financial distress. Rapidly rising prices. The bloodiest communist insurrection in history.

1905. Defeat of Russia by Japan, followed by revolution. The Czarist government hated. Budget unbalanced. Army disloyal. The first Duma. Rising prices. The revolutionary terrorists fight with the terrorists of the reaction. Wholesale murder of the Jews.

1917. Defeat of Russia by Germany. Government in distress. Financial collapse. Mutiny in the army and navy. Czarists abscond and republicans and moderate socialists take over the State. The cost of living rises rapidly. Armed men walk the streets hungry and unemployed. In October came the *coup d'état* of the Bolshevists which was followed by civil war and the Terror.

1918-1926. Armed uprisings in Middle and Eastern Europe. Governments bankrupt. Republicans, socialists and communists take over the States. Nearly all currencies become valueless. Revolutions, civil wars and counter-revolutions. Seventeen countries became republics after the monarchs had fled or been overthrown. Turkey became a republic in 1921 and Ireland a Free State in 1922. Italy became Fascist in 1922 when unemployment was at its maximum. A period of continuous upheaval, of terror, agony and bloody sweat, driving whole nations almost insane.

No attempt has been made, it will be observed, to make a complete list of the insurrections and revolutions which have followed war. The ones I have mentioned are formidable enough and sufficient for my purpose. During seven centuries when the Western world was not only throwing off the shackles of the Dark Ages but was moving into the more progressive and enlightened era of democracy and capitalism and later into the unknown realms of communism and fascism most of the revolutions immediately followed defeat in war. In addition there were many widespread and violent post-war upheavals which were suppressed only after the rioters were massacred. The great revolutions in England and France, as well as the century of exhausting class conflicts in Spain, did not follow defeat in war; but the state of the government finances, the economic disorders and chaotic conditions in all three countries were remarkably similar to those existing after long and unsuccessful wars.

In all the instances I have cited mighty forces were

at work; irritations evidently beyond human endurance were provoking explosions of rage. Were they
always the same forces activated by the same irritations but called by different names?

Historians in the course of their work have passed
through many of these periods of turmoil without having observed any notable uniformities except those
which appear on the surface. The more they have
labored and the more conscientious and dispassionate
they have been the more hesitant they have become.
Like Aristotle, they have been collectors of specimens
—all sorts of ideologies, interests, obstructions, personalities, conspiracies, iniquities, antagonisms and
indignities which may have had some influence in gen-
erating these mass movements. They have gathered
enormous quantities of material much of which has
little value or is not yet clearly classified and understood. Other material of fundamental importance—
such as data upon wages and prices—is now being laboriously accumulated but such work is still in its infancy. If the study of the initiative factors of revolution
has been considered one of the most difficult and complex problems of history, it may be due to this lack of essential material and to the failure of historians to consider, or their inability to assess, the relative importance
of the economic forces. Many books on general history,
fiscal policies, monetary changes, taxation, national

debts, price movements and wage levels have to be consulted and compared before one is able to assemble even the few brief notes which have been set down above, indicating that some of the same provocations arousing discontent and rebellion were active in all the periods mentioned.

2. *The Abortive Revolutions of the Nineteenth Century*

When some of those who have the principal management of affairs lose their fortune, they will endeavor to bring about a revolution; but when others do, nothing of consequence will follow.

—ARISTOTLE

For the systematist one of the periods which seems, at first glance, most irreconcilable is that which followed Waterloo. Preceding the fall of Napoleon, wars and revolutions had followed one another in quick succession for almost forty years. Almost as if by magic the trend turned from thoughts of liberty and democracy toward the restoration of the old regimes. In France the Bourbons returned and the White Terror brought back again horrible massacres much like those which had disgraced the French Revolution. For six years, beginning in 1821, the government of M. de Villele occupied itself with destroying not only the social reforms and liberal institutions achieved in the Revolution but also as much as possible of the *Code*

Napoléon. In England the upper classes, frightened out of their wits by the upheavals on the Continent, settled down with grim determination to deal mercilessly with all seditious groups in the country. At Peterloo in 1819 their position was made clear. Later Sir Robert Peel, feeling that the battles between the classes might get out of hand, established the constabulary to supplement the army. The officers were for many years afterwards contemptuously called Bobbies and Peelers by all trade-unionists. Seismic disturbances continued for over thirty years, the shocks on the Continent being greatest in 1830 and 1848.

Robert Prutz, one of the extremists of the period, writing in ecstasy of the Revolution of 1830, gives us an impression of the trend in Europe after Waterloo: "For fifteen years it had seemed as if the eternal generative power of the world's history were paralyzed. For fifteen years they had been building and cementing, holding congresses, forming alliances, spreading the net of police supervision all over Europe, forging fetters, peopling prisons, erecting gallows—and three days had sufficed to overturn one throne, and make all the others tremble." Unfortunately the revolutions of 1830 accomplished nothing of importance and for nearly two more decades quakes continued to shake the foundations of Europe.

There is hardly to be found in history another period

as black and chaotic as that from 1830 to 1848. Economic disorder was general over most of Western Europe and was at its worst in England which was leading other countries in the use of labor-saving machinery and steam power. One of the arresting pages in *Das Kapital* is Marx's (or is it Engels'?) vivid account of the spasmodic fluctuations in the cotton industry.

From 1815 to 1821 depression: 1822 and 1823 prosperity: 1824 abolition of the laws against Trades' Unions, great extension of factories everywhere: 1825 crisis: 1826 great misery and riots among the factory operatives: 1827 slight improvement: 1828 great increase in power looms, and in exports: 1829 exports, especially to India, surpass all former years: 1830 glutted markets, great distress: 1831 to 1833 continued depression, the monopoly of the trade with India and China withdrawn from the East India Company: 1834 great increase of factories and machinery, shortness of hands. The new poor law furthers the migration of agricultural laborers into the factory districts. The country districts swept of children. White slave trade: 1835 great prosperity, contemporaneous starvation of the handloom weavers: 1836 great prosperity: 1837 and 1838 depression and crisis: 1839 revival: 1840 great depression, riots, calling out of the military: 1841 and 1842 frightful suffering among the factory operatives: 1842 the manufacturers lock the hands out of the factories in order to enforce the repeal of the Corn Laws. The operatives stream in thousands into the towns of Lancashire and Yorkshire, are driven back by the military, and their leaders brought to trial at Lancaster: 1843 great misery: 1844 revival: 1845 great prosperity: 1846 continued improvement at first, then reaction. Repeal of the Corn Laws: 1847 crisis, general reduction of wages by 10 per cent or more in honor of the "big loaf": 1848 continued depression. Manchester under military protection: 1849 revival: 1850 prosperity.

Certainly this is no way for a decent economic system to behave and who can be surprised that Marx and Engels should have thought that capitalism was seeing its last days. Many conservatives agreed with them. Indeed most humane men believed, wished or feared that unless some better economic system were quickly devised the masses would for good or ill take matters into their own hands. It is important to scan this period with some care as most people believe that widespread human misery is the most potent cause of revolution.

That was the view of most of the leaders of the masses in the early decades of the nineteenth century. Indeed they were so sure of it that again and again the impoverished workers were led forth to battle. The uprisings were all failures but they are interesting from many points of view. The developments then taking place in the aims, technique and programs of the revolutionists will help us to understand why they have been more successful since the World War. A study of these abortive revolutions enables us to look into the minds of those bent upon destroying democracy, parliaments, and the capitalist system in order to create an entirely new economic order. We are also enabled to observe some of the irritations which, especially in post-war periods, agitate the masses and make them willing to follow almost anyone who suggests a remedy for the misfortunes which afflict them.

From the beginning of the nineteenth century there were epidemics of bread riots, machine-breaking, incendiarism and insurrection. In 1811 a lad named Ludlam, in a moment of rage, took a hammer and smashed the new machine at which he was working. This act met with a sympathetic response among the operatives and in the following years thousands of stocking frames and lace machines were destroyed in Leicester, Derby, Lancaster and York by groups of rioters prowling about in the night. Theft, arson and murder were other weapons used by the irate toilers in their attacks upon employers. In 1822 the workers began to throw vitriol in the faces of blacklegs and employers. Engels cites a long list of crimes committed by organized bands of laborers during the period from 1831 to 1844. The contagion of violence spread to some rural districts where swing riots and fires, lit by incendiaries, blazed in all directions. Arson was openly advocated as a retort to the soldiers, bayonets and cannon of the government.

There are pages in the diary of Sir Charles Napier, who was sent into the Midlands in the thirties to repress working-class insurrections, which read like dispatches from a seat of war. He reported all the northeast of Manchester riotous and the revolutionists claimed that they had in Lancashire alone 250,000 armed men. The workers had issued a proclamation declaring: "Now or never is the time. Be sure you do not neglect your arms, and when you strike . . . let the blood of all you suspect moisten the soil of your native land, that you may forever destroy the remembrance of your poverty and shame." To meet this challenge Sir Charles warned the gentlemen and yeomanry that they must defend themselves and he arranged his small army in carefully chosen positions to resist a major battle which, however, was never fought. Such was the spirit of the time and rarely if ever before or since has there been class warfare so general, bitter and prolonged.

Men of exceptional emotional power with revolutionary views have always appeared upon the scene in periods of unusual distress. In all countries affected by the post-war upheavals of 1815-1848 poets, writers, men of business, statesmen, clergymen, economists, labor leaders and revolutionists came forward to voice, deplore, quiet or inflame the industrial strife which seemed certain to end in a volcanic eruption of the first magnitude. The ruling powers could no longer expect support from the intellectuals. Shelley, Byron, Crabbe, Landor, and Ernest Jones were as mirrors reflecting the dominating emotional revulsions of the time. William Godwin, Charles Hall, William Thompson, John Gray, Thomas Hodgskin and J. F. Bray found the causes of human misery in political and economic institutions. The mental patterns of Marx and Engels were fashioned in the hungry thirties and forties and influenced all their labors of later years. Southey, Owen, Cobbett, Oastler, Sadler, Joseph Hume, Lord Shaftesbury, Thomas Hughes, Kingsley, Carlyle and many others were seeking to remedy or ameliorate the degradation of the working class which was sickening to all humane observers.

Leading the revolts of the workingmen were some of the most vehement orators ever gathered together in one period. Among those best known were Feargus O'Connor, an agitator and leader of "colossal incoherence"; Stephens, "the greatest mob orator of all time"; G. J. Mantle, whose "sentences seemed shot from a culverin" and whose "throat opened like the mouth of a tunnel"; Bronterre O'Brien, who held his thousands spellbound and wrote *Human Slavery: How it came into the world and how it shall be made to go out*; and Dr. Taylor, who vigorously advocated the "sacred month" in which all workers would refuse to do any labor. Among the more moderate leaders were William Lovett, the cabinet maker, whose calm counsels were never heeded; Thomas Cooper, the Chartist, who when condemned to prison for his activities insisted upon speaking to the Court of the Queen's Bench for eight solid hours; Holyoake, "an agitator for sixty years"; and many others who though unable to calm the troubled seas at the time laid the foundation for the powerful, conservative Cooperative and Trades-Union organizations of later years.

From members of the upper and lower classes came almost every known panacea for the ills of this world. Robert Southey had his plan for increasing public debts in order to provide work for the poor and at the same time a comfortable income for the owners of government bonds. Robert Owen suggested that all land and factories be turned over to unions of workingmen. Carlyle, placing both hands on his great broad sword and belching flames of fiery rage, struck right and left demanding the abdication of all ruling powers and a return to feudalism—a beneficent feudalism. Nationalization of land; State ownership of all industry; voluntary cooperative production; universal suffrage; universal education; trade-unionism; soviet socialism; Christian socialism; "scientific" socialism;

the Dictatorship of the Proletariat; New Harmonies; Fourierism; a return to hand work and domestic workshops; production for use; revision of the poor laws; yielding to labor "the full product of its toil"; labor legislation; prohibition of the labor of women and children; free trade; "salutary" laws regulating money, credit and exchange—each of these and many another remedy for the calamities of this tragic post-war period was offered confidently and often militantly as the only possible cure for what was unquestionably a very sick world. In more or less degree much the same turmoil giving birth to ideas and movements intended to make over the universe was agitating every country in Western Europe.

Every remedy for our social ills—with possibly three exceptions—which has been proposed in any country since the last war can be found in the writings of Englishmen in the early years of the last century. Except for Social Credit, Dr. Townsend's payments to the aged, and the fantastic scheme of thirty "dollars" in warrants every Thursday to every person fifty years of age or older who prefers not to work at a gainful occupation, no new cures have emerged in recent years and even these panaceas are new only in the form in which they appear. All three are forms of outdoor relief and are based on the old theory of John Law and of the Chinese before him that prosperity can be maintained by an ever-mounting volume of money and an increased velocity of spending. Mr. Harry Hopkins was beguiled by the same delusion when he advocated pouring out Federal funds in billions because "the W. P. A. dollar is the fastest moving dollar in the world." The vast public works of the Pharaohs and Solomon increased the velocity of goods, if not money. In fact there could be no quicker way to employ more men, compete less with existing industry and spend more billions than to take the stones out of the fields and build with them great pyramids. Unfortunately there is always some defect in panaceas. Such projects would increase our arable land, create a new era of abundance, reduce eventually the price of food and defeat the deep-laid plans of the Secretary of Agriculture. There might be a *crise pléthorique*, such as the one which disturbed Fourier one hundred and twenty years ago and induced him to advocate a "model prison-type of socialism," called the *phalanstère*.

Production for use is also an idea of ancient vintage. Employed long before the Christian era it appeared again in the reign of Queen Elizabeth and developed into the English workhouse: the most hated of all public institutions even though no work of consequence has ever been known to defile its precincts. At the end of a long journey, it has arrived in Cali-

fornia—new, naked and unashamed. Even the sugges-
tions of some of our more militant reformers that we
destroy labor-saving devices; work only four or five
hours a day; plow under crops and shoot livestock
are not original. From 1819 to 1848 many revolutionists
and reformers believed that too many workers, long
hours, excessive production, steam power and machines were the chief causes of widespread distress
and rapidly recurring cycles of prosperity and depression. As for destroying property, we find that constructive thought voiced by a Methodist pastor, Stephens,
who proposed, in 1830-31, that the children of the
unemployed be supplied with matches and bundles
of straw dipped in pitch to start the conflagration. In
ideas, the reformers of our day have not advanced
much beyond those of a hundred years or even thirty
centuries ago. They are simply products of a post-war
time. When the same old problems reappear they are
always confronted by the same old reformers and
revolutionists offering the same old "irrefutable" nos-
trums. An anthology of panaceas from the time of
Joseph, accompanied by notes of results achieved, if
read along with Aristotle's *Politics*, would supply any
legislator with all he needs to know.

One of the most critical post-war years was 1834.
Terrible insurrections were brutally suppressed in Paris
and Lyons. In England Robert Owen, with his large

means and great influence, decided to launch a gigantic union of laborers which would, without delay,
revolutionize the world. The ideas of Owen were
much like those of a certain section of the labor movement in our day. In fact, they embraced the essential
policies and doctrines of the Industrial Workers of the
World, of the syndicalists of France, and of some of
the leaders of the now active C. I. O. "It is intended,"
said Owen, in the launching of his project, "that national arrangements shall be formed to include all the
working classes in the great organization," which, it
seems, was actually started in January, 1834. Nothing before in the annals of unionism ever approached
the rapidity of the growth which ensued. Within a
few weeks the union was joined by at least half a million members, including tens of thousands of farm
laborers and women. The extension of new unions in
previously unorganized trades and districts was enormous, and throughout the country a mania for unionism swept over the working classes.

Owen insisted at first that the purpose of this gigantic organization was to raise wages and shorten
hours "to an extent which, at no very distant time,
would give them [the workers] the whole proceeds of
their labour." Later he went even further in his revolutionary ideas and declared that he saw in the unions
something more than mere tools for industrial war-

fare. He believed them to be the germs of a new social order. Under the system proposed by Owen, the instruments of production were to become the property, not of the whole community but of the particular set of workers which used them. The unions were to be transformed into "national companies" to carry on all forms of production. The Agricultural Union was to take possession of the land, the Miners' Union of the mines, the Textile Union of the mills. Each trade was to be carried on by its particular union, centralized in one Grand Lodge.

Carried away by the splendor of his new visions of a syndicalist or soviet socialism, Owen was of the opinion that his New Moral World could be established in six months. The change from the capitalist system to a completely new organization of industry, under the control of associations of producers, was to come suddenly upon society, like a thief in the night. "One year," declared a disciple of Owen, "may disorganize the whole fabric of the old world and transfer, by a sudden spring, the whole political government of the country from the master to the servant."

The testing of this early syndicalism was sudden and terrible. The movement spread like a conflagration. It flared up in a manner that brought consternation to the employers. It was a blinding flash that aroused them and the government to make a concerted assault upon the great union. It was smothered out and trampled into the dust by the lockout and the courts. Instantly the union was overwhelmed with the demands for aid from its needy members. What was to have been a general strike became a lockout that left the enormous mass of trade-unionists utterly helpless and impoverished. Enormous subscriptions were raised by the general union; stupendous petitions were circulated. Boycotts and riots were resorted to, but by the end of the summer the revolutionary projects of the Grand National Consolidated and Other Trade Unions had ended in complete failure.

Startling as this upheaval may appear to those unfamiliar with the period following Waterloo, it was merely an incident in decades of labor unrest. The climax, or anti-climax, was reached only after thirty-three years of class warfare. The struggle in England and on the Continent had become so bitter that the year 1848 was ushered in by a series of menacing insurrections. On the 24th of February, Louis Philippe was driven out of Paris and a republic was immediately proclaimed. On the 13th of March, the people of Vienna arose and forced the much hated Metternich to flee hurriedly from the country. On the 18th of

March, the people of Berlin arose and after a bitter struggle the King surrendered himself into their hands.

"Events are coming to the surface," wrote Lord Ashley. "We see the stir on the waves, and we shall soon see the mass thrown up by the volcanoes. Italy is in open revolution; Austria is crumbling to pieces." A few days later he wrote: "Insurrection at Berlin! Insurrection at Vienna! The Prince Metternich deposed! It is astounding at first to see how these great monarchies fall." On March 25th his diary reads: "Revolutions go off like pop-guns! Lombardy is in full revolt." These words of Lord Ashley, who for years had tried to better the condition of the poor in England, will convey some idea of the consternation, perplexity and foreboding which existed among the upper classes as they watched the revolutionary contagion spreading from city to city, from one end of Europe to the other.

In his own explosive style, Carlyle painted a lurid picture of this volcanic period:

As if by sympathetic subterranean electricities, all Europe exploded, boundless, uncontrollable, and we had in the year 1848, one of the most singular, disastrous, amazing, and, on the whole, humiliating years the European world ever saw. Not since the irruption of the Northern Barbarians has there been the like. Everywhere immeas-

urable Democracy rose monstrous, loud, blatant, inarticulate as the voice of Chaos. . . . They [the kings] fled pre-
cipitately, some of them with what we may call an
exquisite ignominy—in terror of the treadmill or worse.
And everywhere the people or the populace, take their
own government upon themselves; and open "kingless-
ness," what we call *anarchy*—how happy if it be anarchy
plus a street-constable!—is everywhere the order of the
day. Such was the history, from Baltic to Mediterranean, in
Italy, France, Prussia, Austria, from end to end of Europe,
in those March days of 1848. Since the destruction of the
old Roman Empire by inroad of the Northern Barbarians,
I have known nothing similar.

And so in City after City, street-barricades are piled, and
truculent, more or less murderous insurrection begins;
populace after populace rises, King after King capitulates
or absconds; and from end to end of Europe Democracy
has blazed up explosive, much higher, more irresistible and
less resisted than ever before; testifying too sadly on what
a bottomless volcano, or universal powder-mine of most
inflammable mutinous chaotic elements, separated from us
by a thin earth-rind, Society with all its arrangements and
acquirements everywhere, in the present epoch, rests!

It was, as usual, in Paris that the epidemic of insurrections started, and no sooner was Louis Philippe
driven out of the city, his palace plundered and the
whole royal family exiled, than a republic was proclaimed. Immediately a Provisional government was

formed, including republicans such as Lamartine, Ledru-Rollin and Arago, with some socialists, of whom Louis Blanc and Albert were the most notable. It was natural that profound differences should arise between the two sections. With different flags, different ideals, and representing as they did antagonistic classes and economic interests, no common action was possible. The republicans had no thought of instituting any far-reaching economic changes. Their aims were purely political and they believed that the working class could be satisfied by certain reforms.

The socialists, on the other hand, considered the republic only as a means of achieving their more radical aims and hoped soon to begin the heroic task of organizing society on a new basis. As soon as the revolutionary forces became dominant many shops and factories were closed down and the workers of Paris were soon in a state of abject misery. Vast numbers were unemployed. The new government was immediately faced with the demands of the workers, led by socialists, that they should be guaranteed "the right to work" and the "unionization of all labor." As these reforms had been advocated for several years by Louis Blanc and his associates, he was called upon to give the following pledges to the populace: "The Provisional Government of the French Republic promises to guarantee the existence of the laborers by work.

It promises to assure work to all citizens. It recognizes that the workers must join together in order to enjoy the benefits of labor."

Here we find the doctrine of the right to work accepted as a governmental policy. A few days later, another popular demonstration demanded a Minister of Progress to undertake the organization of labor. This was proceeding rather too fast for the republicans, and serious quarrels broke out between Louis Blanc and the other members of the government. The second proposition was defeated, although it was agreed that a government commission, under the presidency of Louis Blanc, should be appointed to deal with labor questions. The decree, instituting the commission, was written by Blanc who fearlessly put on record: "The question of labor is of supreme importance and it is necessary without delay to guarantee to the people the legitimate fruits of their labor."

With production for use as a slogan, Louis Blanc overpowered the opposition and all Europe heard for the first time a high official advocate revolutionary socialist doctrines. Some in terror and others with hope and joy heard him proclaim that the workers in the various trades should organize great cooperative productive undertakings and, with the help of subsidies from the State, should begin the work of undermining capitalism. He urged that all the factories, mines and other industrial enterprises should be conducted directly by the workers who would be permitted to select their own superintendents and set their own wages. With the resources and power of the State behind them, Blanc believed the workers would in a short time displace all individual enterprises and individual capitalists.

In the transitory stage, Blanc admitted that it would be necessary to use State capitalism to destroy private capitalism, but once that was accomplished the many industrial unions would be organized on a national plan entirely independent of the government. Blanc promised that the government would act as an intermediary and assure fair play in the battle between private capital and cooperative production. The great capitalist, he asserted, overpowers the little capitalist by "fraud, violence, and all the evils that iniquity carries in its train." And to avoid such violence and injustice, he promised "that the struggle between his new associations and capitalism would be carried on without brutality, without shocks, and with as much clemency as would consist with attaining the desired end, namely, the absorption, successive and pacific, of individual workshops by social workshops."

These are the essential points of Louis Blanc's socialist program, and now, in his powerful position in the government, he undertook to put them into practice. Naturally, such objectives were bound to arouse bitter opposition. They were felt to be subversive and very few of those who were forced at first, by the exigencies of the situation, to support Blanc, agreed with him or wished in any manner to advance his revolutionary ideas. However, with the populace in a very excited state, it was impossible at the moment to oppose openly ideas which represented the aspirations of its militant section; consequently the national workshops were established. Exhibiting their usual slovenly and dull-witted efficiency, the petty officials threw laborers of all professions together and forced them to do all sorts of work for which they were unfitted. Tailors were compelled to dig ditches; bricklayers to make clothes, and all were organized on military lines to carry on various forms of work hastily planned for the occasion. Louis Blanc was, of course, not responsible for this perversion of his exalted plans but it is what often happens when politicians undertake to carry out the ideas of the Utopians.

Government competition with private industry, production for use, the right to work and a "guarantee" that labor should be given the full product of its toil (which in this instance proved to be trifling)—all doctrines proclaimed by the socialists as essential to the peace and welfare of society—became in practice repressive measures which infuriated the workers. By

the end of June a bloody conflict broke out between
the workers and the government. For three days
there was fighting in the streets and, finally, when
the armed forces under General Cavaignac gained
the upper hand, they brutally crushed the rebellion
of employees—no longer the officially blessed. Over
3,000 were killed and later 15,000 were transported.
Thus ended the "Works Progress" experiment of
Louis Blanc.

While these events were taking place in Paris, the
workers of Great Britain were also undergoing a humiliating experience. In fact the most complete revolutionary fiasco of the year occurred in England. Because of superior organization, the enormous masses
of the discontented and the bitterness of the leaders,
it seemed that there if anywhere a revolutionary outbreak would have had the best chance of success.
Following upon years of riot and insurrection; upon
the presentation to Parliament of a petition three miles
long, signed by millions; after decades of indefatigable
agitation carried on by an impassioned band of popular orators; after demonstrations and mass meetings,
assembling crowds so huge that men despaired of
counting them; after strikes that paralyzed all British
industry and forms of repression which fed the spirit
of hate to the point where it seemed unquenchable—
the year 1848 arrived and amidst the most lively emo-

tions and wildest expectations the much heralded uprising of the "universe of workers" was at last to test the powers of the government.

When the news arrived of the Paris insurrection, the British Chartists were carried away with wild enthusiasm. The Marseillaise was sung and all over England the workers organized demonstrations favoring the European rebels. Even the leaders, who bitterly hated each other, forgot their quarrels for the moment and tried to come to some common understanding. It was decided that a convention of Chartist leaders should assemble in London and a huge demonstration of the populace be held on Kennington Common, April 10th. The provinces had been worked up to the highest pitch of enthusiasm and a monster petition was being circulated to present to the House of Commons. The meeting in London was planned to be the most gigantic ever held. At nine o'clock on the day of the demonstration, the Chartist convention assembled. Quarrels again broke out among the leaders and Bronterre O'Brien resigned. In one of those curious fits of inconsistency so characteristic of him, Feargus O'Connor, the leader of the most violent faction, begged the delegates: "In the name of courage, in the name of justice, in the name of God, not to hold the meeting." Terrified when the crisis arrived, he warned them that arrangements had been made by the government to shoot the Chartist leaders. Nevertheless, the delegates undertook to proceed with the demonstration and to present the petition to the House of Commons.

The preparations made by the government to deal with the meeting were immense. The Duke of Wellington was called to take charge of the military forces. Soldiers were hurried from all parts of the country and secreted in every section of the metropolis. The sailors of the Royal Navy, the post-office clerks and other civil servants were armed, and in the city 70,000 special constables were enrolled, among them being Louis Napoleon. Cannon were in readiness and the country breathlessly awaited what seemed likely to be the beginning of a revolution. However, nothing of importance happened and the demonstration was an utter failure. Lord Ashley, always a friend of labor, who had been deeply agitated by the warlike preparations, wrote on the evening of that day: "All was peaceable. The meeting at no time exceeded thirteen thousand. No more actual disturbance than on ordinary days. The procession was abandoned, and the petition came down in a hack cab." O'Connor, with his usual gift for extravagant statement, declared afterward that the meeting at Kennington Common numbered from 400,000 to 500,000 and that the petition was signed by 5,700,000 individuals. This, however, was only his usual braggadocio. When examined, it was found to contain less than 2,000,000 names, of which many were fraudulent including those of the Queen, the Duke of Wellington and other notables.

Very different were the uprisings on the Continent. There were street fights, barricades and bloody conflicts in Berlin, Vienna and other capitals of Europe. University students were actively revolutionary and demanded liberty of the press, speech, assembly and instruction. In Berlin, over 200 barricades were erected, built of stones, gutter-planking and carts. The loyal troops were fired on from almost every roof, and those who could not get arms assaulted the soldiers with whatever they could lay their hands on. Tiles were torn off houses and paving stones were carried up to the roofs in baskets. At first the government appeared victorious. Many killed in the fighting, as well as the prisoners taken, were placed in the cellar of the royal palace. The enraged revolutionists, however, launched new battles, and at last the King found it necessary to address a royal proclamation "to his loving Berliners." He regretted the action of the military and proposed that both parties forget the unfortunate events of the previous days.

An enormous crowd thronged about the castle in response to the proclamation demanding that the corpses of the citizens who had been killed be brought into the courtyard. When shouts arose that the King appear, he came on to the balcony, obviously terrified; whereupon the crowd demanded that all prisoners in the cellar be set free. To this he at last consented. The leader of the mob then gave orders that the corpses be borne past the King, and when the revolutionists shouted "Off with your hat!" the monarch was obliged to uncover.

On the 21st of March the King rode out of the palace, followed by the royal princes and his ministers, for the purpose of assuring his people that he would grant to them liberty, a parliament, and a constitution. He went to the university, where he addressed the professors and students and, after asking them to write down his words, made solemn promises that he would bestow liberties upon the people. At the arsenal, while he was making promises, a piercing voice cried, "Don't believe him, he is lying. He has always lied and he is lying now. Tear me in pieces if you like, but I say he is lying. Don't believe him!"

In Austria the students and masses also demanded an extension of liberty and a constitution. Amidst the battles and revolts, Emperor Ferdinand issued a proclamation promising his people liberty of the press and a convention of deputies for the purpose of "drafting that constitution which we have determined to bestow upon our country." After weeks of wild excitement and revolutionary demonstrations the uprisings in France were suppressed, and later the insurrections in Austria and Germany also subsided. The first German parliament which met at Frankfort was forcibly dispersed by troops on the 18th of June, 1849. The kings had lied and their promises were broken. There is no great political significance in the year 1848. Riots and disorder were general throughout Europe but all attempts at revolution were complete failures.

After 1848 the emotional appeal of the slogans of the Great French Revolution ceased to be effective in arousing the populace. Little was heard of Liberty, Fraternity and Equality after the Marxists began to displace the republicans in the leadership of the radical movement. Although as the years passed, liberal institutions, freedom of speech, of the press and of assembly made headway throughout Europe, the revolutionists were not satisfied and their attacks were directed with increasing force upon the capitalists. The doctrines of socialism and communism had been formulated in the famous Communist Manifesto of Karl Marx and the world began to hear of the coming Dictatorship of the Proletariat. A struggle between capitalists and workers was in the making, and after 1871 it became clear that the battles of the future were to be fought mainly for the control and management of property.

3. *Civil War in France*

*Sooner than be the first victims of the restored democracy,
they were resolved to call in the enemy and make peace
. . . and at all costs retain possession of the government.*
—THUCYDIDES

The upheavals in England and Europe during the
thirty-four years following the defeat of Napoleon
were alarming disturbances; but they should not be
called revolutions. The savage conflict in Paris, which
followed the Franco-German war of 1870, was, however, an ominous revolution; and, while the working
class was only momentarily victorious, nothing so portentous had been seen before in the Western world.
The economic and political situation in Paris in 1871,
though localized, was much like that which existed in
all the defeated countries after the World War. The
people of France had just met with a crushing military
defeat. In less than four weeks the Germans had annihilated the regular armies of France. Most of the
French soldiers were captured and shut up in the
French fortresses which had also been taken by the
Germans. Despite this crushing defeat the German
armies were, nevertheless, held at bay before the gates
of Paris for nearly five months by the citizens organized as a national guard. The only weak heart in besieged Paris was the government, and in despair it
threatened again and again to surrender. But the

slightest suggestion of this enraged the masses who were united in at least one thing, that Paris should be defended to the last man.

The people were disgusted at the cowardice of the government and twice during the siege a revolution threatened—on the 31st of October, 1870, and on January 22nd, 1871. Terrified by these treasonable activities the government decided to fight no longer and Paris was surrendered. The preliminaries of peace were agreed upon at Versailles on the 29th of January, 1871, and the Prussian flag was raised over the forts of the city. In addition to the money indemnity of one billion francs, France was forced to cede to the Germans the entire province of Alsace, excepting Belfort, and a large portion of Lorraine.

It is not difficult to imagine the feeling of outrage that surged through the people of France against terms so cruel and humiliating. They were, however, helpless and for some weeks seemed to be stupefied. At such times business is always at a standstill and tens of thousands of armed men were hungry and unemployed. The unrest in the capital was so widespread that the National government decided for its own security to move from Paris to Versailles. Although the masses were unruly no serious outbreak occurred until the government attempted on the 18th of March to disarm the people, whereupon the working class arose *en masse.* The victory was immediate and complete and the next day the people were in control of Paris. From then until May 28th, Paris was an independent state, surrounded by a hostile France and constantly menaced by such armies as could be mustered by the discredited government of M. Thiers.

Two antagonistic elements were strongly represented among the revolutionists who took control of Paris. The first and most important embraced the radicals and socialists, many of whom were allied to the International Workingmen's Association. This section wished not only to maintain a republic in France but also to carry out certain social reforms. The second powerful group was composed of republicans who cared only "to preserve and purify" the republic. Most of the workingmen, though anti-clerical and anti-capitalist, were ardent patriots, and all suspected that the government and the Imperialists had provoked the disastrous war in order to restore the old regime and crush the young republic. The more impassioned patriots believed that France had been deliberately betrayed and turned over helpless into the hands of the Germans. That there was some ground for such feeling is indicated by the fact that few historians venture to defend the character or the motives of many of the leading statesmen of France at that period. In any case they were thoroughly discredited among the masses, and at all times after the defeat of the French armies their position was perilous.

Although the Internationalists have had to bear and some of them deserve much of the blame for the excesses of the Commune, there were, in fact, among them leaders who discouraged and deplored violence. During the earlier stages a few of them protested against an uprising and urged the workingmen to "fulfill their duties as citizens." Later when the Commune was in control of Paris some of the members of the International belonged to the more conservative section of the revolutionists. They sought to improve the lot of the oppressed and underpaid classes; but they hoped to do this gradually and legally. This was admitted by Thomas March who was one of the most impartial of those who have written the history of the Commune. The most violent group was made up of politicians, syndicalists, journalists and anarchists, most of whom had been thrown into prison under the Empire for their revolutionary or trade-union activities. Some of them were under the spell of Blanqui, the inveterate insurrectionist, and they were responsible for many outrages. They had suffered under the Empire and when their opportunity came they took their full quota of revenge.

The uprising met with almost no resistance. Over 300,000 people in Paris were carrying arms. The government had run away to Versailles and the generals left in Paris found their troops hostile and mutinous. When, therefore, the people arose, the soldiers of the government refused to fire upon them and many joined the revolutionists. In about three hours, as a matter of fact, the insurrectionists were masters of the day and Thiers, escaping from the back door of the Hôtel de Ville, also ran away to Versailles. At half past four in the afternoon the insurgents captured Clement Thomas, a general who had helped to put down the insurrection of 1848. He was placed against a wall and riddled with bullets. General Lecompte, who, in the morning of the same day had ordered his soldiers to shoot the insurrectionists, was given the same punishment, despite his plea for mercy. On the 19th of March the red flag was waving from the Hôtel de Ville and from many other public buildings throughout the city.

Although the Commune had a short life and a terrible ending, and although little of importance was accomplished, nevertheless it is interesting to review some of its acts during the very brief period when it was in control of Paris. The officials of the Commune were almost exclusively workingmen or the representatives of working-class organizations and what they did was intended solely to benefit the working class. One of the first things done was to create a popular

army and to abolish the old professional army. All
rents from October, 1870 to April, 1871 were remitted
and afterward the stalls of the pawnbrokers were
emptied and the goods returned to those who had
pledged them. The highest salary to be paid any public
official was set at 6,000 francs or about $1,200 per
year. The Church was separated from the State and
grants from the public treasury for religious purposes
were refused. All ecclesiastical property was declared
to be national property. On the 12th of April the
Commune ordered the column at the Place Vendôme,
which had been constructed by Napoleon I after the
war of 1809, to be overthrown as it was considered
to be a monument to national vanity and international
jealousy. On the 16th of April a census was taken of
all idle factories and workshops and the workingmen,
formerly employed in them, were organized into cooperative societies to reopen these industries and to
set them going. On the 20th of April the nightwork
of bakers was abolished. Employment offices were
opened for the purpose of getting work for the unemployed.

These are the only important measures, and while
they were in spirit anti-clerical and anti-capitalist,
they gave little evidence that the men in control of
Paris had any fundamentally revolutionary program.
With the few exceptions noted, especially the seizing

of idle factories and workshops and the confiscation of all property held by the religious orders, there was no attempt made by the Commune to abolish private property as an institution, nor did it seek to establish a proletarian dictatorship as has often been stated.

The significance of the Commune is to be found not in its legislative enactments but in the astounding outrages committed by both sides in the struggle for the control of Paris. The government at Versailles executed a number of the revolutionists who had been captured, several of whom were extremely popular among the masses. In retaliation several important hostages were taken by the communists. These included the Archbishop of Paris, a number of priests and a judge of the Court of Appeal who was especially hated by the populace. The Commune offered to exchange all these hostages for the life of one revolutionist, namely the famous Blanqui, but this was declined. Notice was then sent to the government at Versailles that in case any revolutionists were executed, these prominent men of Paris would share the same fate.

Execution of hostages was not, it appears, a French method of warfare. Karl Marx tells us that the custom was revived in modern times by the Germans in the Franco-Prussian War, and later adopted by both sides in the civil war which followed in France. The mere

suggestion that the Archbishop and the other hostages
might be shot aroused not only the rage of the government at Versailles but an uncontrollable fury among
the peasants throughout France who for the most part
were devout Catholics. It was not long before the
government was able to muster enough support outside of Paris to begin its siege of the city and to execute
one of the most frightful massacres in history.

To assist the French government at Versailles in the
restoration of order, the Germans consented early in
April to release the captive French soldiers. This enabled the government to muster 150,000 armed and
trained men for active operations against Paris. The
Commune on the other hand is said to have had about
100,000 of its own men in arms and they possessed
in addition the protection of strong fortifications. By
the middle of May it was clear to the revolutionists
that they could not hold out much longer and along
with their fear and desperation came terrorism. Even
the moderates lost control over themselves. The residence and library of M. Thiers were burned as a warn-
ing to the government that if it continued the siege,
Paris would be reduced to ashes.

However, the government was not deterred and its
army penetrated the first defenses of Paris on May
23rd. Next day many of the public buildings were set
afire, including the Palace of the Tuileries, and while

the city was burning the Archbishop and certain other hostages were shot. The rage of the forces of the government then broke all bounds. They were now fighting fiercely—giving no quarter—in all the streets of Paris, and after a terrible hand to hand conflict in the cemetery of Père Lachaise, the army was at last victorious. The estimates of the number killed in a little more than a week of battle vary greatly. Some have said that 40,000 were slain in the streets but the most reliable authorities agree upon 20,000. The Commune was overthrown and at this point the history of the Third Republic commences.

♣   ♣   ♣

As this book is not a history of revolutions, it may seem that the author has gone far adrift in devoting so much space to the story of some of the insurrections of the nineteenth century. They were, however, omens of a new era in the character and purpose of revolution. The workers, as a class, appear as the disturbing factor and their attacks became increasingly concentrated upon the fortifications of capitalism. During the first half of the century socialist ideas began to make headway among the workers and after the Commune they became the religion of the more aggressive sections of the labor movement. For several reasons, therefore, these insurrections are instructive to the stu-

dent of revolution: (1) The reaction from the excesses
of the French Revolution and the communist program
of the rebels had united the owners of property whose
wholehearted support was given to the repressive
measures of the various governments; (2) deflation
was allowed to proceed without interference; the
United Kingdom was reducing its huge war debt at a
rate never equalled before or since by any other country; (3) the armed forces of the governments were on
the whole loyal and determined to maintain law and
order; (4) the upheavals were due mainly to misery
—misery which wageworkers are usually forced to endure whenever the economic system is unable to function smoothly and continuously; and (5) out of the
experience of the Commune evolved the revolutionary
ideas, programs, organizations and methods of attack
which were so successful in Russia after the World
War.

In France—usually a reliable barometer of revolutionary weather—the critical years were 1814, 1830,
1848 and 1871. In 1814, the people, exhausted by
twenty-five years of war and revolutions, returned
soon to the Old Regime of the Bourbons. In 1830,
another period of revolutionary activity set in and continued with interruptions until 1848, when the socialists began to assume the leadership of the masses.
The dominant note from this point on was the welfare

of the proletarians. No longer were the extremists interested in political power except as a means of acquiring immediately for the workers all land and all industries. Under one name or another most of the militant revolutionists became anti-democratic, anti-parliamentarian and anti-capitalist. To them the Dictatorship of the Proletariat became, after 1871, an obsession.

In thousands of little groups scattered over the world, the socialists read and re-read the story of the Commune. The treatise which Marx wrote upon this revolution became the textbook of the communists who dominated Russia and who led many of the upheavals in Middle and Eastern Europe immediately after the World War. It supplied them lessons in technique and taught them the "art of revolution." After 1871 the militants were convinced that armed forces would decide the issue; that no quarter should be given to any element which might later prove troublesome; that republicans and moderates should be put out of the way as quickly as possible; that representative governments could not be relied upon and that without the support or neutrality of the peasants no revolution of the proletarians could be successful. Lenin, Trotsky, Bela Kun, Mussolini and others had learned these lessons long before the World War and did not forget them when their opportunity arrived. They knew what they wanted and how to get it.

4. *"The Profiteers"*

A study of history would, we believe, confirm the opinion that it is in the changes in the level of prices . . . that the main secret of social trouble is to be found.
—MACMILLAN REPORT

August Bebel rarely missed an opportunity to impress upon his socialist following and his political antagonists that defeat in war is often the forerunner of revolution. The terrifying fulfillment of his predictions astounded Hans Delbrück, the German historian, who wringing his hands in despair amidst the upheavals following the World War lamented, "What mistakes we have made! The Social Democrats have a right to power because they are the only people who have been right about the war." Along with Bebel as an authority upon the causes of revolutionary upheavals we must also place Lenin, whose studies of economics and history taught him a more comprehensive thesis: namely that revolutions are provoked not only by defeat in war but also by rapidly rising prices. As the first section of this chapter was devoted to some illustrations which support Bebel's thesis, let us confine our attention here to Lenin's, which has aroused considerable controversy.

Since the steepest rises in the cost of living take

place in time of war and as revolutions rarely occur during war, many of my readers may jump to the conclusion that Lenin was talking nonsense. But there are special reasons why there are few insurrections during great conflicts between nations. Patriotism is the dominant passion, the able-bodied men and women are employed, wages are high and sedition is treason. After war some of the conditions are reversed. But if the cost of living continues to rise, serious upheavals may be expected. That is what Lenin had in mind and there are many examples in the history of nations to support his view.

A corollary might be added to Lenin's thesis, namely that abortive and counter-revolutions may be expected when prices are rapidly falling. Although there are many cases which can be cited to prove both generalizations, there is no need to rely only upon our readings of history. Reason and common sense confirm these views. However, to prove conclusively that violent upheavals and social revolutions are likely to occur only in periods of rapidly rising prices and that equally violent reactions and counter-revolutions usually occur in periods of rapidly falling prices, it would be necessary to examine minutely the economic conditions which existed in hundreds of cases where the revolutionary cycle was running its course. Needless to say I have not undertaken this formidable task.

Aristotle observed that "the underprivileged," as they are now called, unless they are bearing arms and probably even then, are incapable of sustained and formidable revolutionary action. However, immediately we add to the indigent most of the middle class and others with small homes, modest savings and fixed wages, who find themselves impoverished by a rapidly rising cost of living, a considerable majority becomes eager to join any movement which promises to overthrow the "profiteer." Every country is dangerously exposed to revolution when those who have work cannot live on the wages they receive. In the collapses which follow all inflationary booms in commodities, an entirely different situation develops: the real incomes of the thrifty are rising and the unemployed are bereft of the leadership of the more energetic and capable workers, a majority of whom are employed even during depressions except in certain areas and special industries, and the governments responsible for monetary mismanagement are overthrown. These reactions to economic conditions seem to make sense.

Careful observation leads to the same conclusions. During the months when the last great depression was at its worst, I was traveling around the world. The distress was acute everywhere in the countries visited. There were riots and hunger marches but no definite indications that revolutionary uprisings were in the making. The debtors and farmers were having a difficult time. The worst conditions existed in those countries whose welfare depended upon the production and sale of raw materials. There was almost no demand for their products and the holds of the ships upon which I traveled were empty while docks and warehouses were heavily laden with unsalable goods. If revolutions were caused by an almost complete collapse in the world's productive forces, there would have been in nearly every country during the last depression revolts of the indigent and unemployed.

As we know, from 1931 to 1934 the masses almost everywhere were moving toward the Right. The trend in some of the South American countries as well as in Mexico, Cuba and China may be ignored since for years they had been tossed from one military dictator to another. King Alfonso fled from Spain at the very moment when bravery, patience, tact and intelligence, qualities he never possessed, might have saved his people from civil war. If the countries just mentioned are excepted from the generalization, it may be said that on the whole the rest of the world was in a state of reaction against revolutionary agitators and communism. In Russia, a powerful counter-revolution was gaining momentum and the government defended itself by one of the most extensive purges ever known and by a radical reversal of its communist policies.

One hundred and thirty-eight thousand officials were dismissed from public service and many other prominent leaders were shot or imprisoned. In Germany in 1930, the communists affiliated with Moscow voted for the Nazis while great masses deserted the ranks of the socialists and Bruening, the Catholic, was installed as Chancellor. In 1933, the quarreling factions lost millions of votes and the control of the Republic passed to Hitler. Previously the Labor government in Australia had been defeated at the polls, and in the United Kingdom the Labor Party had been overwhelmed by the Conservatives.

Such was the trend of popular sentiment during the most profound industrial depression the world had suffered in over one hundred years. It is possible that the trend would have been in an opposite direction had the conservative parties been in control; but it is interesting to note that Mr. Roosevelt won his great victory in 1932 by pledging himself to sound money, a balanced budget, a twenty-five per cent reduction in the cost of government and 100 per cent support to one of the most conservative programs ever adopted by a convention of the Democratic Party. Moreover a little later in Canada, the New Deal of the Conservative Mr. Bennett suffered a crushing defeat at the hands of Mr. Mackenzie King, a Liberal, running on a genuinely conservative platform. These political reverses are not entirely convincing evidence that the trend of public sentiment is always toward the Right during a period of deflation. It may mean only that elections are like seditions, against things, not for things, as the wise Aristotle discovered in his time.

A far different picture presented itself to a traveler east of the Rhine after the World War. All forms of liquid capital were completely wiped out in Russia, Germany, Poland, Austria and Hungary by uncontrolled inflation. Savings, insurance policies and currencies became of no value. The middle classes were impoverished and rebellious; labor was on the rampage, including civil servants; anti-semitism in a most virulent form was born, and the communists and their allies were tearing into shreds the prostrate form of capitalism. The cost of living was rising to fantastic heights. After 1921 business was recovering from the first post-war depression but few workmen could live on the wages they were receiving. Many merchants were progressing slowly but certainly toward bankruptcy because the goods they sold one day had to be replaced later at higher prices. Only those who bought foreign currencies in sound countries, invested their funds abroad or hoarded gold were able to preserve their capital. Each one for himself and the Devil take the hindmost was the golden rule in most of Europe for a decade after the war.

France, Italy, Belgium, Spain, Portugal and some other countries managed to check the downward movement before their currencies became worthless but not before much damage had been done. Forces were set in motion which led to serious civil conflicts and in three countries to dictatorships. The United States, the British and their dominions, Holland, Japan, Czechoslovakia and a few other countries undertook immediately after the war to regain control over prices and by deflationary measures managed to stabilize their currencies. The results are of utmost interest and confirm the conclusions of Lenin. In all the countries where inflation became uncontrollable there were all sorts of violent social eruptions. These manifestations of mass madness are of profound significance especially when we contrast them with what was happening elsewhere. Where deflation—an extremely painful alternative—was allowed to take its course there was much suffering and unemployment. The parties in power were displaced by labor and socialist parties in England and elsewhere, but there were no general upheavals of a definitely revolutionary character. As we shall see, this recent history differs in no way from that which relates the story of other times.

As a result of the contrary monetary policies mentioned above, most economists expected political and industrial conditions to develop very much as they did in the various countries. John Maynard Keynes wrote the following critique of the incompetence or malicious intent of what he calls "the belligerent Governments":

Lenin is said to have declared that the best way to destroy the Capitalist System was to debauch the currency. By a continuing process of inflation, Governments can confiscate, secretly and unobserved, an important part of the wealth of their citizens. By this method they not only confiscate, but they confiscate *arbitrarily*; and, while the process impoverishes many, it actually enriches some. The sight of this arbitrary rearrangement of riches strikes not only at security, but at confidence in the equity of the existing distribution of wealth. Those to whom the system brings windfalls, beyond their deserts and even beyond their expectations or desires, become "profiteers," who are the object of the hatred of the bourgeoisie, whom the inflationism has impoverished, not less than of the proletariat. As the inflation proceeds and the real value of the currency fluctuates wildly from month to month, all permanent relations between debtors and creditors, which form the ultimate foundation of capitalism, become so utterly disordered as to be almost meaningless; and the process of wealth-getting degenerates into a gamble and a lottery.

Lenin was certainly right. There is no subtler, no surer means of overturning the existing basis of Society than to debauch the currency. The process engages all the hidden forces of economic law on the side of destruction, and does it in a manner which not one man in a million is able to diagnose.

At the end of his brilliant essay Keynes remarks:

By combining a popular hatred of the class of entrepreneurs with the blow already given to social security by the violent and arbitrary disturbance of contract and of the established equilibrium of wealth which is the inevitable result of inflation, these Governments are fast rendering impossible a continuance of the social and economic order of the nineteenth century.[2]

At the time this was written Keynes was doing the best work of his career. *The Economic Consequences of the Peace* is one of the outstanding books of our time, but it is doubtful if anything he wrote in that prophetic treatise will be quoted so often by future generations as the short essay above. The views which he expresses with such conviction, though more concisely and clearly presented than anyone else has been able to do, are not new. Much the same ideas—upon inflation as a cause of popular upheavals and economic chaos—have been active in the minds of some of the most ruthless and ambitious revolutionists in history.

[2] John Maynard Keynes: *Essays in Persuasion*, New York: Harcourt, Brace and Company, 1932.

A rapidly rising cost of living has been in all ages one of the most potent forces in perturbing and deranging political, social and economic institutions. While one may search diligently through the pages of the historians and find little actual and specific confirmation of this thesis—since they ignore almost entirely the trend of wages and prices—the revolutionists have given the closest attention to this aspect of history. Whenever purchasing power increases so fast as to force the prices of commodities to rise with great rapidity, all sorts of dangerous and unsound situations develop in the economy of a nation. Huge imports of precious metals, governments spending more than they receive in taxation, the lending by banks of funds to encourage speculative movements, civil wars and the printing of money in amounts beyond the requirements of industry and trade, have been the chief causes of rapidly rising prices.

The printing of vast quantities of paper money, as we shall see, has been a far more powerful revolutionary force than the Communist Manifesto. Violently shifting price levels after the Great War caused insurrections, strikes, bloody uprisings, the flight of gold, dissipation of working capital, fear, distress, hatred, revolutions and counter-revolutions. While a passionate love of private property survived in even the most devastated regions, many years of monetary mismanagement combined with the communist assaults unquestionably weakened capitalism and reduced its capacity for usefulness.

5. *Upheavals in Spain and England*

Thus religion was in honor with neither party; but the use of fair phrases to arrive at guilty ends was in high reputation. —THUCYDIDES

Before reviewing the classic example of printing press inflation and its consequences, let us consider briefly two cases of rapidly rising prices due to the influx into Spain and England of enormous quantities of gold and silver from the Americas. In recent centuries no other country has equaled Spain in the dazzling rapidity of her rise to a paramount position among the nations of the world. In less than a hundred years she acquired for herself the most extensive territory that had ever been assembled in one empire. Not only some of the richest areas in Western Europe but North and South America also were dominated by the priests, soldiers and sailors of Spain. Her fleets trebled those of France and England and within her borders great industrial areas had rapidly developed. The products of her soil were being sold all over the then known world and her manufacturers, traders, merchants and landowners were reaping endless harvests of riches from continuous rise in prices. Yet, after less than a century of glory and arrogance she started downward; and once in the abyss of religious and class wars she was unable to extricate herself. What other nation in the world has risen so fast to such dizzy heights or descended so rapidly into such dismal depths?

In the sixteenth century, while Spain was busily at work building her great empire, its foundations were already crumbling and in every decade since the year 1600 a careful diagnostician could have observed an insistent and progressive deterioration taking place in almost every phase of Spanish civilization. Some obscure malady seemed suddenly to have attacked this rich, adventurous, daring and powerful nation and so insidiously affected every portion of its body that for over three centuries its vitality has been continuously waning. The sudden turn in the affairs of Spain has attracted the study of many able historians but none of them, until recently, has ventured to believe that the dominating cause of her ruin was a preposterous discrepancy between supply and demand, creating a hideous mockery of boundless riches, inadequate goods, unproductive laborers and rebellious servants. Perhaps the fog is at last being dispelled by Professor Earl J. Hamilton of Duke University, who, in his minute studies of wages and the cost of living during the two critical centuries, is now throwing Röntgen rays into the opaque region which harbored the germs of Spain's creeping paralysis.

According to Hamilton a sharp rise in prices began about 1519 and in 1601 the price level was almost five times higher than that existing in 1501. With the rising cost of living the rich grew richer and the poor more sullen and rebellious. In 1519 and 1520, the uprising of the *Comuneros* created widespread disorders in Castile. At the same time there were social and agrarian revolts in Valencia. Directed by the *Germania*—the brotherhood—the sailors, the workmen in the towns and the Christian peasants launched their attacks upon the landowners and their serfs. By a series of savage revolts the Catalan peasants obtained emancipation from feudal subjection. In an effort to suppress the growing revolts, David Hannay tells us, the government devised a schedule of fixed prices on everything, and "the weaver, the fuller, the armourer, the potter, the shoemaker were told exactly how to do their own work. All this did not bear its full fruit during the reign of the Catholic sovereigns, but by the end of the sixteenth century it had reduced Spain to a state of Byzantine regulation in which every kind of work had to be done under the eye and subject to the interference of a vast swarm of government officials, all ill paid, and often not paid, all therefore necessitous and corrupt. When the New World was opened,

commerce with it was limited to Seville in order that
the supervision of the State might be more easily exer-
cised. The great resource of the treasury was the
alcabalas or excises—taxes (farmed by contractors) of
5 or 10 per cent on an article every time it was sold—
on the ox when sold to the butcher, on the hide when
sold to the tanner, on the dressed hide sold to the shoemaker and on his shoes." This plan of taxation (advocated these days by Dr. Townsend) soon made Spain
and Portugal the two "most beggarly nations in Europe."

The revolt of the workers in Spain reached a climax
in the uprising of the Moriscoes in 1568 and 1570
which ruined the province of Granada. The Netherlands were in open rebellion and religious wars were
breaking into civil wars in Germany and elsewhere.
The whole country was seething with rebellion and
civil conflicts when Drake, after making a clean sweep
of the Spanish galleons in the West Indies, imperti-
nently sailed into the harbor of Cadiz and burned a
number of vessels. "He singed the King of Spain's
beard!" the English shouted. The next year he dealt a
crushing blow to the "invincible" Armada, which
marked the end of Spain's dominion over the seas.
Murders, massacres, the expulsion of foreigners and
non-Catholics and the cruelty of the Inquisition had
created a state of terror throughout the country and its

dominions. The government was largely in the hands
of lawyers and business men who had profited immensely by the steep rise in prices and the administration assailed the nobles and landlords no less than the
workers and peasants.

Professor Hamilton informs us that,

. . . while universally envied because of her monopoly
of the American gold and silver mines, Spain saw the precious metals driven completely out of circulation by a
cumbersome medium of exchange. Like almost all monetary derangement from medieval debasement of the coinage to the inflation of currency and central bank credit of
modern times, the unbridled alteration of the coinage in
Spain, which began near the end of the reign of Philip II
and gained momentum as the seventeenth century progressed, was largely due to a chronically unbalanced
budget. At frequent intervals in the last three-quarters of
the seventeenth century the evils of inflation called forth
corrective deflation, with sharp declines in the commodity
price level and severe commercial crises as inevitable consequences. From March 1641 to August 1642 wholesale
prices at Seville rose by 93 per cent; and in a few days
following the deflation of September 15, 1642, they
dropped about 87 per cent. In 1680-82 commodity prices
fell by 45.43 per cent as a result of deflation in 1680. From
September 1929 to February 1933 wholesale commodity
prices in the United States fell only 37.86 per cent, and the

drop in the annual index from 1929 to 1933 was but 30.9 per cent.[3]

In any homogeneous country the combination of wars, inflation, high taxation, religious bigotry and despotism prevailing in Spain in the sixteenth century would surely have brought a revolution of the first order. But a widespread revolution could not get under way in Spain, perhaps the most important reasons being that the peasants, serfs and workers were in some areas of foreign origin—Mudejares, Moriscoes, Maragatos and Mozarabs; the small proprietors and artisans were separated by rigid castes; and the nobles, landlords, capitalists and lawyers were at war among themselves. No unity of aim or action was possible and all were devoid of competent leadership. Nevertheless the effect upon the wage unit of inflation, the greed of "the profiteers" and the derangements caused by the political and economic policies of the government were disastrous.

The herds of sheep began to diminish as early as 1560. In less than sixty years the ruin had proceeded to such an extent that anxious inquiries were being made by the government into the growing impoverishment of some of the most important agricultural districts and manufacuring centers. In the early years

[3] "The Decline of Spain," in *The Economic History Review*, Vol. VIII, No. 2, May, 1938.

of the seventeenth century agriculture, industry and commerce declined rapidly. The cities were stricken with famine; sailors were deserting their ships and the ill-paid armies at home and abroad were in rebellion; villages were falling into decay and the fields were becoming deserts. The workers, long rebellious, had become vagabonds. Work had stopped and grass grew in the city streets. Contempt for manual labor, indiscriminate alms, soaring prices, fiscal chaos and oppressive taxation had done their deadly work in Spain and when inevitable deflation set in, the curtain fell upon her day of glory.

After the middle of the sixteenth century the inflationary forces spread to France and England. Wiebe and Hamilton agree that the standard of living of the average laborer fell during the century to half of what it had been at the beginning. Wherever the increased purchasing power of gold and silver was having its effect, the lot of the masses was steadily growing worse. If in the margin of each page of history the author were to place a note indicating the trend of wages and the cost of living, we might find in such data an explanation for conflicts which otherwise seem inexplicable. Turning our thoughts now to England in the first half of the seventeenth century we find a wild inflation coinciding with, if not actually provoking, a conflict of religions, civil wars and revolution. Never before or since have the English of all classes been so disorderly, intolerant and distraught. Is it possible that "all the hidden forces of economic law" were working on the side of destruction?

Many able historians have devoted years of study to this troubled half-century in England and in their books we find all that is known about the military campaigns, the antagonism between the king and Parliament, the class conflicts, the noble and abominable characteristics of the main actors in the great drama, the sins and vices of the court, the battle of religions and the communist doctrines of certain sects; but unless we look sharply we shall not find one illuminating fact: Over a long period the cost of living had been rising with alarming rapidity and persistence. Commenting upon wheat as being "the constant and most general food" in England, Locke considered it "the fittest measure to judge the altered value of things, in any long tract of time..." Taking then the cost of wheat as the best barometer available for judging the impact upon the well-being of the people of the hidden forces of economic law, we find that in 1540 wheat could have been purchased for about twenty-five cents a bushel. In 1600 it had risen to about one dollar a bushel. In 1650 it cost from $1.40 to $1.80, and for the next two decades it fluctuated between that price and $1.00 a bushel. During these years the antagonism of the people to the Church and Crown was developing into a menacing movement. The revolutionary ferment increased in intensity step by step with the rising cost of living. Both the price of wheat and the rage of the revolutionists reached their maximum about the time Charles I was beheaded.

After the steep rise in prices set in, traders, speculators, shipowners and merchants increased immensely their portion of the expanding national income. Following the defeat of the Spanish Armada, the influx of precious metals from the Americas rapidly increased and capitalists formed great companies, assembled huge fleets and constructed great country houses— Knowle, Longleat, Hatfield and Hardwick, among others. Riches were being piled upon riches but underneath the rising and prosperous middle class the hungry masses in cottages, workshops and fields were sullen and bitter, ready for a revolt against the extravagance, drunkenness and debauchery of the *nouveaux riches*, the nobles and the court.[4] Food was dear, but poor people were forced to work for twopence a day; these are the sad words of Gerrard Winstanley.

Lilburne, the Leveller, was immensely popular and

[4] When I visited Eduard Bernstein, before the War, he was excited over the "discoveries" which he had made of the definitely communist character of the English Revolution. Although his views became more moderate before he published his studies, they are valuable as Gardiner, Firth, Trevelyan, Morley and many others confine their attention almost entirely to other aspects.

class antagonism and revolts were threatening to disrupt Cromwell's army. After they were suppressed, Oliver endeavored to appease the rebels by admitting that "the law, as it is now constituted, serves only to maintain the lawyer, and to encourage the rich to oppress the poor." For many decades mighty storms had been gathering and now they had become hurricanes threatening to uproot and destroy the entire fabric of English institutions. King and Parliament were torn from their moorings and for the first and last time in English history a powerful military dictator appeared upon the stage. The chapters in the history of England during the first sixty years of the seventeenth century fall naturally under these headings: The Puritans, the King, the Tyranny, the Revolution, the Civil War, the Levellers, Cromwell the Dictator, and the King Again. A harrowing period of political, religious, social and economic upheavals unique in the history of the English!

The fury once unleashed, how was it possible for England to control the armed and enraged? How was she able to escape the fate of Spain or the devastation of the French Revolution? We need not become involved in attempts to answer these questions, but certain points are of especial interest to us. Although England has suffered humiliating defeats in war, debased her coinage on many occasions and gone through extended periods of inflation and deflation, never have her internal debts and currency become worthless. The government has never destroyed by its own act confidence in the equity of wealth. That is a vitally important point, and may explain the stability of the economic system in England. It is true that toward the end of the seventeenth century, silver began to leave the country at an alarming rate and that despite the intelligence and skill of Sir Isaac Newton, who attempted to reverse the trend, England was forced on to a gold standard. That event marks roughly the beginning of England's march to world-wide empire and to an enormous increase in her foreign trade.

For a hundred years during a period of rising prices and low wages, England was racked by religious intolerance, civil war, rebellions, revolution and counter-revolution. The upheavals did not end with the return of the Stuarts but continued for many decades after. However, deflationary forces began to exert their influence and while there were many erratic movements in the opposite direction the general trend of the cost of living was downward from about 1660 to 1750. The restoration of the Stuarts and the abdication of James II occurred during the long period of declining prices. There was, however, a pronounced upswing after "the glorious revolution" when the price of wheat rose for a few years to the high level reached during the civil

wars which preceded the execution of Charles I. At
the end of a century of upheavals, it was found that
Parliament had remodeled the Coach of State, harnessed the king, taken the reins into its own hands and
was slowly but surely jogging along the broad highway
to liberty and democracy.

Those who have scornfully referred to this era of
democratic achievement as beneficial only to the aristocrats, should consider the words of Guizot: "The
two political changes effected by the Revolution of
1688 are the most popular to be found in history; it
proclaimed and guaranteed, on the one hand, the essential rights common to all citizens, and, on the other,
the active and effectual participation of the country in
its own government. A people so ignorant of its highest interests as not to know that this is all which it
needs, or ought to demand, will never be able to found
a government or to maintain its liberties." To have
been able to accomplish this actual revolution without
destroying any essential part of the framework of
British social, religious, economic and political structures is one of the miracles in the progress of mankind.

Another point is of interest. In times of extreme peril
since the Revolution those in power have not always
relied upon their own abilities but have frequently
had the common sense to call into council, by a Royal
Commission or otherwise, the best brains of the na-

tion. Strange to relate, when these superior minds have pointed out the safe path to take, the leaders in Parliament have sometimes had the wisdom and humility to follow the advice given. Other countries have too often taken the slimy road selected by vote-seeking politicians and most of them have preferred as their advisers, flatterers, sycophants and quick-witted adventurers. In the field of finance they have too often chosen speculators and charlatans such as Law and Necker. Immediately following a revolution, at a time of war and crushing taxation when the financial problems seemed overwhelming, the British turned to two of the ablest minds of all time—Locke and Newton—to reform the currency.

Many school children know a little of what the world owes to Newton; but few know anything about Locke, who endeavored to find a way to end tyranny— the domination of the State. He was among the first to declare that the common weal should be the objective of social progress and that all political authority should rest upon the consent of the governed. He proclaimed the right of resistance to the arbitrary exactions of the State and insisted that heads of State should be subject to the control of legislative bodies elected by the people. At the same time Sir Isaac, through the failure of his experiments, discovered what has since been called the quantity theory of money, which, stated crudely, is that the purchasing power of money is closely related to the quantity in circulation. To monetary science Locke also made important contributions. He was, I think, the first to define the relationship between the rate of interest and the quantity of money. Economists of the present day often find in his keen observations upon monetary and social problems inspiration for their studies and sometimes correction for hastily formed theories, too often unrelated to the facts of life. Cool, clear, classless and penetrating minds are difficult to find in any country and there will always be a dearth of Newtons and Lockes; but the uncommon common sense of British statesmen in seeking and following the advice of the best brains of their country may have been responsible in no small degree for the progressive achievements of Great Britain during the last two hundred and fifty years.

6. *The French Revolution*

The advocate of extreme measures was always to be trusted; his opponent a man to be suspected.

—THUCYDIDES

In all periods of history when society is paying a heavy penalty for its sins of war, misgovernment, speculation or rebellion, countless ingenious methods of relief and avenues of escape are proposed by those wise in their own conceit. The heyday of the charlatan arrives. The fallacies of old days are revived and panaceas have an almost unbelievable power of attraction for extravagant monarchs, weak governments and shifty politicians. As they are usually desperately in need of money, inflation in some form or other invariably allures them although it is, as we have seen, the most effective method which can be employed by governments to make their tenure uncertain, to throw new classes into power and to redistribute wealth. And although it has not yet destroyed the capitalist system it produces what Lenin spoke of as "an imminently revolutionary situation."

There have been many examples of the devastating consequences of inflation, especially since the World War, but an older one, that which raged in France from 1789 to 1797, will always stand out as a classic example. It is useful to review the history of those years because it may help us to judge the soundness of the views of two schools of monetary principles which are in our day contending for mastery. Since the havoc wrought by the Mississippi Scheme and the South Sea Bubble, the leading economists and financiers have warned their governments to keep their budgets in balance and to avoid irredeemable paper issues as they would Hell's fire. After generations had been carefully schooled in orthodox financial doctrines, it created consternation among his colleagues to have

Keynes desert them and actually advocate deficits, doles, devaluation and use of the printing press by the party in power as remedies for industrial depressions. The last proposal was sensational especially as he had so recently declared that there was "no surer means of overturning the existing basis of Society." Abandoning his former convictions, he boldly proclaimed in 1936 that "men cannot be employed when the object of desire (*i.e.*, money) is something which cannot be produced and the demand for which cannot be readily choked off. There is no remedy but to persuade the public that green cheese is practically the same thing and to have a green cheese factory (*i.e.*, a central bank) under public control."[5] If that is the *only* remedy it will be interesting to recall what happened when, after three years of depression, the French in 1789 decided to try this "green cheese" experiment in the hope of reviving trade and increasing employment.

Far too little study has been given to the economic conditions in times of social upheaval, and it is becoming more and more appreciated that for the most part history records only the superficial aspects of such movements. One is particularly impressed with this fact when reading the history of the French Revolution. No great war is associated with that cataclysm.

[5] *The General Theory of Employment, Interest and Money*, London: Macmillan Co. Limited, 1936, p. 235.

It is the classic instance of a rich and powerful country completely ruining itself by an inflation which was wholly unnecessary, undertaken in the hope of dispelling a depression which was no more severe than those which had afflicted France, as well as all other countries, repeatedly.

For some years before the depression of 1786-1789, France was enjoying unparalleled prosperity. Industry was booming. The foreign trade was so extensive that it was not equaled again in volume for well over half a century. While the masses were poor, they were employed and were no worse off than the peasants and workers in neighboring countries. The State, it is true, was heavily in debt and was spending money lavishly on roads, palaces and public buildings. England was at war and the French were profiting from it as did many of the neutral countries during and after the World War.

In almost every way the economic condition of France in the years before the crisis of 1786 resembles the highly inflated period in the United States before 1929. Suddenly from the lofty heights of prosperity France fell headlong, as we did, into the depths of depression. The government added to the intensity of the crisis by suddenly abolishing many import restrictions and embarking upon a policy of free trade. While, in earlier years, this might have prevented the development of an unsound economic situation, it was a vital mistake at the beginning of a collapse. Moreover, a great misfortune then befell France—there was an almost total failure of the harvests for two years, 1787 and 1788. In one important respect our situation in 1929 differed from that of France in 1786, as our Federal budget was balanced; taxes were not excessive and the portion of our national income absorbed by National, State and Municipal governments was not large. When the next pronounced depression arrives we shall not be so fortunate. In the last one many farmers and homeowners refused to pay their taxes; in the next, we may expect widespread rebellions.

If we totally ignore the actors, disregard all other factors and consider merely the economic consequences of the deflationary period from 1786 to 1789 and of the gigantic inflation which followed we shall find sufficient explanation for all that occurred in one of the most delirious periods of human history.[6] No matter what one may think of the child that was born after decades of agony, it is difficult to find another period in history when intelligent and able men were so bereft of their reason.

[6] Serious students would do well to consult Gomel and Stourm. Pierre Gaxotte (*The French Revolution*, New York, Scribner's, 1932) has done a brilliant piece of work. Upon the consequences of the monetary experiments, Andrew D. White's pamphlet is perhaps the best thing that has been done in so short a space. Von Sybel's laborious studies are available in both French and German.

As usual the derangement began at the top. It has
been observed that in all games, great and small—in
sport, war, politics, business and finance—most men
lose their heads when they believe themselves faced
with certain defeat. This is what happened to Necker,
the French Minister of Finance, when the depression
paralyzed all the economic processes in France. For
years he had been making prodigious efforts to balance
the budget and to wring from the people sufficient
taxes to pay the enormous expenses of the government. It was impossible. The nation was in open rebellion against the crushing taxation imposed upon it
at a time when industry was prostrated. But diminishing receipts did not deter him. Instead they produced
in him a feverish anxiety to borrow larger and larger
sums and a part of each new loan was used to pay interest upon those which had preceded. In these days
we call this "priming the pump," or as the Germans say,
initialzündung.

A system of annuities had been introduced in France
in order to tempt out of the pockets of the masses their
little hoards. It was astonishingly successful. Annuities
guaranteed by the government, paying from eight to
ten per cent, were perhaps the most alluring investment ever offered by any State. Compared to the politicians who go in for frenzied high finance which robs
an entire nation, men like Insull and Kreuger are like

little children stealing their neighbors' apples. "Fathers of families," Gaxotte writes, "borrowed at five per cent money which they proceeded to invest in annuities at ten per cent in the name of their infants. At the end of fourteen or fifteen years the debt was paid off, and the child retained intact for the rest of its life the interest at ten per cent on a capital it had never possessed."

It is dangerous to divulge to modern politicians this ingenious method of public finance and no man of public spirit would think of doing so were it not that one which may also prove to be unsound has been devised by those responsible for our Social Security legislation. The money received by Necker could be spent to care for the day to day expenses of the government and the future had to make good the payments upon the annuities guaranteed by the State. The money now being collected by our Treasury to provide payments for insurance against sickness, unemployment and old age can also be used to pay for the immediate needs of the government and its guarantees must be made good, if possible, by taxing in the future those who are supposed to be insured.

In 1789 the King removed Necker from office and when the people heard of this it dawned upon them that the State was bankrupt. Terror and rage swept over the nation. They had been robbed of their savings, in many cases pitifully small. The government had betrayed them and now its ruined creditors—the thrifty, hard-working and enterprising middle class—became violent revolutionists and went forth to give heart and head to the indigent and unemployed—to those whom Marx called the *lumpenproletariat*.

On the 12th of July at midday all Paris seemed to have joined the mob, and here and there it surged not knowing just where to attack the invisible enemy. The next day it began to move toward Les Invalides and later it attacked the Bastille. To appease the riotous masses the King recalled Necker, but the fall of the Bastille, although no serious attempt had been made to defend it, revealed the inherent weakness of the government. While there were short intervals of quiet, disorder was more or less general during the next few months. On October 5th, masses of enraged women started a march to Versailles to beseech food from the King. It seemed at the beginning harmless enough but like the marches of "veterans" and the uprisings of farmers and unemployed, the movement once started developed to alarming proportions. When they reached the palace they overpowered the guards, some of whom were killed and others mutilated. The King and Queen were forced to yield to the mob and were escorted to Paris, where, although the fury of the rabble abated and cries of "Long live the King" arose from the populace, they were from that time on until they were murdered, prisoners.

This was all very serious, but how mild and harmless it seems now compared to the years which followed. In 1789 the revolutionary drama had just begun. Industry was paralyzed, the masses were desperate and hungry, the farmers ruined. The creditors of the government were now being pushed into the abyss. The State itself was helpless and friendless. The bank —the *Caisse d'Escompte*—refused to advance any more money. When the State sought new loans from the public in August, 1789, they were complete failures; yet the State never before had been in such desperate need of money. Relief for the unemployed, purchases of corn, compensation to the holders of suppressed offices, and other obligations of the State required ever-increasing funds and now no more were to be had. Necker himself realized at last the ruin he had wrought. "The most dangerous as well as the most unjust of expedients," he said, "is that of raising loans without having secured the payment of interest on them. . . . Such an administration as this, which is tempting because it puts off the evil day, only increases the harm and brings the precipice nearer."

What happens in all such situations is that the State looks about to find opportunities for pillage. Greedy eyes were now turned toward the lands of the Church.

These were confiscated, and it was decided to issue paper money based on this new asset acquired by the State. Instead of permitting the new issue to be made by the existing bank, which had refused further credits, a new bank was started called the *Caisse de l'Extraordinaire* which was to derive its funds from the sale of 400,000,000 francs' worth of nationalized property. This was the beginning of the famous *assignats*. They were paper money or bonds entitling the bearer to an equivalent value in land, and they were to bear interest at five per cent. The first issue was rapidly exhausted, and in the spring of 1790 the government was once more faced with a deficit. In September of that year a fresh block of 800,000,000 francs in notes (this time not bearing interest) was issued for the repayment of the public debt.

Many of the leading men of France knew perfectly well the danger of inflation. "Both within and without the Assembly," Gaxotte tells us, "Talleyrand, Lebrun, Malouet, Condorcet, Dupont de Nemours, and Lavoisier were prodigal of argument and advice against the issue of this form of paper currency. It would, they said, be impossible to stop the issues without an appalling crisis; there would be a rapidly increasing depreciation of the notes as compared with coined money; fortunes would be wrecked, there would be a rise in the cost of living *pari passu* with the increase

in the media for payment, accompanied by disorgani-
zation of trade and general distress. Scarcely an event
followed that had not been predicted by them. Dupont
gave offense by prophesying that bread would cost
five sous a pound, wine sixteen sous a bottle, and boots
twelve francs a pair. In one respect alone was he mis-
taken, namely, in being too modest in his estimate.
In 1796 bread was to cost fifty francs a pound and a
pair of boots 4,000."

However, the pleas for more money were too alluring to be denied. It was argued the paper money of
earlier days was based on nothing while the *assignats*
were based upon the best of security, good French soil.
Even Mirabeau, who at first opposed the issue, became
a convert to this easy method of financing the State.
"They talk," he cried, "of a rise in the price of commodities, of an increase in the cost of labor, and of the
ruin of manufacturers which is sure to follow. Well!
Do not let them forget the hundreds of manufacturers
who have no orders, the crowd of workmen who are
dying of hunger, the thousands of tradesmen whose
businesses are being destroyed by a stagnation that
consumes their resources! . . . They tell you that
doubling the currency in this way means doubling
the price of everything before long. . . . A false
deduction, if there ever was one! For, the tokens
being doubled, the objects to be represented will be

multiplied, consumption and reproduction will grow, a thousand things now abandoned will recover their value, work will increase, useful enterprises be set on foot, and industry furnish new matter for new expenditure!"

Abbé Brousse became almost ecstatic when drawing his enchanting picture of what more money would do for the people of France. "Who can say," he shouted to the Assembly, "whether a billion more, [billions meant as little in those days as they do now] far from being a crushing burden, will not rather be the germ of life and happiness? Only look and you will see how, as the outcome of this new assistance, the arts and commercial activity will revive and bestir themselves to new enterprises and venture on bolder speculations, how the sea will be covered with new fleets . . . and all manner of prosperity will spread over the favored soil of France!" How little this kindly priest knew to what a catastrophe his monetary plans would lead in a short time.

The French have always been adept at tax evasion, but inflation is a form of taxation which cannot be evaded. As money falls in value, the tax rises and the merchant must find some way to collect the assessment. The politicians escape all blame and the funds available to the government are limited only by the capacity of the presses. Indeed, as soon as the presses are set to work all its difficulties are swept away. Old debts can be paid; hungry and discontented civil servants can be appeased; books need not be kept; budgets need not be balanced; direct taxes need not be levied; and the "profiteers"—not the State—are the victims of the popular rage.

All of this proved true in France, and indeed the first effects of the new currency were favorable. For the first time in years the State had not only ready cash, but courage, and it was heralded abroad that the Revolution was over. While insurrections due to rising prices broke out, they were promptly suppressed by the now loyal soldiers, and some of the revolutionists, including Danton, had to leave France. The secret of the prosperous society, it was thought, had been discovered—it was only necessary for the State to print more and more of those "nice, new, crisp bills," of which we have recently heard so much, and in 1790 an additional 800,000,000 francs came from the presses. In 1791, 1,500,000,000 were printed, and in 1792, 1,000,000,000 followed.

The illusions of the new era were, however, short-lived. Prices were rising ever higher and higher, and all over France there were insurrections. Millions had been ruined by the deflation of 1786-89. Other millions had been ruined at the end of the depression by the defaults in government obligations. The inflationary policies of the State were now adding new classes of victims, laborers, salaried men, government officials, soldiers, investors—in fact all consumers. The Treasury was again pressed for funds, because its soldiers and servants were unable to live on the wages they received and all the supplies required by the government were soaring in price.

Attempts were then made to fix the price of grain and the other foodstuffs, but it required armed bands to induce the owners to give them up. Mills, granaries, houses and barns were looted; shops broken into. Violence spread from one end of the realm to the other; civil war raged in town and country. The franc was daily depreciating in value and those at work, including government employees and troops, were in open rebellion. It was a year of anarchy, and while it seemed impossible that conditions should ever grow worse, the years to follow were even more terrible.

An attempt was made to force a loan from the wealthier classes, but it was unsuccessful and therefore an additional 1,700,000,000 in notes was issued in 1793. Prices soared and the infuriated masses could no longer be controlled. The *Enragés* were now dominant. Paris was in the hands of avowed communists, although they were then called by a different name. Every new insurrection now ended in a massacre. The masses milling about the streets were mown down by grapeshot. Even the inmates of the prisons were butchered. Shopkeepers, farmers, artisans and peasants were denounced as profiteers and brought before the Tribunal for punishment. As most of the producers refused to exchange their goods for paper money, some of the revolutionists then in control of Paris proposed that all private possessions should be confiscated. "Everything is to be common property," said one of the leaders, "there will be only one cellar and one granary from which everyone will take what he needs." Pillage of the necessaries of life was the common order of the day. The Reign of Terror was in full swing. The Revolutionary Tribunal was working night and day. In January the King was beheaded and thousands of others were being sent to the scaffold. The nobles and rich were not the only victims of the French Revolution. In 1794 the prisons were jammed with peasants and shopkeepers, and of the twelve thousand condemned to death nearly eight thousand were farmers, plowmen, artisans, tradesmen and laborers. Only fools would now exchange their goods or labor for the worthless paper.

The State was issuing volumes of decrees. *Assignats* had to be accepted at their face value; goods had to be sold at fixed prices; laborers had to work at fixed wages. Persons having gold or foreign credits were ordered to hand them over to the national treasury in exchange for its paper bills at their face value. The stock exchange was closed. Joint-stock companies were suppressed, and the banks and exchange offices were under the seal of the government. All life and property were rapidly coming under the control of the government and the merciless hands of the terrorists often fell quite as heavily on the working class as they did on any other. Those who defied the government when it demanded either goods or labor were rushed off to the Revolutionary Tribunal and to the guillotine.

Gold and silver had been hoarded in the earlier days; now goods and provisions were hoarded. The severest penalties were inflicted upon those who disobeyed price-fixing regulations either as to goods or labor— ten years in irons for millers and farmers; death for all those who refused to labor, or resisted the confiscation of their goods. Peasants, therefore, would grow no more; factories would produce no more; labor would work no more; and as the ruin progressed a cry arose among the politicians for France to carry the blessings of its Revolution to the rest of Europe. All kings must be destroyed. Property must be confiscated and the crusade begun to carry the high ideals of liberty, fraternity and equality into every foreign land. By 1796, paper money had increased to the fabulous amount of 45,000,000,000 francs.

In that year a new form of paper money was issued

which was, the government said, fully secured and "as
good as gold." Called *mandat territorial*, it could at
any time be exchanged for a portion of the public
domain. Choice public real estate was set apart to an
amount fully equal to the nominal value of the issue.
A law was passed imposing the death penalty upon
anyone who either accepted or offered the money at
less than its par value. The new paper, however,
proved no more acceptable than the discredited *assignats*. All classes had reached the point where they
refused to put any further trust in the money, the
credit, or the pledges of the government. In 1797 the
currency held by the government was burned and all
outstanding was repudiated. It was a cruel remedy
which sealed the ruin of those who had been forced to
exchange their property, goods or labor for these
worthless pieces of paper. All classes were now engulfed in the national wreckage.

While these events were in progress, the statesmen
of England were looking upon France, as they have
been looking upon Europe in the last twenty years—
and as they are looking upon us today—with amaze-
ment and alarm, not always concealing their contempt
for the leaders of other nations who do not read history or seek to learn its lessons. A knowledge of some
of the disasters which have befallen other nations as a
result of their monetary policies would be of ines-

timable value to American statesmen in these difficult
days. Exact historical analogies are rare but it is alarming to set down some of the parallelisms between the
economic conditions and government policies in France
at the end of the eighteenth century and those of the
United States in our day. The timing of the various
developments is no less ominous than the events.

France, 1780-86 (Six Years)

Unexampled prosperity. Immense foreign trade. Industry booming. Public improvements made on a lavish
scale. Public and private debts increasing by leaps
and bounds. Huge credit inflation. Half the gold and
silver of Europe in her vaults.

United States, 1923-29 (Six Years)

Each item approximately the same, except for the
Federal debt, which was materially reduced, and our
holdings of silver which were negligible. However, we
had in our vaults over 37 per cent of the entire monetary gold stocks of the world.

France, 1786-89 (Three Years)

Three years of acute depression and deflation. Widespread bankruptcy. Factories at half-time or closed.
Masses of unemployed. Farmers in rebellion. Bread

lines and hunger riots. Tax strikes. Budget unbalanced. Public debts increasing.

United States, 1929-32 (Three Years)
Each item approximately the same.

France, 1789-97 (Eight Years)
The government, largely to blame for the existing ruin, comes into the control of inexperienced legislators—most of them enthusiastic advocates of a new deal —who propose every conceivable panacea to arrest deflation. Budget unbalanced. Enormous increase in public debts. The State undertakes to save the country. When its credit becomes doubtful and the banks and the public cease loaning, "a green cheese factory" is started. As soon as the paper issues are exhausted depression sets in. All sorts of attempts are made to control wages and prices. Eventually the high cost of living brings chaos. The liberals and idealists destroy the monarchy. The terrorists destroy the liberals. The communists destroy each other. Anarchy and the Terror undermine the entire political, economic and social order.

United States, 1933-39 (Six Years)
Budget unbalanced. Public debts increasing on a vast scale. Devaluation. Repudiation of gold contract.

In 1939, about 60 per cent of the world's monetary gold stocks in our vaults. Baby bonds and Social Security funds helping to finance the daily needs of the government. Banks glutted with government paper. Each time the government stops spending, depression sets in. High government officials advocating class war and forecasting the doom of capitalism. Rapidly mounting taxes, sudden and unpredictable changes in governmental policies, and lack of confidence, deter investors from making long-term commitments. Eleven million unemployed. Inflationists and collectivists contending for mastery. Politicians demand the control of wages and prices. Government competition with private industry. The pump (renamed in 1939, National Investment) was again primed with billions of borrowed money.

While France was digging her own grave and relentlessly pushing her citizens into it, England was, with conservative monetary policies, making slow but steady progress toward recovery just as she has been doing in recent years. If the Federal government of the United States should continue to prime the pump with the last drop of moisture which can be drawn from the wells of the productive citizens, some British statesman may be able to say of us what Edmund Burke said of the French after they had completely wrecked themselves by confiscation, repudiation and irredeemable paper: "The French had shown themselves the ablest architects of ruin that had hitherto existed in the world. . . . They had completely pulled down to the ground their monarchy, their church, their nobility, their law, their revenue, their army, . . . their navy, their commerce, their arts and their manufactures. They had done their business for us as rivals in a way in which twenty Ramillies and Blenheims could never have done. Were we absolute conquerors, and France to lie prostrate at our feet, we should be ashamed to send a commission to settle their affairs which could impose so hard a law upon the French, and so destructive of their consequence as a nation, as they had imposed upon themselves."

What had been only a few years before the richest nation of Europe was now prostrate. Over fifty years elapsed before it regained the prosperity in industry, commerce and national wealth which it had achieved before the depression of 1786-89. It is written in history that "shortly after the paper money was destroyed, provisions in Paris, whose citizens had so often suffered from hunger and thirst and lacked fire and light, had become cheap and abundant; while trade prospered and wages ran high." No explanation is given for this sudden, almost unbelievable, transformation.

It did not mean that France was not still bleeding nor that war was at an end. Indeed France was entering a period of absolutism and militarism far more powerful and exacting than that of Louis XVI. The eighteenth Brumaire was at hand. After a few spasms a dictator was to sit in the saddle and force upon the sons of France a series of wars which ended only at Waterloo. He was the product of a great inflation and knew it so well that he informed his first cabinet that he would issue no more paper money. "I will pay cash or nothing!" he thundered. On a later occasion, when he was urged to use paper to finance his wars, he told his ministers, "While I live I will never resort to irredeemable paper." No matter how hard-pressed he was he kept the faith.

Napoleon had learned the lesson which Lenin again impressed upon us in 1919. He knew that to debauch the currency was as dangerous as to leave sticks of dynamite lying about in a nursery. But like Lenin, Napoleon had his own ends to serve and dangerous weapons were the tools of his trade. Explosives which he refused to permit his minister to play with, he was eager to hand to his enemies. In 1808, he wrote a letter to Count Fouché, Minister of Police, which reveals both his knowledge of the destructive force of paper money and his ingenuity in using every available weapon in warfare. Why should not that which had ruined France be used to ruin Austria?

To Count Fouché, Minister of Police,
Schönbrunn, Sept. 6, 1808.

Maret is sending you specimens of all the different kinds of banknote current here. I enclose a decree dealing with this matter. I want you to organize the printing of these banknotes in all denominations up to a total of 100 millions. You will require a press capable of turning out 10 millions a month. It is by means of paper money that the House of Austria has financed the war against me, and it might do so again. That being so, it must be my policy in peacetime as well as in time of war to depreciate this paper issue, and to force Austria back on to a metal currency. That will inevitably compel her to reduce her army, and to cut down the mad expenditure by which she has compromised the safety of my states. I want this operation carried out secretly, and with an air of mystery; though my object is much more a political one than anything that might be gained by financial speculation. It is in fact an object of first importance. There is no hope of peace in Europe so long as Austria can obtain loans of three or four millions on the security of her paper money.

Send me an intelligent and tactful agent, who can collect on the spot, while I am still here, all the information which I intend, and which will make it so effective.[7]

[7] Lecestre, p. 520. *Letters of Napoleon*, edited by J. M. Thompson. Basil Blackwell, Oxford, publisher.

Histories of the French Revolution usually end with the *coup d'état* of Napoleon when, after ten years of agony, the quarreling incompetents in the Council of Five Hundred, heirs of the mighty Bourbons, were leaping out of windows and running for their lives from the troops of Bonaparte. None of the promises of the Revolution had been fulfilled—work, bread, sound finance, liberty, justice, peace and brotherhood. Instead there had been idleness, starvation, bankruptcy, the Terror, massacre, war, communism and in the end a military dictator, a prototype of Hitler, who sent irate messages to the other Powers that until his ever-mounting demands were satisfied there could be "no hope of peace in Europe." The world is made up of many things but why need it be afflicted with revolutionists, promising but never delivering to the weary and heavy-laden land, bread, work and justice, or with counter-revolutionists wading through seas of blood in pursuit of peace?

7. *Review and Summary*

Glancing back over the entire period from 1204 to 1919, we can count in the limited field to which our attention has been mainly directed in this chapter, nineteen revolutions which have followed immediately after defeat in war. In addition there have been many post-war abortive revolutions—pathetic and futile revolts of peasants and workers against appalling misery. They usually occurred when their employers or masters were most in need of their services and the cost of living was rising. The climax of three of the revolutions specifically mentioned occurred when inflation was running wild. After defeat in war, inflation has nearly always been associated with, or responsible for, the development of a revolutionary psychology in nearly all classes. Since the World War all the revolutions are associated with inflation and a collapse in government while the counter-revolutions of the fascist type have occurred in countries with weak governments during periods of deflation.

Our review of the upheavals from 1814 to 1871 indicates that misery, no matter how widespread and desperate, is not *the* cause of revolution. Russia, Mexico, Spain and China should not be excepted from this generalization, as the masses were of little consequence in the revolutions of recent years, although the indifference, neutrality or sympathy of the proletarians and peasants may have been important as a factor in deciding which group was to be victorious. If depression, poverty, unemployment and enraged masses could "make" revolutions there would have been one every two or three years from 1815 to 1848 in Great Britain and probably elsewhere in Europe.

Slavery, not revolution, is the child of fatigue, poverty and famine; a fact which anyone can verify who reads the records. In the nineteenth century, tens of millions perished from hunger in China, Russia and India, a fact hard to believe in our Western world, but none of these appalling disasters led to revolution. Crop failures, hurricanes, earthquakes, droughts and killing frosts have ruined enormous areas on all continents. Often such catastrophes have made men more kindly and sympathetic toward one another. Class distinctions are accentuated but pity, charity and paternalism are also sometimes intensified.

Humanitarian sentiments languish or depart completely after defeat in war and during rapidly rising prices. Tides of prosperity and depression are normal and inherent in the progress of mankind. It is the unequal incidence, the rapid and erratic recurrences of post-war crises, which drive whole nations almost insane. A few are growing richer while the many are being reduced to poverty. Suspicion, hatred, envy and malice inflame those who are suddenly deprived of their savings or livelihood and terror of the multitude grips those who have managed to salvage something from the wreckage. Even when the latter feel assured of protection from the assaults of the masses the economic fluctuations of the period make their actions as unpredictable as those of the mobs.

If we exclude poverty as a cause of revolution the

next point to be considered is the effect of a collapse of government. Anarchy of many sorts often follows defeat in war but when there has been no defeat, bankrupt and incompetent governments invite all breeds of revolutionists to help themselves. Italy after the war was an excellent example of this hospitality. Historians have dwelt at length upon the prostration of the ruling powers as an incitement to revolution but not adequately upon one of its most serious consequences. The desertion of the intellectuals, of the old leaders, of the armed forces and of the courtiers may be influential factors in revolutionary activity but lying back of all disaffection we usually find that the governments have lost control over their finances and the value of their currencies.

The economic derangements which follow war are well enough known but it may be well to summarize some of them briefly. During the war the cost of living rises abruptly but that is not a disturbing factor since all hands are employed. Wages are rising, other incomes are increasing and the government is buying supplies, equipment and ammunition regardless of cost. Rapidly increasing debts are providing profitable investments for the upper classes. After defeat in war the situation is completely reversed. The purchases of the government are suddenly cut off and while the world price level is falling and often continues to fall

for decades, except for short periods, the incomes of
some groups are falling with even greater rapidity.
Everyone but the moneylender is more or less seriously
affected by a period of deflation. Later, in order to
save themselves and pay their obligations, the old
regimes, if they have survived the storms, and the new
governments, if they hope to keep in power, resort in
desperation to the printing press and quantities of
paper money are issued. After the World War this was
the monetary policy of all the defeated countries. The
inevitable consequence was the confiscation of an
important part of the liquid assets of the industrious,
energetic, thrifty and conservative elements; the very
ones who can be most rebellious when their livelihood,
savings and security are taken from them. In Russia
and most of Europe after the last war, the middle
class, public officials, army officers, large masses of the
working class and all others with inflexible sources of
income were reduced to poverty by the monetary policies of their governments. Many of them helped to
sow the seeds of rebellion: the harvest was gathered
by others.

Those who argue that inflation is a result and not a
cause of revolution will call attention to the fact that
the cost of living always rises during civil conflicts and
international wars. It is true that after long wars defeated countries have rarely felt themselves able, and

probably have not been able, to prevent defaults, devaluations, the depreciation of the exchange value of their currencies and in recent years, the printing of excessive issues of paper money. However it should not be forgotten that some of the steepest inflations recorded in history occurred in Greece, Rome, Spain, France and England as a result of enormous influxes of precious metals. In each case these importations preceded or coincided with economic derangements and internal class conflicts similar in many ways to those which convulsed France in 1789-1797 and Germany, Austria and Russia after the World War. Very rarely has it been possible to produce or tempt out of hiding sufficient quantities of precious metals to force up prices so rapidly as to cause social upheavals; but any government in distress, no matter how incompetent in other ways, can operate a printing press.

Professor R. B. Merriman, who has made "a study of six seventeenth century revolutions in England, France, the Netherlands, Spain, Portugal and Naples, finds that they all had in common a financial origin, all began as protests against taxation."[8] His researches have not been published, but if revolutions have a common origin it is reasonable to suppose that the basis of all transactions between man and man, between

[8] Crane Brinton, *The Anatomy of Revolution*, New York: Norton and Company, 1938, p. 48.

citizens and their government and between country and country should be found to be the most provocative of all known factors. Rapidly and erratically changing prices affect the lives of every human being and while the poor and downtrodden may take their misery as it comes, as they have done in the past, with only feeble and spasmodic resistance, the classes above them are likely to make serious trouble. One need not subscribe wholeheartedly to the Marxian theory of economic determinism to believe that what the productive classes live by, or have lived by, or hope to live by, definitely influences in good times and bad most of their actions. The government which denies them a living should be prepared for revolution.

To state our theses in the simplest terms, the following generalizations may be suggested at this point. For success, a revolution depends upon the conjunction of the following conditions and forces: (1) the collapse of government with all that it involves; (2) the instability of the economic system and particularly of its monetary basis, which is sometimes the cause and sometimes a consequence of (1); (3) "the benevolent neutrality of the populace," as Mussolini once called it; and (4) the militant support of the revolution by armed forces and embittered, aggressive sections or leaders of the middle class. When these are combined and the assault properly timed the success of a revolution is assured. When any one is absent uprisings have been abortive. Those who think the support of a ruined and rebellious middle class is not necessary will discover in chapter four that revolutions are not engineered by proletarians and peasants.

CHAPTER III

A SHORT CYCLE OF REVOLUTION

Whoe'er I know shall shun th' impending fight,
To dogs and vultures soon shall be a prey;
For death is mine. . . .
— (AGAMEMNON) HOMER

1. *The Last Stand of the Czars*

REVOLUTIONS progress in short and long cycles. When
the cycle is in motion no one knows whether it is to be
short or long, when it began or when it will end. Time
alone will tell, for as Thales said Time has discovered
some things already and will discover the rest. Though
we do not know the whole story, we shall assume that
the present cycle is a short one, that it began with the
World War and that it is now completing its revolution. The curtain raiser of this great dramatic trilogy
is *The Last Stand of the Czars*; the interlude, *The
Revolution Triumphant;* and the afterpiece, *The Return of the Czars*. We need not be told as the curtain

falls upon the last act of a drama which has been on the stage for a quarter of a century that it will rise again. For the time being we have enough to think over, which we mean to do, since of all history, that which is most recent is least understood and most easily forgotten.

The curtain rises upon the Kaiser and the Czar, who were confronted in the year 1914 with a tidal wave of democracy which threatened to engulf them. It could no longer be ignored. No one expected the Hapsburgs, Romanoffs and Hohenzollerns to realize what ridiculous anachronisms they had become in a world glowing with democratic ideals, backed by powerful and well-organized movements, but they could not have failed to know that on all fronts they were being frustrated, humiliated or beaten. As war is the last refuge of tyrants, they mobilized their troops, whipped up a fierce hatred against other countries and went forth to battle. The last of the long line of Caesars came out of their trenches and launched their desperate assaults upon enemies abroad in order to quench the spirit of rebellion at home.

In nearly every generation in Russia for three hundred years there have been revolutionists and in nearly every generation many of them were exterminated. Serious attempts at revolution have occurred at frequent intervals. During the two years 1669-1671 the peasant slaves rose *en masse* and with rage such as has rarely been seen in the world they robbed, burned and murdered. Russia was in flames and thousands of nobles were killed before Alexis, the Czar, got the upper hand and suppressed the uprising. Repression followed and the condition of the serfs grew steadily worse.

Another widespread uprising of the serfs occurred in the reign of Catherine II. Again the infuriated people destroyed and murdered and again they were crushed in blood. During the seventeenth and eighteenth centuries the masses were so carefully guarded and so brutally repressed that effective resistance was impossible. Nevertheless thousands of serfs escaped from their masters and organized bands of thieves, brigands and murderers. On the road neither life nor property was safe since at any moment one of these bands might rush out of hiding to exact its revenge. The stories of the robber chieftains, brigands and insurrectionists of these earlier days still live in the folklore of the Russian peasants. There was an old legend that Stenka Razin, who led the insurrection of the serfs against Alexis, and Pougatchoff, who led the uprising against Catherine II, would again come to earth in 1869 to lead a new war of liberation. They did not appear, but curiously enough in that year Bakunin and Nechayeff published their famous book at Geneva,

which advocated robbery, arson and murder as natural
and practical methods of action for revolutionists.[1]

In the sixties and seventies no serious outbreak occurred in Russia although hundreds of revolutionists
were at work and hundreds were imprisoned or hanged.
Nothing in the history of any other country can be
compared to the story of their desperate deeds. The
Nihilism and Terrorism that raged for three decades
would have taught anyone but the mentally incompetent that repression was defeating its purpose and
that the violent crushing of popular aspirations was
bound sooner or later to create chaos. Obvious as this
is, the Russian rulers seemed incapable of such reason-
ing, and Tolstoy, one of the few landlords who foresaw
what was coming, warned the upper classes of the
abyss toward which they were rushing. "The workmen's revolution," he wrote, "with the terrors of destruction and murder, not only threatens us, but we
have already been living upon its verge for the last
thirty years. . . ." Still repression managed to post-
pone the day and it was not until after the Russian
soldiers came back defeated from the war with Japan
that the revolutionists saw their opportunity. Russia
was in a turmoil and in 1905 the masses arose. General strikes were declared and the Czar, forced to

[1] Reviewed at length in my *Violence and the Labor Movement*, New
York: The Macmillan Company, 1914.

yield, promised with all solemnity to give to the people civil rights "based upon the inviolability of the person, and freedom of belief, of speech, of organization and of meeting." These are his own words, but unfortunately, like the kings of 1848, he was only lying.

However, he did permit the first Russian parliament to assemble in May, 1906, and for two months it was allowed to talk. Although it was surrounded by soldiers, the Czar lived in terror of another violent uprising. The representatives in the first Duma were for the most part men from the propertied classes, and when other Dumas assembled each was found to be more conservative than its predecessor. Many socialists, having no faith in the promises of the Czar, refused to participate in the elections, especially when they saw that these parliaments were being used to uncover the dangerous popular leaders. The Czar and his Cossacks remained in the saddle, and within three years all the old forms of repression were again in action. Nearly everyone in the Duma who had shown himself to be an enemy of the Czar was imprisoned, exiled or murdered. Newspapers were suppressed; meetings forbidden; trade-union leaders arrested; speakers, writers, students and others were sentenced without trial to hard labor in Siberia; while the peasants were again flogged if they could not pay the taxes imposed by the government. Repression became so

pitiless that Tolstoy in a frenzy of agony wrote to the
Czar his famous protest: "I cannot be silent!" He demanded that "these inhuman deeds" be stopped; or if
not, that the hangmen put upon him also a shroud and
cap and push him off a bench, "so that by my own
weight I may tighten the well-soaped noose round my
old throat."

Once again repression was successful but only for a
brief time, and in 1914 a new revolution was brewing.
In July of that year a strike was declared by the
workers of the Putilov factories in St. Petersburg. In
the conflict with the police fifty of the strikers were
injured and four were killed. This greatly enraged the
populace and at some large demonstrations and mass
meetings assembled in honor of President Poincaré of
France, who was then on a visit to Russia, these shouts
were heard: "Long live the Republic!" "Amnesty!"
"Down with Autocracy!" "Long live Liberty!" On
July 21st barricades were erected in all parts of the
city and a pitched battle ensued between the people
and the assaulting Cossacks. Serious conflicts also took
place on July 22nd and 23rd. The revolutionists tore
down telephone and telegraph poles, overturned carts
and erected barricades on which they planted the red
flag. It is estimated that at least 200,000 took part in
the battle. Six days later St. Petersburg was under
martial law, and all over Russia the army was being

mobilized ostensibly for the World War; but many well-informed observers believed that the preparations being made were not for the purpose of making war on Germany but to quell the revolutionary movements at home. Mobilization and a flood of patriotism temporarily frustrated the revolutionists.

It is difficult to believe that the Czar and his military advisers could have thought it possible for Russia to keep millions of well-equipped soldiers on its western front. There was plenty of man power but little else. No one who knew the Germans, who had so easily overpowered France in 1870 and who had for years been drilling and equipping both on sea and land the most powerful armed forces the world had ever known, believed that the Russians could fight a successful war against such antagonists. The Japanese had shown them ten years before the weakness of their armies. A country so backward in agricultural and industrial development could not expect anything but disaster from a conflict with a highly mechanized nation such as Germany. Russia could not arm, clothe or feed the millions which were being mobilized. The socialists, who knew best the economic conditions in Russia, prophesied at the beginning of the war that the Czar was committing suicide.

For two decades before the war, the German rulers had been growing more and more apprehensive of the rapid development of the Social Democratic party, which no longer concealed its hatred of the Kaiser and the militarists. From the elections of 1871, when two Social Democrats had been sent to the Reichstag, until 1914, the party had grown steadily in strength until it had become the most powerful political group in the Reich. The local governments of many of the large industrial cities were administered by socialist officials. Over a hundred daily papers and scores of weekly and monthly journals were published. On the eve of the war, the party had over one hundred representatives in the Reichstag and many thousands in the city councils. Berlin was in control of the party and every district in that great city, including the Kaiser's, was represented in the Reichstag by a Social Democrat. In organization and discipline the party was a vast army—polling in 1913 over four million votes—marching steadily, relentlessly toward its goal, defined by Bebel and others as republicanism in politics and socialism in industry.

In Germany, there was only one place, the Reichstag, where men were entirely free to speak their views, and what the members said there could be printed and freely circulated all over Germany. Consequently the major part of all revolutionary agitation was carried on by the rebels from that platform. As the Kaiser was extremely unpopular in Germany the deputies made

the most of this situation and often attacked him bitterly. After the murder of the Russian Czar, Alexander II, Bebel had defended the terrorists and warned
the German government that if it should use Russian
methods to destroy the Social Democratic movement,
there would be assassinations and violent counter-
assaults. He declared that he himself would be one of
the first to lend a hand. On another occasion when
Bebel confessed to "a certain amount of hatred against
the person of the Emperor," there was great commotion in the Reichstag. Bebel made it clear that he did
not believe in the efficacy of assassination but declared
"it is true we are republicans."

The war on the Kaiser's policies was not limited to
mere talk. For years the members of the Social Democratic party in the Reichstag refused to vote any money
intended for the support of the army; and throughout
the country the agitation against militarism was incessant. In 1907 I attended an anti-militarist meeting
where over 100,000 people assembled. A score of orators talked simultaneously in various parts of the immense field. To discredit the war lords every available
weapon was employed by the Social Democrats, perhaps the most effective being the cartoons and the
ridicule appearing constantly in their daily papers.
These methods were so cleverly used that the German

masses roared at the arrogance and stupidities of the army leaders.

The war on German militarism reached its climax in the years 1913 and 1914. The famous Zabern incident aroused Germany to the highest pitch of excitement. A young lieutenant stationed in Alsace had greatly incensed the people by his arrogant, strutting manner, his insults to the French flag and to the Alsatian recruits whom he called *wackes* (blockheads). He also promised a reward of ten marks if any soldier when annoyed would shoot a Social Democrat. When the acts and sayings of this pert fledgling were reported, meetings of protest were held and indignant mobs gathered before the German garrison in Alsace. These were dispersed brutally by the soldiers and several prominent persons were arrested. The Social Democrats all over Germany then set up so great an outcry against militarism that the Chancellor hurried from Berlin to confer with the Emperor who was then visiting at the country estate of his friend, Prince Fürstenberg, and there diverting himself with drinking and cabaret performances. He seemed utterly indifferent to the public clamor and remained partaking of the festivities until one of his closest friends, Von Hulsen, suddenly died of heart failure during a banquet.

Rumors were hastily circulated regarding the Emperor's alleged debaucheries at a time so critical in the affairs of State. To make matters worse the military authorities refused to discipline the officers in charge of the garrison at Zabern and, after they were exonerated, the young lieutenant above mentioned had a dispute on the street with a lame shoemaker whom he cut down with his sword. This brutal act caused a tremendous commotion throughout the Empire and the three parties, the Centrum, the Progressives and the Social Democrats, demanded explanations from Bethmann Hollweg, the Chancellor. General Von Falkenhayn came in person to the Reichstag to defend the military authorities. He said that they had only done their duty; that they were indifferent to popular criticism; that the lieutenant who had offended was a very young man, but that he was exactly the type the country most needed. This impudent statement infuriated the deputies and for the first time in the history of the German Reichstag a vote of censure was passed by the overwhelming majority of 293 to 54.

The Social Democrats were elated by this stupid defense of absolutism and, after the vote of censure, they immediately pressed an important constitutional question—namely, whether this vote of censure did not involve the resignation of the Chancellor. Persisting in their attacks, the Social Democrats urged the majority in the Reichstag to vote against granting the Chancellor's salary and to force him out of office.

The Chancellor treated this motion with contempt. He declared that he was responsible only to the Emperor, that he would refuse to resign, no matter what resolution was passed, that indeed any resolution which might be passed would only indicate to him that a difference of opinion existed between the Reichstag and the government. With utmost frankness he declared that the Emperor and the Chancellor would govern exactly as they pleased.

On the adjournment of the Reichstag, May 20, 1914, a few months after this debate, the Social Democrats staged a sensational demonstration. Although they were the strongest party in the Reichstag, they had always refused to accept the presidency of that body because it was often necessary for the president to confer with the Kaiser and it was thought to be inconsistent for a republican to wear court dress. In other ways they had shown their antagonism to the monarch. It was the custom when the Reichstag was on the point of adjournment for its members to rise and cheer the name of the Emperor. That had never been done by the Social Democrats. On such occasions they had invariably marched out of the chamber. On May 20, 1914, they remained and refused either to rise or to cheer the Emperor. "This occurrence, I know," said Ambassador Gerard, "greatly incensed the

Emperor and did much, I believe, to win his consent to the war."

While the German populace was in a state of indignation over the Zabern incident several other things were happening in the Reichstag which annoyed the Emperor. Toward the close of the session Wendel created consternation when he ended a speech with the cry, "Long live France!" In May, 1914, Karl Liebknecht made several addresses exposing the methods of the big munitions companies of Germany, in which the Kaiser himself was a large stockholder. Liebknecht produced documentary evidence showing that they maintained in all countries spies and agents to bribe high officials, to corrupt newspapers, to arouse suspicion, and to strengthen militarism. The statements of Liebknecht were astounding, and during the two months before the war the Social Democrats at immense mass meetings kept up their continuous agitation against militarism.

The Kaiser could not endure the criticism and insults of his opponents without retort. On one occasion during a great strike, the Kaiser went personally to talk to the men and with his usual indiscretion confessed that "for me every Social Democrat is synonymous with an enemy of the Empire and of his country. Therefore, if there are any tendencies in this movement stirring up to unlawful resistance, I shall act with merciless rigor and bring to bear all the power at my disposal—which is great." From the earliest days of his career the Kaiser felt menaced by the force which was destined to overthrow him; and to some young recruits assembled at Potsdam he once said, "For you there is only one foe and that is my foe. In view of our present social troubles it may come to this: that I command you to shoot down your own relatives, brothers and even parents, in the streets, which God forbid! But then you must obey my orders without a murmur." These were the words of an extremely foolish and arrogant monarch—words which delighted his enemies who eagerly spread them everywhere among the people. After a similar outburst of rage, Bebel remarked quite truthfully that "every time the Kaiser speaks, the Social Democrats add 100,000 votes to their party."

It is clear then that the Kaiser not only bitterly hated the leaders of the rapidly growing democratic forces but he also feared them more than France or Russia and meant to do everything in his power to destroy them. They were growing stronger all the time, and in 1914 they were the most powerful political force in Germany. This could not go on indefinitely without bringing destruction to the Hohenzollerns. The Social Democratic party was hostile to almost everything they stood for. Too little has been written

of another incident which must have infuriated the
Kaiser.

As a delegate of the American Socialist party to the
International Convention at Stuttgart in 1907 and at
Copenhagen in 1910, I was much interested in a resolution proposing that a universal general strike be
called in case Europe should be threatened with war.
Had that resolution been adopted, the strike called
and had the men come out, which we realize now they
would not have done, almost every mine, factory and
railroad in Europe would have ceased to function and
there could have been no war. At Stuttgart considera-
tion of the resolution was postponed but at Copenhagen it was debated at length and no one there will
ever forget the stirring orations of Jaurès, Keir Hardie
and many others pleading with the convention—ten
million workers were represented in that session—to
make this valiant attempt to prevent war.

Late in the afternoon I left the assembly convinced
that the victory had been won. Sometime after mid-
night, Hardie returned to the rooms which we were
sharing and after arousing me recited the story of what
had happened at the convention during the evening.
One could see in his face and eyes that the ambition
of his life had been shattered. Opposition had appeared from unexpected quarters, but the resolution
would have been adopted had it not been for the

pleading of the Germans, who maintained that if such action were taken their organizations would be outlawed, their properties confiscated and their papers suppressed. However, they gave in private their solemn promise—Hardie told me this—that if war were declared the Social Democrats in Germany would immediately join with their comrades in France, Italy, Belgium and Great Britain in a strike that would paralyze all the military forces of Europe.

Upon the outbreak of the war, a few leaders in the German movement risked their lives to keep their promise; but the masses in every country were carried away by their patriotic passions and the socialist leaders, willingly or unwillingly, followed them. Except in England and Serbia, not a vote was cast in any parliament against the declarations of war. "Workers of the World, Unite!" had been proved to be an idle dream. Bebel had died in 1913. Jaurès was assassinated on the eve of the war and Hardie died the next year, unable to survive the nausea caused by his loss of faith in the working class. The German labor movement, which had been made the most powerful the world had ever seen by two sincere democrats, August Bebel and Wilhelm Liebknecht, richly deserved its fate of being consigned to oblivion by Adolf Hitler. In 1914 it betrayed, and perhaps turned backward for centuries, the forces of democracy which had been for over forty years growing steadily and seemed to be on the point of conquering peacefully, legally and with ballots the last stronghold of autocracy in Europe. After the first gun was fired, the threat of Agamemnon could have been uttered without fear by the Czar of Russia and the Kaiser of Germany.

With full knowledge of the "secret" pledge of the German Social Democrats at Copenhagen, it is obvious that there could have been no danger in Europe which the Kaiser and the militarists felt it more necessary to destroy than this movement which was called "*the* enemy of the Fatherland." The Czar entertained, as we know, similar feelings, and while riots, strikes and uprisings were taking place in Russia in July, 1914, the army was being mobilized for war and to deal with the social unrest at home. The war was, as war has always been and may continue to be, a temporary antidote to revolution; but on this occasion it raised the curtain upon the dramatic trilogy, the fatal cycle, the first play of which ended with the extinction of the czars.

2. *The Revolution Triumphant*

> When there is a want of a proper number of men of middling fortune, the poor extend their power too far, abuses arise, and the government is soon at an end.
>
> —ARISTOTLE

The extinction of the czars was hailed by democrats and republicans all over the world as the fulfillment of their dreams. The millions who had perished to make the world safe for democracy had not died in vain. Once more the birds sang as Wordsworth did at the beginning of the French Revolution. But soon again they ceased their warblings. The militants had other things in mind, many of them not at all liked by the republicans and democrats. With arsenals of Marxian dogmas and weapons more substantial, *Les Enragés* after the World War knew precisely what they wanted and with their shock troops they were prepared to take it.

During the war Bernard Shaw said that the only way to end the conflict was for the soldiers to shoot their officers and go home. In some places that actually happened. In the defeated countries many local civil wars followed the World War with the peasants fighting the landlords and the more militant of the proletariat fighting the employers. For brief periods in many places the communist revolutionists were triumphant, many of whom were as violently opposed to democracy as they were to capitalism.

It should never be forgotten that the uprising of the Bolshevists was directed not against the Czar but against the republicans and moderate socialists struggling desperately at the moment to bring order out of social and economic chaos and to found in Russia a political democracy. The Romanoffs had been de-

throned and there was no possibility of them or their
retainers being able to muster sufficient forces to regain their old positions. The world was astonished
therefore when Lenin declared that democracy in
Russia and elsewhere, which he asserted was in fact
only "the dictatorship of the bourgeoisie," had to be
annihilated. That was to be the aim of a world crusade
and when this was announced most of the liberals in
Europe, including a majority of the Social Democrats
inside and outside of Russia, were appalled and has-
tened to sever all connection with the Bolshevists.
Nevertheless for over two decades there have been in
almost every country of the world small militant
groups which have endeavored to imitate the revolutionary policies and tactics of the Russian communists.
The leaders of these groups have been chosen by the
Comintern in Moscow and the professional revolutionists whom they have assembled have been financed
and directed by Lenin, Trotsky and Stalin.

The Bolshevists believed that a world revolution
was imminent and considering the economic disorder
existing in most countries after the war their belief
seemed well founded. Capitalism was in dire straits
not only because the war had deranged the processes
of private enterprise but also because a sustained revival of long-term investment is impossible in any
country where the government is dominated by ele-

ments more or less hostile to the middle class. The
aim of the communists is, as we know, to take possession of the land and the instruments of production
and by means of a dictatorship to force the birth of
a new society. Had not Marx said that physical force
would be the midwife of the new social order? The
Spartacists and Bolshevists remembered that, but they
forgot the retort Marx had made to one of his opponents in tactics who had said to him: "If force is the
midwife of the new social order, why should we bother
with other methods?" Whereupon Marx answered:
"Why if that were so, all I should have to do if I
wanted a child would be to employ a midwife." It is
a pity that he did not instruct his impassioned followers that parents cannot decide according to their
liking the kind of a child that will be born. Republican democracies were in fact born in Russia, Germany,
Austria and other countries, and it is possible they
might have survived had the infants been attended
by competent nurses, admired by proud fathers and
fed by devoted mothers. Instead they were abandoned
and soon perished.

It should be remembered that Karl Marx, born in
1818, lived throughout his youth amidst post-war convulsions and abortive revolutions. Crisis after crisis
occurred and he and many other thoughtful men believed they were witnessing the death agonies of pri-

vate property. At the age of thirty Marx was moved
to deliver the following generous and memorable tribute to capitalism on what he felt certain was the eve
of its burial: "The bourgeoisie during its rule of
scarcely one hundred years has created more massive
and colossal productive forces than all the preceding
generations together. Subjection of Nature's forces to
man, machinery, application of chemistry to industry
and agriculture, steam navigation, railways, electric
telegraphs, clearing of whole continents for cultiva-
tion, canalization of rivers, whole populations con-
jured out of the ground—what earlier century had even
a presentiment that such productive forces slumbered
in the lap of social labor?"

But capitalism declined to let Marx bury it and
shortly after he delivered his eulogy it entered upon
an era of usefulness which was soon to shower upon
all classes the greatest riches they had ever known.
In 1848 the social disturbances which had set in after
the wars of Napoleon suddenly ceased and the freest
and most productive economy ever enjoyed by humanity, lasting for sixty-six years, lay before it. During this period of peace and prosperity, the power of
the State was receding and the energies of hundreds
of millions of free men were being released.

In the democratic countries where capitalism had
been permitted to flourish almost unobstructed, the

Marxians had been unable to attract the working class. Naked facts were refuting every essential doctrine of *Das Kapital*. The masses were not being increasingly impoverished. Property was not being concentrated in the hands of a few. Hours of labor were diminishing and wages rising. Pauperism was declining and while the organized workers were seeking by all means in their power to better their condition they were not class-conscious nor were they becoming more and more antagonistic to the private ownership of property. Where democracy was weakest, capitalism was deprived of much of its vitality and productivity. Where capitalism was retarded or suppressed by the State, democracy was unable to make headway.

Partly, though of course not altogether, as a consequence of democracy and capitalism working in harmony for the greatest good of the greatest number, most of the riches of the world were, in the half century before the war, passing rapidly into the possession of the people of the democratic countries. The incredible productivity of labor, freed from the tyranny of the State, surpassed anything men had ever dreamed of. On the other hand the peoples who remained subject to the decrees, heavy taxation and plans of local lords or of powerful despotic States found that they were being denied the choicest fruits of the most productive age the world has ever known. Indeed in those

huge areas of the world where the State or the local
lords immediately took possession of the wealth produced, hundreds of millions remained on the verge of
famine and there was no inclination for native or
foreign investors to risk their money in enterprises
which were at the mercy of the decrees, legislation
and armed forces of the ruling castes.

Below I have inserted a table of crude descriptive
generalizations which may throw some light upon the
effect of government upon the social and economic
status of the populace in some of the leading countries.
No single term adequately describes the many forms
of production which exist in what have been called
the "Have-not" countries—listed in the lower bracket
of the table—and instead of using the word capitalism
in the top bracket, which embraces the "Have" countries, it might have been better to call it an economy
with the maximum of individual freedom. Capitalism
is used here and elsewhere in this book as a descriptive term for a comparatively free economy based
upon production for profit. In China, Russia, Japan,
Mexico and India one can find small communities
producing their living by methods as antiquated as
those used in the earliest days of civilization. In Russia at present, various forms of cooperation, communism and State capitalism are superimposed upon

vast areas in which the people live and work very
much as they have done for thousands of years.

Country	Natural Resources	Economic System	Political System	Living Standard
U. S. A.	Vast	Capitalism	Democracy	High ($1.36)
Britain	Medium	Capitalism	Democracy	High (1.25)
Australia	Medium	Capitalism	Democracy	High (1.12)
Canada	Vast	Capitalism	Democracy	High (.93)
Sweden	Medium	Capitalism	Democracy	High (.96)
France	Medium	Capitalism	Democracy	High (.75)
Denmark	Poor	Capitalism	Democracy	High (.68)
Norway	Poor	Capitalism	Democracy	High (.54)
Germany	Medium	State Domination of Industry.	Absolute monarchy. Hitler.	High (1.06)
Russia	Vast	State Domination of Industry.	Absolute monarchy. Stalin.	Low (.32)
Italy	Poor	State Domination of Industry.	Monarchy. Mussolini.	Low
Japan	Poor	State Domination of Industry.	Autocracy. Militarism.	Low (.14)
Mexico	Vast	State Domination of Industry.	Despotism. Despotic princes	Low (.09)
India	Vast	State Domination of Industry.	for 2000 years. Autocracy.	Low (.06)
China	Vast	State Domination of Industry.	Banditry. War Lords.	Low (.025)

In all the countries in the lower bracket the people
have been exploited with varying degrees of cruelty
by local, regional or national authorities in possession
of the legislative, judicial and armed forces of the
State. For lack of a better term, State Domination of
Industry is used to describe an economy planned for
the profit of those who govern. In India the native

princes are among the richest rulers in the world while most of their subjects live in abject poverty. Overlords of all types from the earliest days of civilization to Lenin, Hitler, Mussolini, Huey Long and other American political bosses of the present day seized the machinery of government in order to levy tribute upon the productive classes not only to satisfy their personal ambition but also to feed the forces which sustain them in power.

The figures in parentheses in the last column are the most reliable estimates I have been able to find of the average income per head per day in the various countries listed in the table. They have perhaps some value as a basis for comparison in attempting to judge the relative standards of living in many parts of the world. I have found no satisfactory figures for Italy. Without correction for the varying national economic systems and the cost of living, the figures mean very little. It is possible in an economic system dominated by the State for the national income to rise materially while the wages of the workers are falling and their hours increasing. On the other hand in countries such as Denmark and Norway, where production for family uses is extensive, the standard of living may be much higher than the average income per head per day would indicate. In terms of our dollar, the national income in the United States in 1929 exceeded by al-

most eight billion dollars the incomes of the 435,000,-
000 people living in Australia, Austria, Bulgaria, Canada, Chile, Denmark, Estonia, Finland, France, Germany, Hungary, Japan, Norway, Britain and Russia.
During the last ten years our position has deteriorated
when compared with some of the above mentioned
countries. In recent years France and the United
States, the New Deal countries, are slipping while
Russia and Germany, the totalitarian States, are moving forward. However, compulsory labor may increase
production enormously without improving the standard of living.

It is not to be hoped that everyone will agree with
the brief characterizations of the natural resources,
the economic and political systems and the living
standards of the various nations embraced in the above
table. The scale of living in many democracies may
be lower than that in the United States, but it is certainly much higher than that in any of the countries
in the lower bracket, with the exception of Germany.
Regardless of the character of the population and the
existing natural resources, the highest standard of living is to be found in those countries where the people
and their industrial activities have been allowed the
greatest freedom.

On the other hand the lowest standard of living
prevails in those countries which have had and now

have despotic governments. That is true of Russia, China, India and Mexico where the natural resources are amongst the richest in the world. With poor or medium natural resources but with democratic governments, Norway, Denmark and Sweden have higher standards of living than all but one of the countries listed in the lower bracket. Capitalism is a product of the freedom, thrift and hard labor of multitudes and their standard of living cannot be improved when they are the habitual victims of the interference and depredations of a despotic State. If a planned economy administered by a bureaucracy could produce and distribute wealth profusely the people in the autocracies would have been the richest in the world.

Before the war capitalism, although fettered in many ways, was making enormous strides in Germany and as a result the general standard of living there compared favorably with that of many of the democratic countries. It is well-nigh impossible to find out how much it has deteriorated in the last twenty-five years. The figures released by the National Socialist State are not believed to be trustworthy. Furthermore, little reliable information can be obtained in these days concerning the standard of living in Italy and Russia, in both of which countries the masses have always been desperately poor. If Germany is omitted from the generalization, it may safely be said that over 90 per cent of the people in the countries placed in the lower bracket have lived and now live in a condition which Americans would describe as utter destitution.

The achievements of a free economy in the democratic States in improving the standard of living among the masses were ignored by the communists and when the power of the Russian State fell into their hands they were not content with having rid the world of a Czar but immediately organized their forces to exterminate republics, democracies and capitalism wherever they existed in any part of the world. "Under the banner of the Workers' Councils, of the revolutionary fight for power and the dictatorship of the proletariat, under the banner of the Third International, workers of all countries, unite!" Ending with these words, written by Trotsky, a manifesto was issued announcing that the rulers of Russia intended to carry their fight for communism into every country. It was issued at a critical moment in Europe when the communists in Germany, Austria, Hungary and Finland were at the height of their power and seemed likely to join the ranks of the Russians.

The communists in the defeated nations were determined that no economic system should be permitted to survive which bore the image of the bourgeoisie. They wanted a child of a different type, indeed one quite new in the history of creation. It was to be

brought into existence by decree and the most astonishing series of proclamations ever issued by a government came from the Bolshevists, defining what
were to be the physical, mental, social and religious
characteristics of their prospective offspring. While
the Bolshevists were demolishing as fast as possible
every vestige of capitalism in Russia, a new social and
economic system was hastily designed. Fortunately or
unfortunately, the material basis for the new life was
lacking. Private industry had already collapsed and
instead of attempting to revive it the powerful government assaulted what was left of it with every
available weapon, even though the Bolshevists knew
that the new economic system with which they sought
to displace capitalism had not yet been born.

After the World War the people in Germany, Austria, Italy, Poland, Bulgaria, Roumania, Czechoslovakia, Yugoslavia, Finland, Estonia, Latvia, Lithu-
ania, Greece, Portugal and Turkey drove out their
lords and masters, altered their various forms of government and revolutionists of one sort or another came
into possession of the State. In a few of these countries,
private property was socialized and in most of them
inflation confiscated an important part of the wealth
of their citizens. "Throughout the Continent," Keynes
wrote in 1923, "the pre-war savings of the middle
class, so far as they were invested in bonds, mortgages

or bank deposits, have been largely or entirely wiped out." The extinction of a score of monarchs and their retainers was no loss and might have opened the way for universal democracy but the extinction of the middle class was fatal to any such prospect. After that, no large group was left powerful or intelligent enough to create strong republican states and no funds were available to revive vigorously the capitalist system. By direct assault in Russia and by monetary and other weapons in Europe, the revolutions had devoured the class which in previous centuries had carried on the fight for liberty and democracy.

It is not to be expected that revolutions should be guided by reason. In any case the able mariners who had been so clever in handling their tiny craft in the wild seas which immediately followed the war, lost no time, after they became masters of the great battleships of State, in burning their entire fleet of merchant vessels. In one way or another, in the terrible twenties the economic basis of life was destroyed for hundreds of millions in Europe and Russia. Many of the moderate socialists warned the communists of the suicidal nature of their policies. "It is impossible," said Kurt Eisner, "to turn over industry to the ownership of the community at a time when the productive strength of the country is nearly exhausted. You cannot socialize when there is nothing to socialize." The slaying of democracy will end in "the dictatorship of the reaction," declared the Congress of Socialists at Berne. That is a prophecy worth recalling. Nothing so disastrous and unexpected, involving entire nations, had ever occurred before with such swiftness as the extinction of the middle class and the destruction of the necessary economic basis for democracy. The triumphant revolutionists, who called themselves Marxists, refused to look at the world about them or abroad and believed that the wisdom of all ages was contained in the few pages of the Communist Manifesto of 1847. Most of them lived in countries where democracy was unknown and where capitalism was in its infancy.

Marx, as we have said, condemned capitalism mainly because it was, as he thought, increasingly impoverishing the masses. In his opinion this tendency was inherent in the system. Democracy was, he maintained, the political State of the most aggressive capitalists; it was one of their best tools for clamping upon the masses the chains of wage slavery. Nearly all the militants of the revolutions believed Marx and refused to admit that conditions had altered since 1847 and that the nations which were making the most rapid and substantial progress in the material well-being of the workers were those in which democracy was strongest and where capitalism had been allowed the greatest liberty to create industries and to carry on commerce.

As economic conditions in the United States are a complete refutation of the main doctrines of Marx, it may be worth while to consider briefly some of the facts. We are informed by the *Westminster Bank Review* that with a little over five per cent of the world's territory and about six and one-half per cent of its population the United States has more purchasing power than that of five hundred million people in Europe and consumes more of the world's goods than a thousand million Asiatics. During the decade of 1927-36—in which there were five years of falling incomes, widespread unemployment and industrial depression—our six and one-half per cent of the world's population have been consuming annually on the average 48 per cent of the world's coffee, 44 per cent of its tin, 54 per cent of its rubber, 21 per cent of its sugar, 72 per cent of its silk, 36 per cent of its coal, 42 per cent of its pig iron, 42 per cent of its copper, 24 per cent of its cotton, and 69 per cent of its crude petroleum. The United States operates 60 per cent of the world's telephone and telegraph facilities, 33 per cent of the railroads, and owns 78 per cent of the motorcars in use. It produces 64 per cent of the oil, 64 per cent of the corn, 51 per cent of the cotton, 39 per cent of the copper, 30 per cent of the lead, and 38 per cent of the coal of the entire world.

Dr. A. A. Potter of Purdue University estimates that Americans have the equivalent in mechanical power of more than 400 human slaves for each of the 30,-000,000 families in the country. In the last thirty years, he says, "the volume of production has doubled and the wages of the workers have increased four-fold." In a country greatly favored by its rich natural resources these are some of the achievements of capitalism and democracy. In America every prophecy of Marx has been refuted and that is true also in all other democracies.

There are two standards by which we can best judge the utility of any particular civilization: first, the volume of production and second, the distribution of the wealth created. Recently the National Resources Committee has issued a report which embraces its studies of the "Consumer Incomes of the United States." The figures presented are estimates based on data gathered from 300,000 families by a house-to-house canvass of W.P.A. workers. Several pages of this book could well be devoted to a criticism of the work done by the committee, but it is not necessary since it confirms what has been said above. Defective as the study is in many respects, a report of this sort is an effort in the right direction. If we had comparable data for, let us say, 1925-26, 1912-13, 1905-06, 1891-92 and 1881-82, we should know whether or not the money incomes of the poorer classes have increased with the passing years. As to real incomes, which are of course what we require before comparisons can be of value, we are left completely in the dark. It seems to be forgotten by government experts that "The labourer is rich or poor, is well or ill rewarded, in proportion to the real not the nominal price of his labour," as Adam Smith pointed out in his time.

Without having comparable data for earlier years in our own country or of the incomes of the various classes in other countries, it is, of course, impossible to judge when reading this report whether or not there is any reason to be proud of what has been accomplished in the United States. It is estimated that 69 per cent of our families have a *net* income of less than $1,500 a year. Those with an income of that amount or less are classed as "continually fighting poverty." If it is true that over two-thirds of our people are continually fighting poverty, how is it possible for our 131 million inhabitants to consume more goods than a thousand million Asiatics? How can a nation with 69 per cent of its families "continually fighting poverty" afford to consume 72 per cent of the silk and own 50 per cent of all the wireless sets and 78 per cent of all the motorcars in the world? Surely these figures are indications, not of poverty, but of a comparatively abundant life.

In 1936 there were 28,000,000 automobiles registered in this country of 29,400,000 families. A population of about 1,600,000 in the small state of Connecticut owns more cars than 170,000,000 Russians. The residents of Rhode Island own more cars than all the people of Mexico. Evidently the communist nations with their vast natural resources do not rank high in the abundant life. The state of Illinois has more cars than 84,000,000 Germans and the state of North Carolina more cars than 44,000,000 Italians. Obviously the totalitarian states are not moving very fast toward the land of plenty. If the wage earners of the United States are continually fighting poverty it can at least be said that they own more cars than all the inhabitants of Germany, Italy, Russia, China, Japan and Mexico combined. It would be interesting to know what Marx would think, if he were now living, to see unskilled laborers coming to their work and the unemployed arriving at the offices of the W.P.A. in their own motorcars. When Marx wrote his Communist Manifesto, even women and children were permitted to work twelve hours a day in factories and there was no limit, except human endurance, to their hours in domestic industries and on the farms. The money wages of all laborers (except agricultural) increased in the United

States seven-fold from 1840 to 1920. The wages of one day now equal the wages of seven days at the time Marx was beginning his study of *Das Kapital*. Although we remain in the dark as to the purchasing power of money now and then, it can hardly be disputed that capitalism has not increasingly impoverished the workers.

Let us return to motorcars. They are the best indication we can find of the standard of living now as compared to past years and in the United States as compared to that of other countries. A motorcar is an expensive, heavily taxed form of luxury which quickly depreciates. Many would prefer to see families with incomes of less than $1,500 a year building better dwellings for themselves as the Dutch, Swedes and English do, or buying farms where they could produce a measurable part of their livelihood and perhaps enjoy a fair degree of comfort when their breadwinners are unemployed. It is quite possible they would get more substantial satisfaction out of life than they can possibly get from the products which they are now purchasing. Two or three motorcars consume the value of a small house or farm in a few years. However, as there is no Stalin, Hitler or Mussolini in the United States, no one can issue decrees outlawing those tastes of consumers which may or may not be laudable. In a democracy the people can spend their money as they like and *Das Kapital* as it actually exists in a free State, lives to please and must please to live, which is not true of Bolshevism and Totalitarianism. This thought leads us to consider a conception of democracy and capitalism, the importance and implications of which have not been sufficiently emphasized.

The sovereign power in a capitalist system rests in the hands of the consumers and the sovereign power in a democracy lies in the hands of the voters. These tremendous levers would enable the people, if they were properly employed, to make this world their paradise. Ignorantly or improperly employed, they can make this world the poor thing it is. If the consumers want opium there will be traders who will find ways to get it for them. If the voters want criminals to run their government, plenty will be found to undertake the task. The money of the consumers will decide whether we are to be a nation on wheels or a nation of charming homes. Their votes will decide whether we are to have a government administered by honest and competent servants or one administered by bands of looting politicians. In a democracy the people can have what they want. Those capitalists who defraud them can be ruined as soon as the people withdraw their patronage. The politicians who deceive them can be retired as soon as the people withhold their votes. In the democracies the weapons in the hands of the people are all-powerful and the world is what the people make it.

The capitalist system is, as we have seen, enormously productive, but it has many of the defects of democracy. In order to maintain it as a sound economic basis and as an efficient force for promoting the welfare of the people, it must be kept on a truly competitive basis. Genuine competition between capitalists for financial success, between workmen for advancement, and between parties for political advantage would solve most of the problems of democracy. When capitalists obtain special privileges, when trade-unionists restrain ambition or restrict other men from working in their trades and when politicians use public funds to keep themselves in power, both democracy and capitalism are on the way out. The politicians, not the capitalists, are in these days the outstanding enemies of democracy. The voters are offered intangible promises, often forgotten, while the capitalist must turn over to the consumers in return for their money something which they can taste, feel, handle and use —in some manner test and pass judgment upon. If they continue being swindled, it is no one's fault but their own.

In a despotism, communist or totalitarian, the fate of the people is in the hands of the State. In a democracy the fate of both politician and capitalist is in the hands of the people. Elections occur only at stated times but the capitalist must face a continuous plebiscite of the consumers. Everyone who buys or refuses to buy an article is, so to speak, casting a vote. He approves or disapproves, buys or refuses to buy, and that settles the matter. If he thinks he has been cheated he will condemn the guilty. There will be no pardons and no probations. The people may be, and often are, deceived by clever advertising and high-pressure salesmanship, but over a period of time they are competent to decide which is the best article obtainable at the lowest price. This is not folklore; those capitalists who cannot satisfy the demands of their customers enter upon the road to ruin. And many of them are being forced all the time to take that road.

Manufacturers, farmers and merchants succeed by carefully watching costs, by offering a little better quality or a greater quantity of goods, and by these and other means actively and intelligently competing with their rivals for the pennies in the pockets of the consumers. In the long run the ones who get the most pennies are those who "deliver the goods." Except in a few industries the capitalist is at the mercy of the buyers. The exceptions are noteworthy: industries protected by some form of monopoly; the politico-criminal alliances in many cities; and the employment of corrupt public officials by racketeers of high and low degree to assault legitimate business. A book could be devoted to this practice which is one of the most insidious and menacing evils in a democracy. In a despotism a division of the spoils is unnecessary because the entire Council of State is in business for itself.

Extensive and deplorable as they are, the exceptions above mentioned need not overconcern us. They are diseases which can be cured. For the most part business subscribes to the dictum of Cicero: "Whatever is profitable must also be honest, and whatever is honest must also be profitable." A good trade name is a precious asset, difficult to acquire and easy to lose. It is earned by useful and faithful service to the public. What sensible man of business ever forgets that he is a servant of the consumer? Newspapers, motion pictures, foods, clothes, motorcars, houses, materials—everything for sale—must satisfy the buyer. The United States Steel Corporation, the public utilities and the railroads are buyers as well as sellers and they, no less than the workingman with a few dollars, must be satisfied. Capitalism issues no decrees. It cannot force the public to buy Ford cars, Ivory soap or Camel cigarettes. The public can buy what it likes. Although the general price level is beyond the control of the consumer—and over the long run beyond the control of bankers, producers and politicians—whenever the price of any particular article seems too high, the buyer can and will choose something else. Beef steaks and pork chops found that out when the planned scarcity of the New Deal was intensified by an unexpected drought.

A project owned by the government deals with the people on a different basis. If the consumer does not like its prices or the goods it offers, he must go without. There is no other choice. If he attempts to buy elsewhere he becomes a criminal. What capitalist would not like to be in the position of the government which decides arbitrarily what wages it will pay, what service it will give, what prices it will charge, and if the pennies of its customers will not pay its bills, the money required will be taken from them in taxes. No citizen can escape the direct and indirect exactions of the government. What it wants it can take.

In the United States the employees on government projects are, as we know, rarely selected because they are efficient or desire to please and serve the public. Wherever possible the jobs are given to those who can do most to re-elect the party in power. In the industries owned by the government we find "democracy displaced by varying degrees of despotism, merit displaced by patronage and straightforward dealing displaced by intrigue." There is no new revelation in these words of Arthur Morgan, dismissed by President

Roosevelt from his position as chairman of the Tennessee Valley Authority. The last word in the title of this project is well chosen. The old term Authoritarianism has not been used before in this book. It embraces the principle of enforced obedience to authority as opposed to individual liberty. The Bolshevist and totalitarian States are founded upon this principle and in economics as in politics its other name is Despotism.

The economic basis of democracy is a system of profit and loss in which multitudes risk their savings. In the long run the consumers decide which capitalists win or lose. But the system remains democratic only when proper laws and an incorruptible judiciary insist that the race be "free for all" with no favoritism shown to any of the contestants. Wherever the race has been run with little or no hindrance from government, the total earnings have been enormous, and while the profits of the few have been perhaps for short periods excessive, the benefits reaped by the masses have been prodigious. The building of automobiles has been one of the freest and most competitive of industries. Individual capitalists engaged in this business have come and gone. A great many entered the race and most of them lost, but each year more and more men have been employed at high wages and more and more millions have found it possible to buy the product as the quality has been improved and prices have been reduced.

Upon some forms of private industry here and abroad, the government has laid its inexperienced and shiftless hand. When it has bought outright certain industries, its successes, which have been few, are due almost entirely to the management of carefully chosen civil servants who cannot be removed from office by the party in power. Without subsidies, public ownership has rarely been the victor when faced with the competition of private industry. It may be useful where competition and profitable operations are not in the interest of the public, where the work is mere routine and innovations are not desirable, or where the community has taken care to choose competent administrators. In a limited field socialism may be beneficial, but this we know that wherever the State has attempted to control the hours, wages and prices of private enterprise, capitalism has languished, the people have been impoverished and the government has become more and more despotic. That has been true not only in the past but is also true in the present, as we have seen in Russia, Germany, Italy and Mexico.

Capitalism and democracy appear most attractive —perhaps one should say they are only attractive— when they are compared to other political and economic systems, past and present. In pre-war days when a socialist presented his visions of an ideal social organism, a critic was placed in a difficult position because no one can attack effectively something which exists only in another's imagination. That was true in the democracies and, of course, in Russia and many other countries, there were a hundred reasons why the ideals of the Utopians should have gained converts. Certainly there was little or no resistance to communism in Russia in 1917. The people did not know what it meant. They wanted the land and the workshops because they were propertyless and they were told they could have them. But opposition to State interference immediately developed as soon as the masses obtained possession of the confiscated properties. As a result of their hostility the communist system of production has never been able to function with any marked degree of efficiency.

Democracy is a clumsy, awkward thing and capitalism is too often a game of chance in which millions lose and win. Yet with all this and much more admitted, it is strange, in the twentieth century, the revolution triumphant should not have known that those areas which have permitted democracy and capitalism to bear their fruit have given to the people of high and low degree the highest standard of living ever known to the inhabitants of this earth. The entire world today is confronted with an old problem which has appeared again and again after long and exhausting wars. A decision must be made, is in fact being made. At the moment almost every indication leads to the belief that the "many-headed multitude" and their political leaders are convinced that only the State can solve the problems of our time. If this view prevails, the decision cannot be reversed without a bloody revolution in which the rebellious will have to fight the armed forces of government. Hitherto in the world's history revolts of this sort have not been fruitful except when new and independent classes have regained from the despots by centuries of toil some of the power and wealth which their ancestors had lost. The communists, Fascists and Nazis have permitted themselves to be made prisoners in wellguarded penitentiaries and they may like their new workshops, but if they do not, it will be no easy task to overthrow their jailers.

In the democracies the people are the supreme power. They choose their governors, legislators and judges; but what now frightens thoughtful democrats is the readiness with which people evade their duties and relinquish their rights and privileges. In the United States many million voters will not trouble to vote. The consumers make little if any attempt to organize and oppose those fiscal policies which increase their cost of living. The taxpayers seem only mildly interested in economy or the proper use of their funds. The citizens can rarely be aroused to turn out vicious public servants and select honorable and efficient ones. Most astonishing of all is the indifference of investors who own shares in large industrial enterprises. Few of them ever attend a meeting of stockholders. By proxies, they turn over to employees or to a small coterie of directors the management of their property. Voters, consumers, citizens and stockholders do not appear to have any conception of their duties or to realize that they are the sovereign power in the capitalist system and the democratic State. Nevertheless they remain the master who keeps in check to some degree the appetites of his servants, not because he is attentive to his interests but because he may one day become irritated and cause no end of trouble to those who swindle him.

We can never expect to be free from fraud, adulteration, politico-criminal alliances and malpractices of other sorts so long as people are permitted to make their fortunes by them. Laws already enacted, if properly enforced by an independent and upright judiciary, can protect the indolent masses in a democracy from both corrupt politicians and fraudulent capitalists; but unless the people are vigilant nothing will save them in the long run. We know the multitude of evils more or less inherent in a democratic-capitalist system but at their worst they are insignificant compared to those afflicting nations which have become the victims of the revolution triumphant. "Why," asked Cicero, "do we gather instances of petty crime—legacies criminally obtained and fraudulent buying and selling? Behold, here you have a man [Caesar] who was ambitious to be king of the Roman People and master of the whole world; and he achieved it!" Cicero also warned us that we can "never expect to be free of civil wars so long as people hope to make their fortunes by them." At the moment I am writing these words another name, that of General Franco, must be added to the long list of adventurers who in recent years have made their fortune by civil war.

The ancient art of the *coup d'état* and the technique of the revolutionists have been for twenty years the two most absorbing studies of the leaders of the warring groups in many countries. When the revolutions got under way after the war, the militants of Right and Left began to read of the methods and exploits of Dionysius, Agathocles, Sulla, Caesar and other dictators down to Napoleon. As soon as the books of Trotsky and Lenin were published, they became the textbooks of all classes of militants. Dreaming day and night of the time when that meaningless slogan of Marx—the Dictatorship of the Proletariat—would take form and substance, the communists swept away wherever possible every vestige of democracy and capitalism. Infatuated by the Communist Manifesto, which

had forecast the doom of private property and representative government long before they had begun to
bear their choicest fruits, the disciples of Marx in the
revolution triumphant destroyed the economic basis of
the only classes which might have withstood the armed
forces of the new brood of despots. The middle class
was crushed, the republicans and democrats were
thrust aside and the socialists and communists, fighting among themselves, prepared the way for "stern
men with empires in their brain."

3. *The Return of the Czars*

*I know from whom I flee without knowing to whom I
flee.*

—CICERO

Was ever feather so lightly blown . . . as this multitude?
—SHAKESPEARE

When Carlyle said of the uprisings of 1848, "im-
measurable Democracy rose monstrous, loud, blatant,
inarticulate as the voice of Chaos," he was talking
sheer nonsense. As we shall see in the next chapter, the
upheavals in his day, as in our own, have been inspired, organized, turned this way and that by small
bands of zealots. When conditions favored them daring
leaders followed by a few fanatical and well-disciplined converts have been able to foment revolutions.
As those who have looked beneath the surface know
this to be true, it is curious how widespread is the

conviction that the overthrowing of governments and economic systems is a product of mass uprisings.

The people of the present day differ little from the Romans of two thousand years ago. The man who expresses the mood of the public and has the right technique can lead or drive the masses wherever he likes. Lenin drove them into a Communist State, Hitler led them into a National Socialist State, and Mussolini into a Fascist State. It is the old story. When in poverty the people seek a benefactor. When they have been punished they seek an avenger. When they are fighting class or other wars they seek a hero. In the last twenty years men highly skilled in the arts of mastery have appeared on the scene. Like lion tamers they have called forth their beasts to do the tricks required and then with whip in hand they have sent them back to their cages again.

The most singular, disastrous, and humiliating years the European world ever saw were perhaps those following the Great War; but they were not singular, disastrous, amazing and humiliating because—to continue with Carlyle's words and thought—the people or the populace took their government upon themselves. Millions of armed men, hungry and unemployed, were crowded in the cities, towns and villages. Had they been capable of taking over their governments no one could have stopped them. Had they been disposed to murder, burn and pillage, no force then existing could have stayed them. The republican governments which first came into power immediately after the war begged the soldiers and sailors to give up their arms and ammunition, which few were willing to do. That is not surprising. The astonishing fact is how few serious offenses were committed by these armed and destitute masses. Except where some bandit or terrorist led them they did nothing at all. In Russia, where the misery was indescribable, they waited eight months for the Republic to solve their problems before some of them turned without much warmth, faith or sympathy to the Bolshevists.

Dirty, hungry, cold and bitter, they were sleeping in the streets or, in their waking hours, listening dumbly to the fiery speeches of Kerensky, the anarchists, the Bolshevists and the Menshevists. They were waiting, waiting, waiting; hoping, hoping, hoping. Hope deferred maketh the heart sick, and eight months was a long while for the empty stomachs of armed men to be denied. Nevertheless the communist revolution, when it came, was not of their making. A handful of insurrectionists, despising "the people," as their own words tell us, organized the successful assault. When Trotsky later drove the representatives of the people out of the Taurida Palace, they went home just as they would have done under the czars. Although elected by the votes of all Russia and backed by a large majority of the population, a few troops under Trotsky sent them scurrying into the cellars in terror of the treadmill or worse. That was the most fatal blow given in our time to progress and the hope, cherished by the Friends of Russian Freedom, for a peaceful birth of democracy in Russia. For those who relish grim irony and tricks of fate, that crime has exacted its appropriate penalty. Only one of those who planned that massacre of the Republic remains alive, Joseph Stalin.

Within less than a year after the first revolution, Lenin was seated on the throne of the Romanoffs, the people or the populace were being driven like sheep, Trotsky was in high command of the Red Army, and Zinoviev was graciously or ungraciously giving audiences to his people in the carriages and chambers of the Czar. It was not long before purges were begun to clean out of the party the moderate socialists. In 1918-19 over 128,000 were arrested. Later when the cities were on the point of starvation because the small peasant landowners refused to produce food on the terms offered them by the government, Zinoviev declared that it would be imperative "to crush them in the economic and, if necessary, in the physical sense." Lenin's address before the Congress for School Extension (May 6, 1919) is the most bitter attack ever made by the head of a government upon the habits and customs of an overwhelming majority of its citizens. With his words ringing in their ears, the Bolshevists tried every available method to make the peasants of Russia the serfs of the State.

There is no need to dwell upon the massacres, the terror, the Cheka and other measures and instruments required to subdue the nation. Disillusioned socialists, communists, anarchists and labor leaders have supplied us with an extensive literature upon this phase of the revolution. For our uses, Lenin's own words to the All-Russian Central Committee in 1921 are sufficient: "We made the mistake of deciding upon an immediate transition to communist production and distribution. . . . We counted (or, to speak more accurately, we assumed without counting) upon our ability to organize a system of nationalized production and nationalized distribution communistically in a petty-bourgeois country by means of a direct command on the part of the proletarian State. Life has shown us our mistake . . . In the spring of 1921, on the economic front, our attempt at the transition to communism sustained a defeat more serious than ever before."

Millions of peasants ("petty-bourgeois") passively and actively, so far as they dared, resisted with all their power the designs of the Bolshevists. In order to

save the Russian cities from starvation, the Dictatorship of the Proletariat has had again and again to
abandon parts of its economic program, and at times
it has been on the point of discarding communism
altogether. Under both Lenin and Stalin all sorts of
capitalist methods and incentives have had to be introduced in order to increase production. The stubborn
resistance of the people to the policies of the State
has been astonishing to those who knew what ruthless
methods have been used by the bureaucrats to enforce their decrees. The peasants have at times refused
to plant their land; they have hidden their grain; they
have killed their cattle; all because they bitterly re-
sented the communization of their produce, which was
only another word for confiscation.

Whenever the Bolshevists have attempted to na-
tionalize the land, which in 1917 they had instructed
the peasants to wrest from their landlords and divide
among themselves, thousands of small holders (Kulaks) each with a few acres of land and some livestock, have had to be exiled or shot. During three different periods the "comrades" in the cities were threatened with famine because of the antagonism of the
peasants to the Bolshevist regime. Again and again
Red soldiers were sent into the huts to confiscate whatever small hoards of foodstuffs could be found. By
every form of resistance the workers and peasants have

tried to wreck the economic system and today, despite the many years of incredibly brutal penalties, the *saboteurs* are so numerous in Russia that the system can be kept going only by having the agents of the government periodically shoot a few officials, peasants, and workers as a wholesome example to the others. This is called in Russia the "Workers' Paradise."

To a student of history and human behavior the experience of the Bolshevists in Russia is most illuminating. A small group of zealots may make a revolution; install themselves in the palace of the czars; and rule the people by every force at their command; but there are certain instincts, habits and desires which they cannot eradicate from the mind of the worker, the most tenacious being the love of family and of home, the desire to own property and to enjoy as he likes the reward of his labor. Tremendous efforts have been made by socialists and communists to convince the workers that they will receive larger rewards if they will all cooperate to produce wealth, pass it on to the State and later have "the full product of their toil" returned to them. They won't believe it. They are often persuaded to believe that it is to their advantage to have the State confiscate the property of the rich, but nowhere has anyone been able to make them think that they themselves would be benefited if their own small possessions were taken.

When a State is planning to confiscate the property of the people it should start at the top and proceed gradually downward. It should permit the peasant to own and feed all the cows he can raise providing he turns over most of the milk to the government. That is the policy of the Fascists and Nazis and as we know there has been no collapse of production in Germany and Italy such as occurred in Russia. On the contrary, the people in the totalitarian states are enormously productive and may continue so for many decades, if their wars are successful. But it is doubtful if industrial activities in these nations will be directed toward improving the standard of living of the many millions who have thus far shown no ability to resist the growing tyranny of the dictators.

Outside of Russia and Mexico, Germany is probably most advanced in the process of absorbing the earnings of private undertakings and in the growth of State financing. In 1928, less than 30 per cent of the total loans were for the account of the government. In 1936, 93 per cent of such issues were designed to provide funds for the State and its enterprises. We have no figures for Italy, but in France the same trend is to be observed. Only three million francs were invested in new enterprises in the first ten months of 1937, against about forty millions in 1931. An enormous decrease in private investment has also taken place in the United States. If the cause of this withdrawal of private capital from private enterprises is due to the antagonism of the State and if it persists for long, capitalism which is the only possible economic basis for democracy will perish.

Marx and other students of *Das Kapital*, as it lives and has its being, should have learned one elementary lesson about the conditions which are essential to its growth. The process of production requires the laying out of capital long before, in some cases many years before, any returns can be expected from the investment. No intelligent man of business will take such long risks with his savings or borrowed money when conditions are unsettled, and even the most venturesome are fearful of what lies ahead. Without confidence in the future, without trust in the government, without faith in the courts, and without some assurance that the laws of the game will not be changed, capital will not seek investment. "Nothing so cements and holds together in union all parts of a society as faith or credit," wrote Cicero at the time the Roman Republic was destroying both. No statesman before or since Cicero has pointed out so clearly as he did, at the moment of their occurrence, the causes of a nation's ruin. Every criticism he uttered at the time

Caesar and his allies were crushing capitalism, democracy and republican institutions in Rome could be repeated with justice and without the change of a syllable in many nations of the modern world.

The communists can be criticized for their ignorance and for their attempts to destroy capitalism, but it must be said they have never concealed their intentions. For decades they have published their programs, books and papers which left no one who read them in doubt as to their aims. It is true that each of the many sects which advocated the confiscation of private property presented its program to the public in a form as attractive as possible. And each time the sect acquired a bad name, the name was changed. The Marxists first called themselves communists. Later they became socialists or social democrats. After the war they appeared again as communists. In Russia they called themselves social revolutionists, communists, sovietists, bolshevists and menshevists. The Fabians presented an anemic, sapient prodigy particularly well suited to its intellectual environment, while the Syndicalists of France and Italy gave birth to a lusty, mischievous *gamin* who was fed and fostered by a sterile intelligentsia. By giving the Artful Dodger a new name he was able to come in at the front door immediately after he had been thrown out of the kitchen. When he was cast out as Despotism, he returned as Democracy. No human intellect ever came into this world better fitted to be this Devil's advocate than Bernard Shaw's. When this crafty counsel was present, no one was ever able to convict the changeling of any ignoble design. The prosecutor was invariably proved to be the knave until Lenin undertook to fashion Russia according to the plans of Marx. Fortunately for the enlightenment of the world this great adventure was undertaken and anyone who cares to study the results in Russia where the revolution was triumphant can learn some useful lessons.

It is stupid to say that the battle of this age is a warfare between ideologies, dreams and manifestoes. The absolute masters of nations cannot afford the luxury of ideologies. The conflict is one of appetites, personalities and national interests, and all of them stand naked before us. The revolutionists have taught us many valuable lessons, one of the most important of which is that two compact and well-disciplined minorities, by fighting with each other, can often assemble on either side of the conflict mobs of irate warriors, very few of whom know or appear to be interested in the ultimate aims of their leaders. Their only thought is to crush those gathered on the other side. A small body of militant communists bent upon the slaughter of a small body of militant Fascists can involve a whole nation in civil war, despite the fact that the millions who fight for the Fascists do not seek Fascism and the opposing millions who fight for the communists do not seek communism.

To start a fight is an old game of revolutionists, and it has been played with great success in recent years. A few Fascists in Italy, bent on the destruction of the communists, gathered behind them great masses of Italians who found that when they had won their battle they had lost their freedom. A few Bolshevists got enough support from the armed workers and peasants to destroy the young Republic and now all Russians find themselves under the rule of Stalin. The millions of Germans who feared communism and backed Hitler find themselves with a totalitarian State. It is absurd to believe that the Russian, German and Italian masses had the slightest conception of the real objectives of their leaders. They were interested only in what they were fighting to destroy. Sir Oswald Mosley has been using for years this technique in the hope of dividing the English people into Fascists and communists. It is also being used in the United States and many other places. That only a few thousands have become involved, despite many attempts to stage a battle, is a credit to the intelligence of British and American citizens. However, since the Great Depression, the conflict in France and the United States between the politicians, brandishing the overpowering weapons of State, and the industrialists, big and little, dominated, we are told, by Economic Royalists, Tories and Feudal Barons, has been fanning the flames of class warfare to the point where capital has ceased to be venturesome and democracy is in peril. Under the socialist, M. Blum, industry in France became stagnant and in the United States, the man-days lost in strikes and lockouts increased from 4,463,000 in 1932 to over 28,424,000 in 1937.

For many centuries the economy of a nation created a political system suited to its needs. Feudalism had its own peculiar political order which was sufficient for its day. "Bourgeois individualism," to use a term employed by Marx, necessitated liberty for the masses, and eventually that arrived. Capitalism and democracy were peacefully and rapidly spreading throughout the world, as we have seen, when the Great War placed the State in the saddle. Ever since, it has been riding, as they say in the cattle country, high, wide and handsome. Autocrats, Fascists, Nazis, Communists, Socialists, New Dealers, Popular Fronts, National Salvationists (Daladier's happy thought) have today this one thought in common that the State must regulate the affairs of mankind, although they quarrel bitterly over the man, the group or the sect best fitted, in their opinion, to serve their ends. We are now well advanced in a new epoch where the attempt is being made to reverse the old sequence of things. Instead of economic systems creating States suited to their needs, the States are endeavoring to create economic systems suited to their needs. This is a revolution in our approach to social problems which may herald the coming of a new era in the world.

John Law and many money managers since his time have told us that money is not the result but the cause of wealth. In some of the democracies, especially in France and America, the dominant political parties have accepted this credo. The communist, Fascist and Nazi dictators believe—most of them are students if not disciples of Marx—that labor is the source of all wealth, and they are using every power at their command to employ all the energies of their millions of laborers to produce wealth. If one had to choose between the two doctrines—more money or more work— most sensible men would have to admit that the dictators are right. Additions to the wealth of the world can come only from work and an exchange of goods and services. If the workers rely upon siege, sit-down and slow-down strikes to combat their employers, and the democracies upon paper money, taxes on enterprise and relief in exchange for votes to solve their economic problems, there can be no doubt that they will grow weaker and poorer as the years pass.

We are told that there is no unemployment in Russia and Italy. In Germany there is a shortage of labor.

Six million more Germans were at work in January, 1939 than in 1929. If the world could be assured of half a century of peace and if the wealth produced in these busy hives of over 300 million workers were used for improving their standards of living, there could hardly be any question about the future in Russia, Germany and Italy. However nothing of this sort can be expected. Aristotle, who knew much more about tyrannies than we do, found in them all that is bad in all governments, mainly because whatever is not absolutely essential to feed, clothe and house the working citizens is absorbed by dictators to support their armed forces. Moreover they must waste the produce of the workers upon military adventures. This we see also in our day and no less their supreme arrogance. According to Mussolini, their doctrine is, "Everything within the State, nothing against the State." "My leadership," said Hitler, "is quite absolute. I can even adopt unpopular measures if necessary." Stalin's purges speak louder than words. Law's scheme for increasing the wealth of a nation leads to economic ruin. The policies of the dictators lead toward serfdom.

A year before the end of the World War, a czar had returned. Others followed and in January, 1939, there were twenty or more ruling over as many countries with far greater powers than those possessed by the monarchs of pre-war days. We are beginning to see what the people have lost and we know, unless the trend changes, that the people of the future will have no opportunity whatever to decide upon the kind of government they are to live under or in what manner the production and distribution of wealth shall take place. Except in the democracies the day of the liberals, rebels and revolutionists is, for the time being, past. To one who has known many of them in the last half-century the change in their prospects is almost un-believable. Hundreds of them who fought all their lives against the Kaiser and the Czar lived to a ripe and usually less dangerous old age.

It is not difficult to collect a great mass of data to prove the contention of the revolutionists that the old autocrats well deserved their fate. It is easy to collect evidence of the brutality of many of the French and Russian rulers before their dynasties were overthrown. It was not, however, Louis XVI but the revolutionists who sent tens of thousands of opponents to the guillo-tine. It was not the Czar but Lenin, Trotsky and Stalin who stood every enemy against a wall and filled his body with bullets. "Don't you understand," said Lenin to Balabanoff, who was protesting against the reign of terror which he had inaugurated, "that if we do not shoot these few leaders we may be placed in the posi-tion where we would need to shoot ten thousand workers?" Why ten thousand workers in a "Republic of the Workers"? Tyranny from the beginning of time has excused itself on that ground. And so terror became a habit. "These crimes did not begin with Stalin. They are links in a chain that had been forged by 1920. They were implicit in the development of the Bolshevik method—a method which Stalin has merely amplified to incredible proportions."[2] In truth the czars had returned.

Hundreds of rebels have been destroyed by Hitler and Mussolini for every one imprisoned by their predecessors. It was not the guards of the Kaiser but those of the Social Democrats who shot Karl Liebknecht and Rosa Luxemburg. Bebel and Liebknecht were imprisoned in their early days but later both were allowed freedom to shout defiance at the Kaiser. Marx was exiled from Germany but he did not have his throat cut. I walked the streets of Berlin with Karl Liebknecht the entire night before he went to prison for his attacks upon German militarism. He told me he had been given several months to collect his library and to arrange his private affairs before he was called to serve his sentence. He was grateful for the opportunity he would have in prison to read, write, and work upon *Antimilitarismus*. Many of the Russians I knew thirty years ago had been banished to Siberia

[2] Angelica Balabanoff, *My Life as a Rebel*, New York: Harper & Brothers, 1938.

for their political views. Almost all of them had escaped. Thousands—including Bakunin, Nechayeff, Kropotkin, Plekhanoff, Lenin and Trotsky—lived afterward in exile, free to carry on incessant agitation not only against the country of their birth but also against the countries which gave them shelter.

From almost every country in the world old Russian revolutionists rushed back to their native land in the spring of 1917. There were thousands of them. Had they been treated in their early days in the same manner that Stalin now deals with his opponents, there would have been for them only Heaven or Hell in which to preach their doctrines. Stalin was sent five times to Siberia and each time escaped after a short period of imprisonment and returned to Russia to fight the Czar. So far as can be learned the present Czar has permitted no outspoken critic or opponent in Russia to escape the firing squad.[3] Compared to the modern dictators, Louis XVI, Nicholas II and the Kaiser were benevolent rulers.

And what about Germany? Trade-unionists and socialists enjoyed almost complete freedom. Bismarck, the Iron Chancellor, after trying for years to suppress the rapidly growing Social Democratic party, capit-

---

[3] Among the notables who have recently been put out of the way are: Zinoviev, Kamenev, Rykov, Bukharin, Radek, Sokolnikov, Tomski, Serebriakov, Smirnov, Piatakov, Yevdokimov, and almost the entire general staff of the Red Army.

ulated in 1890 and for twenty-four years the revolutionists were allowed to fight their industrial and political battles almost without hindrance from the State. In its effort to combat the Social Democrats, the German State had organized a system of social insurance, more comprehensive than that in any other country before or since, to protect the workers against poverty due to unemployment, sickness, invalidity, old age and death. State and municipal socialism was taking over many forms of industry. Slum areas were being demolished and large apartment houses were being built about parks and playgrounds. The effect produced by these reforms of the State seems to have been the reverse of what was expected. The working class became more discontented and the Social Democrats more powerful.

Other countries in Europe adopted similar measures to appease the workers. In Italy, the government was corrupt and inefficient but the masses were allowed complete freedom to carry on revolutionary propaganda and to organize their syndicates and socialist parties. Mussolini and Balabanoff when menaced by mobs were protected by the police and rushed to safety in a cab provided by the authorities. Today in Germany and Italy no individual is permitted to express an opinion which is objectionable to the party in power. The people are not permitted to have their own papers, parties, unions, elections, leaders or legislative bodies. In these countries as in Russia only one view may be expressed and only one interest served. It is well not to be indifferent to a trend that is affecting the lives of hundreds of millions on this planet. Repetition of facts we all know grows tiresome and we become so inattentive that most of us do not seem to realize that in the last twenty years the democratic achievements of centuries have been wiped out.

Those who set violent upheavals in motion are usually the first victims of their folly. Every change of scene brings forth a new set of actors with objectives often diametrically opposed to the ends desired by the rulers who preceded them and always opposed to those sought by the ones who led the revolt in its earliest stages. If one were an insurrectionist as incorrigible as Blanqui, he would be wise to go forth to meet the boastful Kaiser and the frightened and superstitious Czar, if they were about to return, with music and flowers, because he would have the comfort of knowing that were he to squall with rage at their conduct of affairs he might be spanked and sent to bed, or he might be asked to leave the country, or again he might be condemned to some unwholesome spot to do hard labor, but he would not suddenly be stood up against a wall and riddled with bullets.

Anyone who ever attended an international gathering of the socialists in pre-war days must forever be recalling to mind old friends who had beautiful dreams of a better world for all humanity. At each recurrent purge in Russia, Germany and Italy some of the old kindly faces reappear. The "better world" has no place for them now, and let those who remain alive in their "ideal societies" utter no sigh of protest for that will be treason and their comrades will give the orders to the firing squad. To the young rebels of the present day the advice of an indulgent father would be to practice their Art (that is what Marx called it) solely in the democratic countries. In such political climates they will live longer and enjoy better health. It is true that where there is "universal suffrage" there is no need for a violent revolution, but one cannot expect a revolutionist to believe it. No one could wish to offend those ardent, impatient young idealists who think that an active and daring minority, without the consent of the governed, can make a better world or one nearer to their hearts' desire. The best one can do is to assure them they are wrong, if there are lessons in history worth remembering.

The impoverishment of Russia, the reign of terror and the despotism of "the dictatorship of the proletariat" produced a violent reaction throughout Europe. The tyranny of the Czar had been largely if not entirely directed against political rebels. The tyranny of the Bolshevists was directed against every type of rebel. Their main attacks were made upon those who differed with them in politics but this warfare was a minor affair compared to their attempts to force the entire Russian people to accept the official view upon religion, education, family life and private property. Rarely has terrorism like this been known in the world before. The revulsion throughout Europe was not confined to the upper classes. Most of the trade-unionists and socialists also expressed their abhorrence. The reaction was running high after Mussolini led his legions to Rome. The next year Hitler tried his *Putsch*. The vicious cycle, which began to operate with the declaration of war, entered its second phase with the *coup d'état* of the Bolshevists in Russia and passed into its third phase when Mussolini prepared the way for the return of the czars into Europe.

In resorting to war to prevent revolution the autocrats created what they had tried to destroy. In the revolutions which followed, the communists created what they had fought to destroy. Apparently they who take the sword perish with the sword. It reminds one of the outcry of Prometheus:

> Whilst I behold such execrable shapes
> Methinks I grow like what I contemplate.

Another simile comes to mind, dramatically pictured

by Dante in the revolting conflict between a man and a serpent. Eventually each combatant is transformed into the likeness of his antagonist. The serpent stands up, a man, and the man slinks down, a serpent.

In recent years it has been demonstrated that as soon as a socialist becomes a democrat he ceases to be a conspirator and insurrectionist (Engels, Bebel, Briand, MacDonald, Vandervelde, Branting and many others) and as soon as a socialist becomes a conspirator and insurrectionist he ceases to be a democrat (Lenin, Trotsky, Stalin, Bela Kun, Pilsudski, Mussolini). In every one of these successful revolutionists we find the instincts and characteristics of a czar. When Lenin realized that the Bolshevist insurrection could not win the active support of the masses he said to Trotsky, "There is only one rule: Succeed. You prefer Napoleon to Kerensky, don't you?" There is a logic here which cannot be denied. As we shall see in our next chapter Trotsky and Lenin were right. In every war—civil, revolutionary, or foreign—the people must be classed and treated as human zeros, and every independent mind turned over to the firing squads. In the story of her life as a rebel, Angelica Balabanoff has made this perfectly clear.

And more than that appears. When posing as democrats, the modern revolutionists have been imposters. Balabanoff depicts herself "as a nerve o'er which do creep the else unfelt oppressions of this earth," and this she was, but in her entire book not one word of sympathy is expressed for the thousands of peasants who have been shot and the millions who have had the produce of their labor confiscated. Believing that all evil is the product of private property, she suckled what she now pictures vividly as a litter of wolfish bandits, the betrayers of democracy who have become the czars of the present day. She loves the socialists who died before the revolution and reveres many who failed, but she has nothing but contempt for those who were successful. Inscribed upon the title page of her book should be the words of that venal, bloodthirsty, self-adoring product of the gutter, Danton, who lamented, as he was led to the guillotine, "At last I perceive that in revolution the supreme power rests with the most abandoned."

CHAPTER IV

STUDIES IN TECHNIQUE

Men are guilty of the greatest crimes from ambition, and not from necessity. No one, for instance, aims at being a tyrant to keep himself from the cold.

—ARISTOTLE

---

1. *The Catalines*

WE HAVE seen that favorable economic and political conditions must exist before a country is ripe for revolution; but they alone are not enough to assure victory for those who are bent upon overthrowing a government. Realizing that revolution is war, the more intelligent insurrectionists, before attempting their assaults, have carefully developed for themselves and their agents a more or less complete technique in the use of the instruments and arts of war. Both the strategy of the campaign in general and the tactics of employing effectively the units of action have been often minutely worked out in advance. The methods cannot always be the same, as each situation, nationality, and field of battle presents its own peculiar problems. The forces to be combated also differ, even though the economic derangements torturing the populace and creating the internal strains and convulsions may be almost identical.

The techniques which interest us can be classified under these headings: The Militarists, the Catalines, the Bolshevists, the Termites, and the Demagogues. With histories and biographies available it is not necessary to dwell here upon the methods used by generals in their *coups d'état*. Technically the movements of Agathocles, Hieron, Gelon, Sulla, Caesar, Cromwell, Napoleon, and others too numerous to mention, were much the same. With armies at their command they were direct, brutal and irresistible.

Farthest removed from the successful assaults of the war lords have been the feeble, though often sanguinary, rebellions led by those who may be classed as Spartacists or Catalines. Their attacks have been ill-advised and mis-timed, while their inadequately armed followers have been destitute, unruly and irresolute. Without any carefully planned method of warfare, their mad revolts have been utterly disastrous; and without the sympathy or support of the populace in general, their attempts at revolution have been easily suppressed. A few pages are alloted to abortive revolutions because they taught the Bolshevists what not to do.

More space will be given to Lenin and Trotsky because of the originality and simplicity of their technique. As a result of their success a new school in revolutionary tactics developed. Although his aims were different and the legions he led were anti-communist, Mussolini employed his forces on the same lines as the Bolshevists. Hitler profited from the experience of both the Russian and Italian revolutionists.

The conditions in Italy in 1922 and in Germany in 1933 differed greatly from those in Russia in 1917 and, therefore, it has been necessary to allot special sections to the Fascists and Nazis. The story of Joseph, the Termite, is taken as an outstanding example of those who bore from within while Plato's outline of the technique of a demagogue has been used because nothing superior to it can be found in literature.

As we are not dealing with the Militarists we can turn our attention first to the Catalines. They have relied upon the indigent as a revolutionary force. Cataline, it will be remembered, undertook to form a party of the propertyless and gathered about him peasants wanting land, the unemployed, the bankrupts and the large number of impoverished veterans who had returned to Rome penniless from the wars. All the discontented were welcomed into the fold, including criminals, outlaws and slaves. The rage aroused by

Sulla's brutal executions and reprisals had created a host of rebels who also looked to Cataline, secretly supported by Caesar, for leadership. Heavily in debt he was desperate when he lost his election to the Senate and, in an attempt to seize the State, died fighting at the head of his bedraggled army. Many servile upheavals had occurred in earlier days and many more were to come in the centuries that followed, but, menacing as some were at the time, none of them was successful in the Western world.

All of the Catalines have made the same mistakes. Thinking that revolutions were the product of depressions and that the forces to be employed were the "down and out," they organized mass uprisings of the lowest classes, only to find that they could neither direct nor rely upon them. What Marx calls "the passively rotting scum" or "the *lumpenproletariat*" was to them hopeful material out of which to assemble the cohorts of rebellion. This class was numerous at the time of Cataline's insurrection. It was, I think, Plutarch who said that the man who first ruined the Roman people was he who first gave them gratuities. Revolutions from below need not be feared when a majority of the people have become mendicants. Battles for power will continue between those who rule and those who hope to rule the State; but the conflicts will be confined to the court and the army. When Cataline launched his insurrection, the masses were rebellious but a large proportion consisted of the pauperized wards of the Republic and there is no possibility of recruiting from such material first-class, fighting revolutionists. Marx understood this perfectly.

There have been hundreds of Catalines Some of them aristocrats and nobles, dissolute and disreputable, much like their famous prototype; others, like Nechayeff, were downright criminals; most of them were peasants, serfs or slaves such as Spartacus, Jack Straw, Wat Tyler, Hans Mueller, Stenka Razin and Pougatchoff. Religious zealots such as John Ball led widespread revolts while anarchist or socialist fanatics such as Babeuf, Bakunin and Blanqui were the forerunners in aim, though not in strategy, of the communist revolutionists who led the uprisings which immediately followed the Great War.

Babeuf was a journalist who had enthusiastically supported the "share the wealth" ideas of Robespierre, "The Incorruptible," who had slaughtered rich and poor alike as "the enemies of the people." Conditions in Paris seemed to be overripe for an assault upon those who had sent this hero of the communists to the guillotine. A majority of the population had been ruined by the insane decrees of the criminals and demagogues then in control of France and there was an abundance of indigent material at hand to encourage those who desired to lead an insurrection. Born of a union of terrorists, communist theorists, unemployed workmen and destitute members of the lower middle classes, Babeuf's secret *Société des Egaux* hopefully published its program advocating equality of wages, the abolition of poverty and the common ownership of all the necessaries of life. By means of an elaborate and minutely planned conspiracy, Babeuf was collecting his forces to overthrow the government when the authorities got wind of his activities. He and thirty of his comrades were arrested and shot. Veteran revolutionists were then in control of the State and they knew instinctively how to deal effectively and finally with disaffected allies. Although Babeuf was executed, his ideas could not be buried with him and again and again they were revived by the insurrectionists of later days.

There were many upheavals during the nineteenth century but there were no revolutions in Europe. There were many Catalines but no Lenins. Two of the most notable of those who sought to arouse the impoverished to revolt were Bakunin, the exiled Russian anarchist, and Blanqui, the French insurrectionist, who had within them a spirit of rebellion which could not be quelled. I shall not repeat here what I wrote of Bakunin in *Violence and the Labor Movement*, but Blanqui must be given a few words. He was an incurable insurrectionist who came to be called *l'Enfermé*, because so many years of his life were spent in prison. As soon as the authorities released him and an opportunity arose he was leading a mob to storm the fortifications of government. His life was a series of unsuccessful assaults upon authority, launched in the hope that if he could place the power of the State in the hands of a dictator, a communist system of production could be organized immediately. He was a man of the street, who had only to shout his orders to an army of thousands who were always eager to follow him. Blanqui used to say, so Kropotkin relates, that there were in Paris fifty thousand men ready at any moment for insurrection. Again and again he arose like an apparition among them, and on one occasion, at the head of two hundred thousand rioters, he offered the dictatorship of France to Louis Blanc.

In their earlier days Marx, Engels, Bebel, Liebknecht and other intelligent socialists thought that the working class in a period of widespread unemployment would overthrow the existing capitalist system. At a singularly inappropriate moment (in 1845) Engels delivered himself of this prophecy: "The people will not endure another crisis. . . . By the time this crisis arrives the English people will have had enough. . . . A revolution will follow with which none hitherto can be compared. The proletarians, driven to despair, will seize the torch which Stephens has offered to them; the vengeance of the people will come with a wrath of which the rage of 1793 gives no true idea. The war of the poor against the rich will be the bloodiest ever waged."

Similar opinions were expressed by other leaders. However the failure of every uprising in Europe from 1819 to the crushing of the Commune in 1871 and the tragedies attending the many violent assaults upon the established order, such as those of Blanqui and Bakunin, taught the socialists that nothing of value could result from these ill-timed attacks of the indigent upon organized society and forced them to alter their views completely. Another development also was having its effect. They were astonished at the electoral successes of the socialist parties after the eighties. What Marx in his early days had scornfully called "parliamentary *cretinism*" no longer met with criticism. The leading socialists became politicians and thought their entire program could be carried out legally and peacefully.

When the powerful trade-unions and cooperatives combined their political efforts with those of the socialists, the voting strength of the united movements increased enormously. By 1913 this coalition had attracted over 11,000,000 votes. In no less than twelve parliaments they had over ten per cent of the representatives. In Great Britain the Labor party had over one million dues-paying members, and in Germany alone in 1913 the Social Democrats had polled 4,250,-000 votes. Now on the crest of the incoming tide the outlook for the socialists was very different from that in earlier days. In the nineties Engels had come to this conclusion: "The time for small minorities to place themselves at the head of the ignorant masses and resort to force in order to bring about revolution is gone. A complete change in the organization of society can be brought about only by the conscious co-operation of the masses; they must be alive to the aim in view; they must know what they want. The history of the last fifty years has taught that." Engels had become a democrat. In method he had ceased being a revolutionist. He had discarded the weapons of the Catalines —conspiracies, barricades, and insurrections—although socialism remained the goal. The oustanding parliamentarians of the socialist movement in Europe fell into line.

2. *The Bolshevists*

When in consequence of their disputes and quarrels with each other either the rich get the better of the poor or the poor of the rich, neither of them will establish a free state.

—ARISTOTLE

Romanticists who relish the discovery of some apparently trifling incident as a turning point in history

would do well to study the proceedings of the second
conference of the Russian Revolutionary Socialist and
Social Democratic parties. They held their sessions in
Brussels and London in the year 1903 and the delegates were almost exclusively intellectuals, loquacious
doctrinaires and exiles, representing hostile groups
always eager for sectarian warfare. However, they
made a favorable start toward harmony when they
adopted unanimously the stereotyped Marxian program drafted by Plekhanoff and Lenin. Later they
were torn asunder by a bitter conflict over the revolutionary tactics proposed by Lenin, who maintained
that it was preposterous to believe that the masses
could be converted to socialism, or that their active
support was required in a revolution. The only imperative was the organization of compact, fighting units
of secretly chosen professionals working under the
direction of a completely trustworthy generalissimo.
When the vote was taken and it was found that the
majority (Bolshevists) supported Lenin, the minority
(Menshevists) were infuriated. To understand the
reasons for the violent conflicts aroused by this decision of the conference, which have continued unabated
to this day, the reader would have to know a great
deal more than has a place here of the history of Russian revolutions, of the Okhrana, and of the titanic
battles between Marx and Bakunin for control of the

International Workingmen's Association.[1] It is doubtful if the Menshevists believed with Engels that in
Russia a beneficial reorganization of society could be
accomplished *only* with the conscious cooperation of
the masses but they did believe that within the socialist movement itself the principles and machinery of
democracy had to be preserved.

Lenin's victory was an omen of immense significance.
It meant that the Bolshevists had abandoned democracy and the hope of converting the masses to socialism. It was an act of despair, based on the conviction
that if czarism and capitalism were to be overthrown,
the work had to be done by a small minority of the
population. Lenin had no ambition to be another Cataline leading a bedraggled army of the indigent. He
was not a general and did not expect to become one
but he did want to begin at once to muster fighting
troops which would conquer Russia for the socialists
in the same manner that the armies of Caesar, Cromwell and Napoleon had conquered Rome, England and
France. No dictator of the past had won his victories
by a vote of the people or because of their active support. If the socialists hoped for success they had to be
realists and adopt the techniques of their opponents.
When Lenin emerged from the conference as the master of the most militant section of the Russian revolu-

[1] The history is given at length in *Violence and the Labor Movement*.

tionary movement, a turning point had been passed in its history and his conquest in October, 1917, marked a turning point in the history of many nations in Europe.

After Lenin's death, two books, which had been his most intimate companions for many years, were found by his bed. Both were studies in the technique of war. They were Marx's *Civil War in France* and Clausewitz's *Concerning War*. As a student and instructor in the strategy of class conflicts, Marx is little known outside the inner circles, but Lenin, Pilsudski, Bela Kun, Mussolini and others were graduated *cum laude* from his school of revolutionary tactics.[2] Upon world developments, *Das Kapital*, the work best known of Marx, has had far less influence than his brochures, pamphlets and letters devoted to the timing, the employment of man power, the conditions and the tactics which he thought were essential to the success of revolutionary movements.

Lenin's greatest achievement was his complete mastery of what was called the art of revolution. To the study of this art, he devoted his best talents and as the

[2] In the hope of fomenting revolutions and civil wars, the Bolshevist "master technicians" in Moscow selected agents to carry their messages, disburse their money and organize their forces in many parts of the world. As leaders, most of them have been failures and as *provocateurs*, they have usually been the forerunners of reaction. The names of these agents are well known: Radek, Lukacz, Rakowski, Borodin, Thores, Pollitt, Diaz, Thaelmann and Browder.

years passed he found himself more and more at odds with the leaders of the International Socialist Movement. Engels' conversion to the processes of democracy, Lenin considered convincing evidence of senility. When he realized that Plekhanoff could not free his mind from the Marxian dogma that there was a sequence in the evolution of civilization which could not be altered, Lenin broke with him. If it were true that all nations had to pass from feudalism to bourgeois individualism and from that stage to full-blown capitalism, before it was possible to have proletarian communism, it was obvious that a revolution in Russia could not be expected for a century or more. Lenin was determined to have a revolution in his time and he meant that nothing should be allowed to stand in his way.

Lenin had not been able to collect his invisible armies or to instruct them in his technique in preparation for the Russian Revolution of 1905, but he was on the ground as an observer learning many useful lessons. When two years later he returned to exile in Switzerland, he was more convinced than ever that only by the use of the methods which he had so carefully and systematically developed could the socialists be successful in a period favorable to revolutionary action. While Lenin was formulating and refining his views, an interesting new development was under way in the labor movements of France, Italy and Spain. Many groups in these countries were actively opposing the democratic policies of the socialist political parties. The most vocal of these Latins were the old anarchists and the revolutionary syndicalists who were influential in the trade-unions during the decade preceding the war. Siege, sit-down, slow-down and general strikes, accompanied by various forms of sabotage, were being advocated in those days as the most effective weapons which could be used by the proletarians. Aristide Briand and many other ambitious young lawyers began their political careers by advocating the use of these instruments of war. Arturo Labriola, Émile Pouget, Guérard, Griffuelhes and others found one outlet for their revolutionary views in the columns of the handsomely printed *Le Mouvement Socialiste*, which was edited and financed by a small coterie of the intelligentsia. This new school of syndicalists was unfolding a social philosophy and a technique of revolution which attracted many of the most ardent of the younger socialists.

Some of the ideas of the syndicalists are worth recording here as they show the trend in opposition to democracy which was causing serious concern to the leading socialists. "Syndicalism and Democracy," said Émile Pouget, "are the two opposite poles, which exclude and neutralize each other. . . . Democracy is a social superfluity, a parasitic and external excrescence, while syndicalism is the logical manifestation of a growth of life. It is a rational cohesion of human beings, and that is why, instead of restraining their individuality, it prolongs and develops it." Democracy is, in the view of Sorel, the regime *par excellence* in which men are governed "by the magical power of high-sounding words rather than by ideas; by formulas rather than by reasons; by dogmas, the origin of which nobody cares to find out, rather than by doctrines based on observation." Lagardelle declared that syndicalism is post-democratic. "Democracy corresponds to a definite historical movement," he said, "which has come to an end. Syndicalism is an anti-democratic movement."

These are three out of the many criticisms of democracy which might be quoted from the writings of this school of revolutionists. Expressing as they do the antagonism of the syndicalists to democracy, these ideas developed rapidly into a new technique for controlling the movements of the working class. The minority must drive the majority. Guérard suggested, in his advocacy of the general strike, that if the railroad workers struck, many other trades "would be compelled to quit work. . . . A daring revolutionary minority conscious of its aim can carry away with it the majority." Pouget declared that, "The syndicalist has a contempt for the vulgar idea of democracy—the inert, unconscious mass is not to be taken into account when the minority wishes to act so as to benefit it. . . ." He referred in another place to the majority who "may be considered as human zeros. Thus appears the enormous difference in method," he concluded, "which distinguishes syndicalism and democracy; the latter, by the mechanism of universal suffrage, gives direction to the unconscious . . . and stifles the minorities who bear within them the hopes of the future."

Although Lenin did not call himself a syndicalist his program of action was in harmony with these anti-democratic or post-democratic principles. In fact his doctrines and technique of warfare were becoming a curious composite of what the leading socialists were denouncing as fundamentally anti-socialist. As he proceeded to piece together his synthesis of conspiracies, storm troops and the Propaganda of the Deed, formerly advocated by Bakunin and Nechayeff, of the direct action and industrial formations promoted by the syndicalists and of Marx's ancient myth, the Dictatorship of the Proletariat, Lenin was forced at the same time to discard altogether the programs and methods which were then cherished by the socialist parties of Europe.

It is true that Lenin had never been a Utopian, but he had the reputation of being one of the most bigoted defenders of the Marxian dogmas. However, no one had a keener or more critical mind and he realized that many of Marx's forecasts had failed to materialize. For instance it was clear that capitalism was not increasingly impoverishing the workers and that big-scale, mechanized agriculture was not ruining the small landowners. Consequently, as a realist and incorrigible revolutionist, Lenin was forced to adopt the technique of a demagogue. When he promised land to the peasants and factories to the workers, many socialists agreed with Rosa Luxemburg that a program of that sort would retard communism indefinitely. The peasant would become as he had in France *un petit bourgeois* and the trade-unions, *syndicats* and soviets would develop into corporations or guilds warring incessantly over hours, wages, prices and the distribution of their products.

Upon the great strategist these criticisms had no deterrent effect. Lenin's aim was revolution and, as he had not forgotten that the peasants had been of no use in the Russian Revolution of 1905, he knew that they and the factory workers had to be bribed to win their sympathy and support. To offer them communism or socialism, the meaning of which they could not understand, would not win them. What they wanted were specific pledges of immediate and tangible benefits such as bread, land, work and peace.

What was given them could be taken away when the Dictatorship became master of the situation.

With every detail of his technique carefully formulated, Lenin awaited his opportunity, which would come the moment the Czar's armies were defeated in the war. Lenin had made it clear at Stuttgart in 1907, that a European war would open the door for the socialists and so, immediately after the vast armies began their conflict in 1914, he issued his famous broadcast: "Yes, we hope for the defeat of Russia—the abolition of her slavery, her liberation from the chains of Tsarism." The Menshevists believed that Lenin's statement was an open invitation to the German secret service to come to his support with money, men, transportation and other essentials for promoting sedition in the Russian army. Each for his own ends, the Kaiser and Lenin were of one mind in their desire for the defeat of the Russians.

The great Bolshevist was truly a man of destiny. His opportunity came in precisely the manner he desired. His technique worked out to perfection and his plans and specifications proved to be faultless. As a conqueror, his conquest was complete; but, as he later confessed quite frankly, his excursion into the realm of communism by the slimy path usually chosen by demagogues made it necessary for him to subdue the populace by becoming the most truculent of tyrants.

However, had Lenin not lured the peasants, workers and soldiers by pledges which he had little or no intention of fulfilling and which were, in fact, in opposition to his designs, the Bolshevists would not have been victorious in Russia.

In dealing with plans and theories we have got ahead of events. Let us now see how Lenin's ideas worked out in the revolution. When Lenin arrived in Russia in 1917, the whole country was in chaos. Probably two hundred thousand deserters, with arms and cartridges, were milling about the streets of Petrograd, and somewhat the same spectacle, in less degree, was to be seen in every city, town and village in Russia. Liberals, Republicans, Social Democrats, Social Revolutionists, Bolshevists and Menshevists were haranguing the masses. Soviets were forming in all the larger centers and these included not only all classes of workers but most of the soldiers and sailors. Colonel Polkovnikov was issuing military orders and seemed to be under the delusion that he could whenever he desired arrest and imprison all the discontented. That was nonsense. All that was required at the time was to imprison or exile Lenin, Trotsky, Kamenev, Zinoviev, Sverdlov, Smilga, Stalin, Djersinsky, Bukharin and two or three others, not one of whom was a workingman.

The new cabinet of the Republic moved farther and

farther to the Left until eventually Kerensky, the impassioned orator and moderate socialist, was put forward as a pledge to the people that their demands would be granted. Lenin and his *enragés* were planning their *coup d'état*; but their plans were not matured when, in July, troops of mutinous soldiers and reckless rebels seized some strategic positions and fought for three days to defeat the loyal troops of the Provisional government. As soon as Lenin saw that the insurrection was doomed, he fled into hiding. Trotsky, Lunacharsky and Kamenev were arrested, but whether because of fear or of the high ideals of democracy which Kerensky professed, they were set free after a few days.

Had Kerensky been a first-rate revolutionist, instead of a sentimental democrat, he would have known instinctively what had to be done with the leaders of the ill-timed uprising. He would have sentenced to death all the leaders who had had any part in it. When Cromwell heard there was mutiny in one of his regiments his orders were: "You must cut these people to pieces or they will cut you in pieces." That is the way Lenin, Trotsky, Stalin, Mussolini and Hitler, the real revolutionists, dealt with their antagonists. Tolerance, liberalism and democracy avail nothing in a revolution. As Machiavelli said, "in seizing a State, the usurper ought to examine closely into all those injuries which it is necessary for him to inflict, and to do them all at one stroke. . . ." Mercy is considered a sign of weakness and cowardice. Ruthless, swift and unexpected purges are imperative in a revolution if *the leader* is to survive.

It has been said that if ten men had been shot after the July insurrection the history of Russia, and perhaps that of all Europe, might have taken a wholly different course. There is an obvious fallacy in this supposition. Had Kerensky purged the land of his enemies he would have destroyed Lenin, Stalin and many others but in the process would have himself become the czar of Russia. In Russia, as in France a hundred and twenty-five years before, the moderate elements yielded to the more violent until the only ones fitted to survive were Lenin, through the first Reign of Terror, and later Stalin, the Man of Steel. There is no use trying to imagine what might have happened had Kerensky managed to keep in control of the situation. There is a logic in history, as in a cycle of revolution, which has a way of asserting itself, no matter what steps are taken or what men play the leading roles.

The failure of the July insurrection sobered the revolutionists and weeks were spent by the Bolshevists in heated discussions upon the program and the strategy to be employed in the next uprising. Lenin was disturbed about many phases of the problem. The ghosts of the Catalines were tormenting him in his sleep. He began to examine all aspects. Inflation was rampant. The currency was rapidly becoming valueless. The number of rubles in circulation had increased during the ten months from 9,103,000,000 to 18,917,000,000. In a time of widespread unemployment, general distress, a rapidly rising cost of living and a shortage of foodstuffs, Lenin had little fear of the masses turning actively against him. But would they be for him? Four groups of the unorganized had to be attracted: the deserters; the soldiers and sailors who, though loyal, did not want to fight any longer; the peasants begging for the land; the unemployed seeking work and the hungry wanting bread.

Each of these groups had to be offered something, bribed in some manner to support the Bolshevists until the Republic was overthrown and the Dictatorship got control of the machinery of government. Lenin knew well how often in Russia a handful of loyal troops had suppressed mass uprisings and how the peasants of France had been the bitterest opponents of the Commune. Peasants had usually been counted upon as the main support of the conservatives and the counter-revolutionists. The following slogans were phrased and all over the country Lenin's agents were impressing them on the minds of the multitudes: All power to the Soviets! Land for the peasants! Factories for the workers! Bread for the hungry! Peace with Germany! No other revolutionists in history have had a more favorable moment for offering so alluring a program to tempt the masses to give armed support to their designs.

As programs do not make revolutions most of Lenin's time in hiding was spent in writing long letters to Trotsky and the Central Committee of the party, carefully outlining the methods which should be employed before making another attempt. Revolution should be considered as an art, he cautioned the Central Committee, and begged them to recall the rules laid down by Marx. "Applied to the present situation in Russia," Lenin wrote, "these rules include: (1) a swift and sudden general offensive on Petrograd; (2) an attack, both from inside and out, from the workers' districts in Finland, from Revel and from Kronstadt; (3) an offensive with the whole fleet; and (4) the concentration of troops greatly superior to the government's forces which will not exceed 20,000 Cadets and Cossacks. Our three chief forces, the fleet, the workers, and the military units, must take over the telephone and telegraph exchanges, the railway stations and the bridges and hold them at any cost. We must recruit tenacious storming troops whose duty it will be to occupy all the important bridges and to take part in every decisive engagement. We must also form gangs of workers armed with rifles and hand grenades who will march on enemy positions and on the officers' training schools and surround them. The success of both the Russian and the world revolution depends on a two or three days' struggle."

Lenin's program of action, while desirable, was beyond the capacity and resources of the Committee, and Trotsky retorted: "As far as strategy is concerned, Marx himself could be outdone by Kornilov. We must concentrate on tactics, move in selected areas with a few men, concentrate all our efforts on the principal objectives, strike hard and straight. It is not so complicated. Dangerous things are always extremely simple! But we must not challenge an unfavorable circumstance nor trust to a favorable one. Hit our adversary in the stomach and the blow will be noiseless. Insurrection is a piece of noiseless machinery. Your strategy demands too many favorable circumstances. Insurrection needs nothing. It is self-sufficient."

Evidently Trotsky did not intend to follow the instructions of Lenin nor the rules of Marx. He was in a powerful position as President of the Petrograd Soviet and also of the Revolutionary Military Committee, the authority of which was acknowledged by the garrison. The sailors of the Baltic fleet were restless and eager to support with their arms any program of action proposed by the Bolshevists. Kerensky had only two battalions of troops and one company of women. Under such favorable military conditions Lenin's plea for a direct assault was sound but Trotsky was faced with at least two problems which seemed to him personally of great importance.

The Central Committee of the Bolshevists was dominated by Stalin and his friends and they disliked and distrusted Trotsky. Moreover they had their own plan of campaign and were at work organizing their forces for a mass insurrection supported by a general strike. With the armed forces at their disposal a mass upheaval such as they proposed gave every promise of being irresistible. However, Trotsky was annoyed by the hostility of the Committee and was by no means sure that the workers in the essential industries would strike whenever he chose to issue his commands. In some of the Soviets the Bolshevists were decidedly in the minority. Trotsky alone knows whether or not at that advanced stage in the preparations for revolution he sincerely believed what he wrote to Lenin or was being forced by unfriendly elements to adopt the perilous tactics which he actually employed. In any case he declared: "What we need is not the bulk of workers, deserters and fugitives, but shock troops."

The strong point in Trotsky's technique was that with small, well-disciplined forces he could keep all movements under his own control. Mass upheavals have never been controllable or effective in revolution.

A general strike can be the means of destroying those who set it in motion. While he welcomed the emotional support of the surging masses they would serve him best if they were ignorant of his specific objectives. He encouraged everywhere infuriated, disorganized and chaotic demonstrations, but his own actions must be directed against a few vital points and entirely invisible not only to the government but also to the populace. "Insurrection," he said, "is an art. It is an engine. Technical experts are required to start it and they alone can stop it."

Hitherto only the militarists had known how to stop a revolution after it had placed them in power. Trotsky, a master of all forms of revolutionary activity, could have taught the militarists, who in other periods had placed their mailed hands on the State, all the tricks of their trade including some which they had never known. Napoleon lost his nerve at the critical moment. He stammered, nearly fainted and was ejected from the Council of the Five Hundred in a state of mental and physical collapse. His brother Lucien saved the day for him. All of which is related in the histories.

Before the crucial hour arrived Trotsky had prepared his blueprints of every important step to be taken before and after the *coup d'état*. His storming parties and shock troops were being schooled and in charge of their movements he placed a former officer of the army, Antonov-Ovseënko. From the mass of revolutionary workmen, soldiers and sailors, he selected with care about a thousand comrades who could be trusted under all circumstances. He then organized them into small groups according to their skill for the jobs in hand and instructed them minutely in what he called "the invisible maneuvers." Most of them were directed to go about their work unarmed so as to arouse little if any suspicion. They moved quietly through the mass of deserters, camping or milling about in the streets, and lounged about the barracks, the important bridges, government buildings, post offices, railway stations, telephone and telegraph offices, in order to make notes as to the best methods to employ in taking complete possession of these services and all strategic points as soon as Trotsky gave the signal. For weeks they discussed and practiced "the art of insurrection." As technicians they were expected to learn not only the best method for paralyzing all the means of communication and transportation used by the government but also how to put them immediately, when instructed to do so, at the service of the Bolshevists. As time passed, Lenin and Kamenev became more and more impatient and fearful. There seemed to be no common purpose among the various Bolshevist groups, each following its own theory as to the best method of launching the revolution.

Eventually the momentous hour arrived and the armed troops and technicians of Trotsky took control of the railways, the telegraph, the telephones and other essential services. All orders came now from the Bolshevists. The members of the government could not send a message which did not pass through the hands of Trotsky. They were unharmed and thought they were still at the head of the State, unable to realize for some hours that they were no longer the ruling power. They huddled together in the Winter Palace, guarded by Cadets, rejoicing that there had been no *coup d'état*. They still had their heads on but their arms and feet had been cut off. The essentials of life, activity and power were now in the hands of Trotsky's shock troops. The next day Trotsky ordered his forces to attack the Winter Palace, and the members of the Council of the Republic were taken prisoners. Lenin and most of the leaders of the Soviets could not believe, until after the Palace had fallen into their hands, that the State had been captured and all Russia was theirs to do with as they liked. [3a]

An account of the activities of the revolutionists throughout the vast area of Russia would serve no useful purpose here. Detailed descriptions of minor battles, civil wars and the movements of the various conflicting forces can now be found in many books. More useful to us is a knowledge of the methods used

by the leading surgeons. Their technique was the
acme of simplicity and effectiveness. In the writings of
Lenin, Trotsky, Stalin and others there can be found
no impersonal, unbiased and objective account of the
operation. Each one is convinced that he alone conceived the strategy and tactics which placed Russia,
swooning, prostrate and helpless, in the hands of the
Bolshevists. Lenin may be excepted partially from
this generalization as he gave a great deal of credit to
Trotsky. Perhaps this was due to his fear of Stalin or
to his habitual policy of inciting vain, powerful and
jealous subordinates to direct their plots and conspiracies against each other rather than against him.
Lenin had no good reason to fear Trotzky but many
reasons for fearing the Man of Steel, as later history
proved. Of the Committee which Stalin claims organized the revolution, he alone remains alive. All the
others have been his victims. Some of them have been
shot. Others have committed suicide. Trotsky, not a
member of the Committee, was assassinated in Mexico.

After the *coup d'état* there remained one important
operation still awaiting the surgeons. They had cut
from the social structure every institution but one
which might menace their dictatorship. The Republic
had decreed that all citizens of both sexes who had
reached the age of twenty should elect by popular vote

their representatives to a Constituent Assembly. During the widespread disorder following the Bolshevist victory these elections were being held but despite the bribes, pleadings and threats of the communist officials and soldiers, their opponents obtained a large majority. When the elected representatives assembled in Petrograd and endeavored to enter the Taurida Palace they were confronted by guards who forced them to leave. Some were arrested as "enemies of the people."

Eventually, however, the other representatives of the people were permitted to meet, surrounded by Trotsky's troops, as the members of the Duma had been surrounded eleven years before by the troops of the Czar. Ignoring this attempt to terrify the members, the Assembly, after overwhelmingly defeating the Bolshevist candidate for the Presidency, Marie Spiridonova, refused to vote its approval of some of the communist decrees issued by the new government. This was treason and the Constituent Assembly was ejected from the Taurida Palace. The new czars then solemnly announced that they could not permit the people to make decisions in a period of revolution or to obstruct the minority which bore within its breast the hopes of the future. As Trotsky said, "In a revolution, the people are of no use." At a single blow the young Russian democracy was decapitated. One hundred and sixty million Russians had no conception of what had happened to them nor of what the new regime had in store for them.

3. Mussolini

He who builds on the people builds on the mud.
—MACHIAVELLI

During the years immediately following the war, Italy was ripe for revolution. Although she had not been one of the defeated countries, the communists were winning many recruits and some of the leaders were familiar with the methods used by the Bolshevists. The economic system was prostrated by strikes, mutinies and rebellions. The government was impotent. Some of the factories had been seized by the workmen and converted into fortresses, stored with arms and ammunition. Had there been in Italy a communist tactician with Trotsky's talents the course of events might have taken a wholly different trend.

Prices were rising and the value of wages was falling. The high cost of living and the "exactions of the profiteers" had infected the army, police and civil servants with the fever of sedition. High-ranking officers of the army were spat upon and the crowds in the streets often attacked and beat them. Parliament, under the control of the Parties of the Left, was supporting the revolutionary activities of the communists. The police

3a It seems at this writing that Trotsky's tactics have been used with paralyzing effect by Hitler in preparation for his invasion of Norway, Holland, Belgium and France. (May, 1940)

would not, or dared not, attempt to control the mobs, and, when in 1920 some peasants and workers took possession of the land and the factories, holding the owners as hostages, the judges were too terrified to interfere. When Giolitti, the Prime Minister, was appealed to, he answered: "Let the workers see for themselves how difficult it is to conduct an industry. Let them find from experience how bad is the state of trade! Let them run their heads up against economic laws! Besides, our troops are all needed to protect the public buildings."

In the midst of this turmoil the lonely and portentous figure of Mussolini was emerging from the mass. Dictators usually arrive on the scene in the later stages of a revolution when the people are prostrated by the fury and hatreds of class and civil wars. Mussolini appeared before the revolution had got under way. The shock troops employed by him to conquer Italy were fashioned after those used by Trotsky and Lenin in Russia. But the situation in Italy was different and, so far as I have been able to learn, the performance of Mussolini is unique. To overthrow a democracy—called in Italy a socialist monarchy—was without precedent, especially as the country was in the early stages of a civil war similar to the one which later devastated Spain. In a masterly manner he carried out a turning movement and without a major battle directed the cohorts of rebellion into a path which led them into an all-powerful one-man State consciously designed by the plain-spoken Mussolini to force upon the Italians abject obedience to every command which he was pleased to proclaim.

The dictators mentioned by Aristotle were demagogues or generals or both. Mussolini was neither a demagogue nor a general. Caesar, Cromwell and Napoleon were backed by armies when they seized the powers of the State. Napoleon, Hitler and other despots arrived as counter-revolutionists and then only after the people were sick unto death with the internal chaos prevailing at the time. Lenin and Trotsky came into power after defeat in war when inflation was running wild. In Russia the Republican government was new, weak and inefficient. In Italy, the government was seated in the saddle and with the forces at its command could have maintained order had it made an effort to do so. Italy had been on the winning side in the World War, and although the lira was rapidly depreciating, it had not become valueless. In the election of 1919, Mussolini had polled only a few votes and the paper which he had edited before the war described him as a corpse ready for burial. The rapid rise to power of this undaunted spirit—unaided by the army, an established party, money, family prestige, or posi-

tion—is one of the most incredible achievements in
history.

Mussolini did not use any of the wiles of the Greek
Tyrant to attract a following. As he was not in power,
he could not bribe the people with their own money.
He did not offer them land, factories, or the property
of the rich. He did not flatter or beguile them. On the
contrary he often berated and insulted them. On one
occasion he said: "I do not tell you, O people, that you
are as gods. As I love you truly, so I should say to you
that you are dirty, you must arise and cleanse yourselves; you are ignorant, therefore set yourselves to
gain instruction. . . . Horny hands are not enough to
prove a man capable of guiding a State. . . . You can
make a revolution in twenty-four hours, but you cannot
in that time create a new social order for a nation
which is part of a world order."

These are not the words of a demagogue and in
fact Mussolini had at this time no connection with
the corrupt and supine politicians of his country. He
had no patronage to distribute. He was not in Parliament and even held himself aloof from membership
in organizations which might have helped him. He
used none of the baits which demagogues in his own
and other times employed to attract the masses. He
had been one of the most intelligent and well-informed leaders in the powerful socialist movement.

He resigned from it and poured upon it torrents of
rage and contempt. With his own refinements he employed the methods—technicians and shock troops—
of the Bolshevists but scorned their appeals to the
mercenary and rapacious instincts of the masses. He
never at any time promised them the abundant life.
Work, order and peace between capital and labor
were the main points in his program for a united
Italy. He was not in a position to offer bread and cir-
cuses, and in fact such were not in his line. Mussolini was the outstanding phenomenon of the early
post-war period. He believed himself, and his conviction has not changed, to be the reincarnated and
distilled essence of Caesar and Augustus with all the
charm and intellect of Marcus Aurelius thrown in,
destined by the gods to recreate in some heroic manner the Roman Empire.

Circumstances were favorable and Mussolini knew
how to make use of them. The political Termites had
so undermined the foundations of the State that it
was disintegrating. There was a corrupt, pusillani-
mous government and a parliament of cretins. One
of the revolutionists had said that most of the members would take their daughters to the brothel if this
would obtain for them money or votes. The more
intelligent and high-minded Italians were nauseated
by the corruption and political impotence of the gov-

ernment. The socialists and trade-unionists voted for their "friends," but they despised them and thought of Parliament as the House of Prattlers. Mussolini made the most of this antagonism. In the industrial sections the communists were constantly at work stirring up senseless disorder and the greatest sufferer, the working class, was becoming disgusted. The demand for some sort of interference with their malicious activity was rising and in many groups the conviction was growing that only a dictator would be courageous enough to suppress them. For two years Italy endured all sorts of violent outrages but definite signs of an anti-Bolshevist reaction did not become manifest until the communists had murdered some of their political opponents in Bologna, Modena and Ferrara.

Mussolini, as a student of history, knew that disorder is the most dangerous enemy of democracy. Like other aspiring dictators before him he denounced mob tyranny and like many of his predecessors he organized mobs to fight mobs. The areas infested by armed communists were systematically invaded by armed Black Shirts. At times as many as fifteen thousand Fascists would march into a town and not only attack the meetings of the Reds but also destroy their offices, printing presses, Labor Exchanges and Cooperatives. The clashes became more and more savage between those who had property or wanted to work and those who had nothing and did not want to work. There was war in Italy for four years between land-lords and peasants, capitalists and workers, Fascists and communists. Many outrages were committed and a great deal of blood was shed. With the police intim-idated and many high officials unwilling to align themselves openly on either side, Mussolini's program of "beating up" the communists eventually broke their spirit and more and more workmen, small tradesmen and ex-soldiers—who wanted to work or to sell their wares—fell in behind the militant Benito.[3]

Organizations of Black Shirts were forming all over Italy. In 1921, the socialists and communists were astounded when they lost to the Fascists thirty-three seats in Parliament. Mussolini, thrilled by his victories at the polls, dramatically rebuked his own unruly forces who could not be kept in check by their local chiefs: "The nation turned to us when our movement appeared as a liberator from a tyranny; the nation will turn against us if our movement takes on the guise of a fresh tyranny. . . . The nation needs peace in order to recover, to restore itself, to fulfill its highest destinies. You do not understand, you do not wish to understand, that the country wishes to work without

[3] Approximately 40 per cent of the Fascists were trade-unionists. Some of them had taken to heart the words of the Italian Socialist delegates who reported after their inspection of conditions in Russia: "The only equality which has been achieved is the equality of universal misery."

being disturbed. I would enter into alliance at this moment with the devil himself, with Antichrist, if that would give this poor country five years of tranquillity, of restoration, of peace."

Mussolini was too well schooled in the methods of revolution to expect the populace to be moved for long in any direction by sentiment alone, and he continued to organize his fast-growing following into a hierarchy which would have made Bakunin envious. Although he declared that a revolution has no chance of success unless "it is surrounded by a halo of sympathy by the majority," he maintained that it could *only* be carried through to completion by small groups under perfect discipline, and he proceeded with care and persistence to build up his armed shock troops and technical experts. He had taken a page out of Trotsky's book and used adroitly the technique of the Bolshevist to destroy Bolshevism in Italy. Nearly every move made by Italy's man of destiny and his legions was attended with success, and as success attracts the multitude, tens of thousands of recruits rushed to enroll themselves for service in an organization which was soon to be the dominant power in the State. Under the name of Law and Order mob tyranny was victorious. To attack in others what you propose to do yourself is one of the maxims of a dictator.

In August the opponents of the Fascists combined to stop the progress of Mussolini by calling a general strike. Immediately Il Duce sent forth his technical experts to capture strategic positions and within a few hours all of Italy was in the control of his 200,000 Black Shirts. This was the final blow to all serious opposition, although it was not until October that the hour came for "the march on Rome." At a congress in Naples Mussolini spoke with definite authority to his troops, confident at last that nothing could stand in the way of their victory: "Today, without striking one wounding blow, we have conquered the burning, vibrating soul of Naples." All Italy now seemed aflame and he demanded that "the government must be handed over to us, or we shall seize it by marching on Rome!" In every part of Italy the cry was rising, "To Rome! To Rome!"

In many places the Fascists were already taking possession of the local governments. At Cremona the Black Shirts seized the telephone, the telegraph, the postal services and the public offices. Barricades were being erected in various parts of the country and Mussolini, knowing the hour to strike had come, summoned his troops to mobilize for the attack. Remarkable for the fervor and breadth of its appeal, the manifesto reveals also his absolute confidence in himself and in his forces:

Fascists of Italy!
The hour for a decisive battle has struck! Four years

ago, the National Army entered upon the supreme offensive which was to lead to Victory: today the Army of the Black Shirts grasps that incomplete Victory and, marching with determination on Rome, leads her back to the glories of Campidoglio. Today, Leaders and Legionaries have been mobilized. The martial law of Fascism has been put into force. Under the orders of the Chief, a secret Quadrumvirate has been formed, with a mandate to concentrate all the military, political and administrative functions of the party in their hands.

The Army, as the supreme reserve and safeguard of the Nation, ought not to take part in the struggle. Fascism lays renewed stress on the deep admiration it feels for the Army of Vittorio Veneto. Nor does Fascism march on the agents of the public administration, but against that class of imbecile and mentally deficient politicians, who, during four long years, have not known how to give a Government to the Nation. Those classes which compose the productive bourgeoisie know that Fascism wishes only to impose discipline on the Nation and to aid all those forces which assist its economic expansion and its well-being.

The working classes, the people of the fields and of the factories, the transport workers and the civil servants, have nothing to fear from the Fascist rule. Their just rights will be loyally observed. We shall be generous to our unarmed adversaries. We shall be pitiless towards the others.

It is interesting to observe that Mussolini at the most critical moment of his life offered no bribes or panaceas. Economic expansion, discipline and national glory were his slogans. No other dictator had ever conquered a nation with a program like that. He asked the army to remain neutral and assured the civil servants, capitalists and workers that they had nothing to fear; but he did not plead for their support. The only group attacked were the "imbecile and mentally deficient politicians." Interesting also is the sequence of the crises which made it possible for Mussolini to gain his recruits: Widespread unemployment after the war; inflation which forced up the cost of living; deflation and depression which again threw multitudes out of work. A prolonged epidemic of strikes paralyzed industry, and fear of the revolutionary prattlers and socialist incompetents in control of the government so completely disrupted the capitalist system as to make dictatorship the only alternative to civil war.

Aristotle tells of democracy being destroyed and the power of the people lost at Thebes, Megara, Syracuse and Rhodes through anarchy and disorder. That is what occurred in Italy. The government not only permitted Mussolini to build up his own private army but refused to discipline the Bolshevists who by their riots were vindicating the counter-assaults of the Black Shirts. The leading socialists of pre-war days—Marx, Engels, Liebknecht, Bebel, Guesde and Jaurès—issued many warnings to the effect that anarchy and disorder are the forerunners of reaction. When Marx was battling with the Bakuninists, he permitted his agent, Moritz Hess, to denounce them in these words: "Between the collectivists of the International and the Russian communists there is all the difference between civilization and barbarism, between liberty and despotism, between citizens condemning every form of violence and slaves addicted to the use of brutal force."

Either the "Socialist Monarch" and the politicians of the Left had not studied Marx or they were hoping that if they permitted the two private armies to destroy each other they would escape being cast out of their high positions. The same illusion possessed the politicians of Spain and Germany in later years. The result in the first instance was civil war and in the second, Hitler. *L'expérience* Blum created similar disorders in France and while most of his projects were discarded when the war with Germany united the snarling factions, one would be overly optimistic to believe that prosperity will continue if when the war ends, the class feuds should once more appear.

In Italy the reaction was rising like a flood tide.

On the 28th October, Mussolini, still in Milan, had brushed aside the proposal that he should take office under Salandra. "Tell him I will not come to Rome to discuss and compromise. Unless I am given an absolute mandate to form a government—my own ministry—I will not leave Milan, save to place myself at the head of the legions."

At midday, on the next day, October 29th, General Cittadini, *aide-de-camp* of the King, called up Mussolini on the telephone.

A silence fell upon the room.

"Yes, certainly. I thank His Majesty. I should like to receive confirmation of the official mandate by telegram. I will leave for Rome at once."

Half-an-hour after, the yellow envelope was delivered.

"His Majesty the King begs you to come at once to Rome. He wishes to offer you the task of forming a ministry. Signed—General Cittadini."

Notified by telegrams, telephone, messengers, the legionaries cheered and shouted, "To Rome! To Rome!"[4]

From the train carrying him to Rome, Mussolini informed the immense crowds gathered about the stations: "Tomorrow Italy will not have a ministry. She will have a real government. . . . We have won a great victory. It is our victory, we must not spoil it. Until the new government has been formed, you will remain under arms. What we have taken we shall hold. I insist upon the strictest discipline, the most complete order and absolute sobriety. Italy is in our

[4] Margherita G. Sarfatti, *The Life of Benito Mussolini*, New York: Frederick A. Stokes Co., 1925, p. 312.

hands and we swear to lead her back into the ways of her ancient greatness."

The Fascists had accomplished their task with little or no violence against the State, although they were prepared to use it in case of need. Great stores of arms and ammunition had been placed at many strategic points and large sections of the Italian army were believed to be sympathetic. "Revolutions will be accomplished," said Mussolini before his march on Rome, "with the army, not against the army; with arms, not without them; with trained forces, not with undisciplined mobs called together in the streets." Later he returned to the same thought: "For my part, I prefer fifty thousand rifles to five million votes!"

Dictators must always have their fingers on the trigger and when they reach their goal they know that their first task is to put out of the way everyone offering the slightest criticism or opposition. Mussolini began his purges as soon as he came to power and every man or organization threatening in any manner to be a source of danger was wiped out. It is the irony of fate, sardonic and derisive, that the revolutionary technique of all the counter-revolutionists since the Great War was bequeathed to them by Lenin and Trotsky. Mussolini refined it and Hitler profited from the experiences of his forerunners. The Bolshevists fashioned the tools and their enemies found that they could use them with even greater skill than the inventors.

4. *Hitler*

A tyrant is chosen out of the meanest of the populace.
—ARISTOTLE

My father embarked upon his venture at a time when democracy was hated.
—DIONYSIUS THE YOUNGER

Most of those who have written at length about the rise of Hitler have directed their studies too much to his personality and far too little to the conditions which produced him as well as to the character of those Germans who find in him a mirror of their own souls. Whether or not he has an authority complex or an Oedipus complex or is psychopathic, matters less than what appears to be the most tragic fact of our time that he expresses in thought and action the desires and passions of a majority of Germans. The German people are on trial, despite all that can be said by their defenders. If Hitler is mad, so are his idolators, as he is at the moment the visible sign of emotions, rational and irrational, which are dominant in millions of them.

The Greeks observed that people do not easily change, but love their ancient customs. Tacitus, two thousand years ago, gave to the Romans his valuation of the "fierce and independent spirit" of the Germans, and they are now as they were then, militant, orderly, disciplined and efficient. They are self-centered, emotional, vain and intensely patriotic. They believe in their own castes. No power is great enough to save those who lead them to defeat; no god higher in their hearts than he who leads them to victory. In times of peace and plenty they quarrel among themselves, but let outsiders threaten the Fatherland and they will obey any command of their rulers. The ruthless, unshackled family of Wotan will not be enchained for long by another people.[5]

The Germans have always thought themselves surrounded by enemies threatening their Kultur. For centuries they have been taught in their cradles to dread "The Barbarian Hordes" in Russia which would one day swarm into their country and try to crush them. That is a national complex, born of an old experience, from which they have never been able to free themselves. Moreover defeat in war is to them

---

[5] When Hitler became the dictator of all Germany, largely due to his vehement denunciation of the "barbaric penalties" of the Treaty of Versailles, many friends of the German people were inclined to think, as I did, that if only Clemenceau and Lloyd George had understood the character of the Germans they would not have condemned them to the black regions of despair which were sure to produce a Lucifer. In May, 1940, one is horrified to recall that in the space of seventy-six years, the Germans (among whom the Prussians were the chief offenders before 1870) have invaded the territories of their neighbors no less than twenty-five times, robbing them of land and possessions and in some cases of their political independence.

the greatest of all humiliations and it was inevitable that sooner or later they would find someone to do for them what Joan of Arc did for France.

It may seem far-fetched to compare Germany after 1918 with France in the early years of the fifteenth century. Yet the conditions and the mental state of the Germans which enabled Hitler, a brooding, passionate fanatic, to assemble his vast legions and take possession of the throne of the Hohenzollerns were not unlike those which existed in France when the fanaticism of La Pucelle aroused that battered nation to revolt against the English. With the support of Philip of Burgundy, the English armies had conquered most of France north of the Loire. In 1412, the infant English King, Henry VI, had been proclaimed King of France, and the native heir to the Crown stood helplessly by as he watched the progressive dismemberment of his country. The French army had degenerated into bands of robbers, and class strife had divided the people into bitterly hostile groups, each bent on the destruction of the others. The nation was torn asunder by social upheavals resembling those which afflicted Germany after the World War. National leaders of indomitable courage, fanatical zeal and unfaltering purpose were called for and in both cases, as often happens, they appeared.

If to think of the anarchy in France in the fifteenth

century as in many respects like that in Germany after the war seems far-fetched, it will appear ridiculous to believe that the role of Hitler today has any resemblance to that of the Maid of Orleans. But when arousing a nation to arms a Sadist may serve as well as a Saint. Had the President of the German Republic sold Hitler to the French to be burned at the stake the comparison might not seem so absurd. Instead of a Saint, he has become in the eyes of the world a rival to His Satanic Majesty, with a matchless talent for infecting and reinfecting multitudes of Germans with his unquenchable thirst for the blood of his most vulnerable and defenseless neighbors at home and of all abroad who will not meekly pass under the yoke of his imaginary Wagnerian race of Nordics. That is the common judgment of the hour, if not the verdict of history. And as a matter of fact it is beside the point, which is that Joan and Adolf did appear when their nations were torn by internal hatreds and, interesting as it is to speculate about their true characters, far more important than they are the conditions which produced them, which in fact made them inevitable.

When driven to despair men often turn in their search for satisfaction or relief to some form of cruel fanaticism. The man of the hour if he is to express the chaotic emotions of the masses must be rabid, im-

petuous, fervid. He must reflect in himself as in a
mirror the hope, love, yearning, pride, hatred—all the
passions good and bad which burn in the souls of
the populace in a time when they are the victims
of overwhelming disasters. As a register for the rising
and falling emotions in the hearts of the Germans,
Hitler is an instrument of acute sensitivity. In his own
being the popular passions run riot and he plays upon
the raw hide of the populace with the same certainty
of obtaining the exact response he seeks as a master
who bows the strings of his violin. With his control
over the press his point of view is now the only one
which can be conveyed to the public and with his
loud-speakers in every street his shrieks of complaint
and denunciation are the only ones which can be
heard by the entire multitude.

It is doubtful if any other nation would have endured for twenty years such agonies, such continuous
and unmitigated suffering, without having them cli-
maxed by a bloody civil war. A generation or more
had been almost completely wiped out. The young
were mostly starvelings brought up by terrified
women. Four years of that explains much. Later, uncontrolled inflation confiscated the savings of the
thrifty. Gone was the financial independence of the
sanest and most intelligent of the middle class and
later in the depression the shrewdest of the entrepre-

neurs were engulfed in the ruin. A traditional enemy was occupying the Ruhr and billions in penalties had been levied upon them by the Treaty of Versailles. While these catastrophes were hitting the Germans like sheets of icy hail, a parliament of prattlers was tossing from one group to another the government of the Republic.

And yet, onward they took their weary way in comparative peace, interrupted only by enemies within the Fatherland. And who indeed was not an enemy? There were thirteen political parties and every voter believed that twelve of them were antagonistic to something he cherished—his Fatherland, his religion, his property, his profession or his class. The socialists were allied to the International; the Centrum to Rome; and the communists were largly financed by the most dreaded of all enemies, the leaders of Red armies and the vast Russian hordes. The Bolshevists in the democratic countries deny vehemently a statement such as that, but did not Lenin write to Balabanoff in Sweden: "Spend millions, tens of millions, if necessary. There is plenty of money at our disposal."

Three bonds were holding together the German nation: (1) The hatred of the people for France and their instinctive, primordial fear of Russia. Every party which gained control of the government was diligent in keeping the voters informed, by every means in its power, of the appalling misery which the Bolshevist regime had produced in Russia; (2) the distaste for armed uprisings. The rebellions of the Spartacists, the Kapp *Putsch* in 1920 and the Hitler *Putsch* in 1923 failed to win any considerable support; (3) the discipline which has always been a strong characteristic not only of the upper classes, but also of the powerful German Social Democratic party and of the Trade-Unions, both of which were mainly anti-communist. Moreover the workers had been taught by their leaders to rely confidently upon legal, electoral and parliamentary methods to achieve their objectives. These teachings were so ingrained that even Hitler, mad, passionate and vehement as he was, could not ignore them and after he was released from prison he dared not attempt another armed assault upon the State.

Therefore, in his efforts to attract the masses and not too confident that his own emotions were shared by the majority of Germans, Hitler launched a political party, shrewdly designed to lure into his net as many votes as possible. That was his technique as a politician. Its name, the National Socialist German Labor party, was a net big enough to catch millions including some Jews and communists. National and German attracted everybody while the great mass of proletarians liked an avenging patriot who was a

friend of labor and an advocate of sane German State
Socialism. Denouncing passionately all forms of in-
ternationalism, his fury was magnificent when he flayed
those Jews and communists who were "bribed by foreign bankers and subsidized by Moscow" as the organized enemies of the Fatherland.

In a period of rapidly changing price levels, when
the whole economic basis of life is shifting perilously,
the unrest of the masses often expresses itself in religious as well as class wars. John Morley says that
religion has ever been one of the prime movers in
revolution. Although that is a superficial view born of
a period he knew well, one of the many unexplained
mysteries of human behavior is the ferocity of religious hatreds which often accompanies revolutions.
Many instances of this intolerance come to mind: the
increased intensity of the Inquisition in Spain; the
antagonism to the Church of England in Cromwell's
time; the confiscation of the lands of the Church in
France during its great Revolution; the shooting of
the Archbishop of Paris in 1871; the persecution of
the Jews in Germany in the last few years and at other
times from the year they were expelled from Egypt.
Without clearly understanding why these forms of intolerance should so often become virulent, it is nevertheless clear that many ambitious men use these occasions to further their own ends. That is an old

technique, known not only to crusading despots but also to the most ignorant politician. When Hitler began his campaign to turn the rage of the Germans against the "profiteers" into animosity against "foreigners," the Jews were, as they so often have been in other countries, especially vulnerable.

In almost all countries at some time or other the Jews have been assailed as aliens. Some of them were, of course, communists and others had been enriched by the gigantic inflation which had impoverished the German middle class. Many Jews were merchants and traders who sold their goods at soaring prices and, although they did not always benefit by this, they were denounced as profiteers.[6] Others more intelligent knew that when prices are rising the value of money is falling and had wisely exchanged their German marks for jewels, silver, gold or stable foreign currencies. Many pure-blooded Germans had done likewise but most of them had put their savings into banks, bonds and insurance policies. Some of them had even hoarded the old marks of the Imperial regime, unable to believe that they would ever become valueless. These Germans were, of course, ruined. Stupid people are not fond of those who have been wiser than themselves and nothing could have been

---

[6] Merchants rarely profit in a period of rapid inflation, because what they sell must be replaced at higher prices. The result of this is a continuous depletion of their working capital.

easier for a crafty politician, especially in a country chauvinistic to the core, than to convince those who had suffered most that the "foreigners" at home and abroad were united in a conspiracy to bankrupt the Fatherland. Jews, communists, some Roman Catholics and others having international connections were denounced as traitors and thrown to the wolves.

Anyone who can formulate a theory which seems to solve our problems is sure to become our priest. Anyone who can point out to us men or things and make us believe they are the causes of our misfortunes is sure to become our leader. The creature who can lead us to our quarry, whether it be man or beast, will be treasured. Hounds of this sort have always been in demand and nowhere could the demand have been more insistent than among a people which for years had looked upon everyone who was not a German as a beast intent upon devouring them. Every turn of events favored Hitler. Attempts to deal with their conquerors in the World War had ended, the Germans were told in further humiliation. Political and economic irritants were opening deep wounds and into them the Nazis were rubbing doses of salt. This technique was pursued for years before Hitlerism attained the status of a unified national movement which no other political force in Germany was strong enough to combat. His opponents were fighting among themselves. Many elections had been held and a few able men had dominated to some degree the affairs of State but not one of them was able to bring order out of chaos. It was the old story from Right to Left and from Left to Right until the people were dizzy.

All the successful modern revolutionists have been first-rate propagandists. Hitler excels in this field, perhaps because he came out of the masses with contempt for their intelligence—a contempt which he does not conceal. "By clever and sustained propaganda," he wrote in *Mein Kampf*, "an entire people can be made to believe that heaven is hell and the most miserable existence a paradise." Such statements have been made by others but Hitler has proved that what he wrote is true.[7] Although he captured the machinery of a State by words, Hitler had in his hands other more substantial weapons. In 1933 the Nazis had over one million dues-paying members and about half a million Storm Troopers. Their nerve centers, militant groups, were scattered all over Germany. Their munitions, rifles, machine guns and trench mortars were stored at

---

[7] In fact he has proved it again and again. In 1939 there was great rejoicing throughout Germany, it was reported, when the Minister of Propaganda released the news of the signing of the mutual assistance pact with Russia. The Russians were no longer ruthless barbarian hordes; the Bolshevists no longer frenzied incendiaries with flaming torches in their hands; and the Great Bear of the North was no longer a ravenous beast intent upon devouring Der Fuehrer and his people.

strategic points and their forces were being trained by skilled officers for unified revolutionary action. Awaiting *Der Tag* they amused themselves by employing against the communists the terrorist tactics which had proved so successful in Italy.

Although the privately owned army of young unemployed workers ready to obey any command of the *Oberster Sturmabteilung Fuehrer* cowed the government, words proved to be Hitler's most effective weapons and millions of the populace were reading his book and standing spellbound before him as he pictured to them the dark cells of Hell in which they worked, they, the superb Nordics, driven by the lash of the dwarflike foreign Alberichs. In the hands of a dramatist such as Hitler this theme was enough, and more than 17,000,000 Germans fell in line to give battle to the throttling plutonic power which propaganda had personified as the foreigner. No other party in the history of Germany had attracted so many followers. No other revolutionist had come to power with an army of that size. Not only Hitler's opponents in the great democracies but his adversaries at home and the smaller countries in his vicinity may well be fearful so long as he can retain the loyalty of these millions.

The power of Hitler was underestimated until it was too late. Relentless and cunning, he is willing to await his opportunity. His movements are stealthily planned and then enacted with the rapidity and precision of a cat. He is always happy to make non-aggression pacts with his enemies until he is prepared to conquer them. The revolutionists of other parties scornfully called him Adolf Légalité. The street fights and parades of his Storm Troopers made little impression upon his opponents, few of whom realized the slow but steady progress he was making in building up his well-disciplined "Socialist" and "Labor" party. Each year brought new recruits and his opponents were astounded when, in 1930, the Nazis polled 6,-400,000 votes. Bruening then prepared the way for Adolf Illégalité. He dissolved the Reichstag and governed by decree. Like Kerensky, however, he did not have the essential quality of genuine dictators; he did not understand the necessity for their most powerful instrument—the purge.

In a depression the party in power is almost invariably voted out of office and for this reason the world-wide economic collapse was to Hitler a gift from Valhalla. It might be well for those who consider Hitler merely as a ruthless usurper to spend a few minutes looking up the facts. When he took control of the Reich he was backed by the huge vote of 17,-269,629 citizens. The Social Democratic party polled the next largest vote but it totaled only 7,177,294. He beat his nearest opponents by over ten million votes. In the same depression Mr. Roosevelt did not do as well as that in his contest with President Hoover. In Germany, it is true, there were thirteen parties in the field. Of these the Catholic, Social Democratic and Communist parties were the most powerful but they were bitterly opposed to each other and no one knows how their following would have voted had the issue been definitely Hitler or anti-Hitler. However, had all their votes been combined they would have been beaten by over 800,000.[8]

In any case the long battle of Der Fuehrer was over. Hitler had a mandate from the people of Germany. With exhaustless rhetoric; with a sleep-robbing theme of great dramatic power; with the primitive emotions so well phrased by Wagner, the disciple of Bakunin; and with shock troops far exceeding those of the Bolshevists, one of the meanest of the populace had made himself Tyrant, an achievement not new in the world

[8] It might interest Americans to know that the Nazis in 1933 were supported by about 27 per cent of the total population of Germany while Mr. Roosevelt was elected in 1932 by about 18 per cent. Please note that I am not referring to the electorate. Germany had at that time roughly a population of about 66,000,000, the United States about 123,000,000. In both countries all citizens, male and female, are entitled to vote. In Germany those of twenty years or over had the franchise and more than thirty-nine millions of them went to the polls. In the United States, with almost twice the population, the vote was smaller by about one hundred thousand than that of the Germans. In America there is an astonishing number of the unburied dead walking about who will not trouble to vote.

if the words of Aristotle can be trusted. At a meeting
of the new Reichstag, Hitler was given dictatorial
powers. Wholesale arrests of communists, Jews and
Social Democrats immediately followed. Over 40,000
political opponents were thrown into prison by a carefully planned and concerted action. The headquarters,
funds, papers and properties of the trade-unions were
confiscated. In Germany, as a result of fifteen years of
seismic disturbances, a granite ridge of immense proportions, menacing all Europe, had risen above the
conglomerate.

Lenin, Mussolini and Hitler! Magnates of revolution and masters of great nations! No wonder they
should always have despised the millions of industrialists and shopkeepers with their small armies of
workmen, petty profits and parochial outlook. How
mean compared to themselves, intent upon conquering nations, are the richest of economic royalists. What
Rockefeller or Ford ever dreamed of subjecting to his
will the lives and property of all the people in a nation?
Bernard Shaw expresses on every possible occasion the
contempt which these potentates of revolution have for
middle-class religion, middle-class morality, middle-
class mediocrity, middle-class vulgarity, middle-class
family life and so on to the end of his book, indeed of
his many, many books. There is nothing middle class in

the modern Caesars. They play only for the highest
stakes and when they win they sweep into their hands
the entire pot—the State, the Church, the land, the
industries, the schools, the press, the banks and the
people themselves. Compared to them the naughty
capitalists resemble a circle of little boys playing craps
for pennies, with one of their number placed in position to watch for the policeman. When the revolutionists win the policemen belong to them.

In the comments of Thucydides upon the march of
the revolution in Corcyra, over twenty-three centuries
ago, can be found the most concise diagnosis ever
penned of the rage, moral depravity and bestial passions aroused in the combatants during that bloody
war of the classes. When law and order are cast aside
and the tyranny of naked force takes their place, we
find that those who are contending for mastery in our
day have the same characteristics as the chieftains of
the mobs in the pre-Christian world. At Corcyra, Thucydides found: revenge was held of more account than
self-preservation; success by treachery won . . . the
palm of superior intelligence; frantic violence became
the attribute of manliness; and cautious plotting was
thought to be a justifiable means of self-defense. He
observed "the cunning of their enterprises and the
atrocity of their reprisals." Those who survive the carnage of revolution and particularly those who kill
wavering comrades with vindictive delight, are slayers

by nature, or, if not that, acquire during their frenzied battles for survival the cunning of foxes and the
hunger of wolves. Tyrants, whose passion for power
has driven them to massacre their own countrymen,
are not likely to become trustworthy, high-minded and
humane when making treaties with foreigners. The
following words of Thucydides are as true of the fuehrers of our time as they were of the revolutionists of
his day: "Oaths of reconciliation . . . only held good
so long as no other weapon was at hand." So long as
oaths mean nothing more than that in the moral code
of the modern Caesars, an insuperable obstacle will
stand in the way of peace.

However, we have had quite enough, for the time
being, of the magnates of revolution and so we turn
to the Termites and Demagogues, who, not having
to fight for power and "without bowels full of wrath,"
are perhaps the least pardonable of the several varieties of destroyers.

5. *Joseph*

*It is also advantageous for a tyranny that all those who
are under it should be oppressed with poverty . . . and
that being employed in procuring their daily bread, they
may have no leisure to conspire against their tyrants.*
—ARISTOTLE

We must go back thousands of years to find nations
which have been impoverished by their rulers to such
an extent that the populace has been reduced to slav-

ery. If this is happening in our time, as it may be in
the Fascist and communist States, it will not be known
until after many generations have passed away. Democracies are rarely overthrown by force; they are
usually undermined from within by demagogues. It
is also rare for independent farmers and freeholders
to be deprived of their property by force. The Bolshevists found out very quickly how difficult it is to
take by arms the land or produce of the peasants. But
there are other ways known to revolutionists by which
a free State can be turned into a slave State.

The militant communist and Fascist leaders of popular upheavals neglect to tell their followers that the
violent seizure of the State develops inevitably into
some form of dictatorship, with an individual or small
group in complete possession of the main instruments
of political and economic power. Once a dictatorship
is firmly established the work of undermining an economic system is not a difficult matter. The same
result may be achieved gradually in a more or less
democratic social system by demagogues. Those State
Socialists who prefer the methods of peaceful penetra-
tion and bloodless revolution should give serious con-
sideration to the technique of Joseph.

Like Trotsky, whose methods we have already discussed, Joseph was a genius in his field of action, and
if the machinery built by Trotsky to capture the State

was almost noiseless, that of Joseph to transform the economic system of Egypt was as silent as the stars. It wasn't necessary, in order to make it work, to have war, inflation or deflation supply it with fuel. Famine following a shortage of grain started the motor and after that it ran automatically and achieved a more fundamental, enduring and comprehensive revolution in a shorter period of time than any other we know of, excepting only that of Dionysius in Syracuse —a despot of quality. His attacks upon the rich so delighted the populace that he "was thought worthy of being raised to a tyranny" where "in the space of five years he collected all the property of his subjects into his own coffers" (Aristotle). In Egypt the multitudes were not hostile to Joseph after the revolution, as the Russians were to the Bolshevists. Rather they adored him and called upon the Lord to bless his name.

The technique of Joseph requires the use of only two simple tools: one-man control over the monetary policies of the State and the food supplies of the nation. In order to make the scheme work perfectly, a State-owned granary and a State monopoly of precious metals must be, as Joseph prescribes, completely under the control of one wise man.

Joseph was an impoverished soothsayer, a clairvoyant, who could look into the future and interpret all sorts of mysterious signs. He wormed his way into the sacred precincts of the Pharaohs, where he got control of the State. With this mighty mandible he was able, under the guise of providing food for the famished, to destroy a primitive social order of independent farmers and craftsmen and establish a totalitarian state under the domination of an all-powerful despot. Although the story is to be found in the Old Testament, what follows is condensed from an article on Joseph in Smith's *Dictionary of the Bible*.

Pharaoh was much troubled, so the story runs, because he could not understand the meaning of two dreams which had disturbed his sleep. He dreamed that he stood by the river and beheld, coming up out of the river, seven heifers beautiful in appearance and fat-fleshed; and they fed on the marsh-grass. And behold, seven other heifers came up after them out of the river, evil in appearance and lean-fleshed. These ate up the first seven and yet, when they had eaten them they remained as lean as before. Then Pharaoh had a second dream. Behold, seven ears of corn coming up on one stalk, fat and good; and behold seven others, thin and blasted with the east wind, sprouting forth after them. These devoured the first seven ears.

Pharaoh sent for the scribes and wise men of Egypt, but they were unable to give him an interpretation. He then called for Joseph, an interpreter of dreams. The King related his dreams, and Joseph declared to him that they were sent of God to forewarn Pharaoh. They were essentially but one dream. Both heifers and ears symbolized years. There were to be seven years of great plenty in Egypt, followed by seven years of consuming and very heavy famine. The doubling of the dream denoted that the events it foreshadowed were certain and imminent.

Joseph then counseled Pharaoh to choose a wise man and set him over the country, in order that he should take the fifth part of the produce of the seven years of plenty and preserve it to provide for the years of famine. To this high post the King appointed Joseph. Thus, when he was thirty years of age, he was placed in a position of the greatest honor where he was able to establish in all Egypt an ever-normal granary, a reservoir of supplies with the outlet in his own fair hands.

Pharaoh, seeing the wisdom of Joseph, whom he perceived to be under God's guidance, made him not only governor of Egypt but second only to the sovereign. And Pharaoh took off the signet ring from his finger and put it upon Joseph's hand, and arrayed him in vestures of fine linen and put a collar of gold about his neck; and he made him ride in the second chariot; and the people cried before him, "Abrech!" And they wished to set him over all the land of Egypt.

Joseph's first act was to go throughout all the land.

During the seven plenteous years there was a very abundant produce, and he gathered the fifth part, as he had advised Pharaoh, and laid it up. The abundance of this store is evident from the statement that Joseph gathered corn as the sand of the sea.

When the seven good years had passed, the famine began. And when all the land of Egypt was famished, the people cried to Pharaoh for bread; and Pharaoh said unto all the Egyptians, "Go to Joseph, what he saith to you, do." And the famine was over all the face of the earth. And Joseph opened all the storehouses and sold unto the Egyptians. And other countries came into Egypt to buy corn, because the famine was so sore in all lands.

After a time, apparently two years, there was no bread in all the land, so that the people of Egypt and Canaan fainted by reason of the famine. And Joseph, in exchange for the corn which he had stored, gathered up all the money that was found in the land of Egypt and in the land of Canaan, and placed the precious metals in Pharaoh's house. When all the money of Egypt and Canaan was exhausted, barter became necessary. Through barter Joseph also obtained all the cattle of Egypt and, in the next year, all the land (except that of the priests) and apparently, as a consequence, the bodies and souls of the Egyptians themselves.

Thus we find in Joseph a revolutionist of the first rank with a flawless technique. His shrewd economic and financial policies laid all the possessions of the people of Egypt at Pharaoh's feet. First the corn, later the money, then the cattle and the land, and last of all the Egyptians themselves became the property of the sovereign. In their gratitude the people shouted: "Thou hast saved our lives; let us find grace in the sight of my Lord, and we will be Pharaoh's servants."

6. *The Tyrant*

The generality of tyrants were indeed mere demagogues, who gained credit with the people by oppressing the nobles.

—ARISTOTLE

Many fair democracies in the world known to the Greeks were seduced and abandoned by tyrants. Socrates, Plato and Aristotle were well supplied with historical data upon the rise and fall of States. Before Aristotle published his *Politics* he had carefully examined one hundred and fifty-eight different constitutions. At the time he was writing, revolutions were transforming many of the old States bordering on the Mediterranean, the Adriatic and the Aegean Seas. Twenty-seven years of war had exhausted the Athenians and when disaster followed disaster, the Greek scholars began to turn their minds to the pursuit of the ideal State. Like other teachers before him, Aristotle endeavored to formulate the principles upon which the perfect State should be founded. However it is evident that Aristotle, the idealist, could not convince Aristotle, the realist, and as he turns to his records of the world as it is, he seems to say to his students: "So much for the ideal, my children, but as I know you will not like it, make the best of what you have, whether it be a democratic, aristocratic or oligarchic State, and take heed, therefore, of the mistakes which have been made in the past."

Having become disheartened by the deplorable condition of political life in Athens, Plato hoped that reason combined with a picture of what he believed would be an ideal commonwealth might induce humanity to see the error of its ways. He presented his conception of a model republic in a series of dialogues which no doubt were as dull reading for the Athenians as they are to a modern reader. Ideal States seem to appeal only to those who conceive them. Certainly they have never attracted for long any considerable body of disciples nor have they influenced in any noticeable degree the activities of statesmen. Aristotle was as severe in his criticism of Plato's *Republic* as others have been of Aristotle's ideal State and also of his advice to legislators. William Morris, provoked by Edward Bellamy's *Looking Backward*, in which the *phalanstère* of Fourier was expanded into a hideous form of State socialism, wrote his *News from No-wher*e, a picture of a pastoral romantic Utopia, as a protest against the views of most socialists that the organization of life and labor "can be dealt with by a huge national centralization, working by a kind of magic."[9] Marx attacked as Utopians all the socialists who had preceded him. Plato and Aristotle attract readers in these days not because they were schematists but because they teach us how little man has changed in the last twenty-four centuries and when we study their discussions of social and political instability, we find about us perfect specimens to illustrate their conclusions.

In the struggles which have recently occurred between the absolutists and the many varieties of democrats, the latter have invariably been beaten. What have been called granite ridges have thrust themselves upward ominously. Although all but one of the battles won by the dictators up to 1939 took place in countries which have had but little experience in popular government, many people, who are deeply concerned over these defeats, are fearful that democracy everywhere is doomed. It may be well for us to look about and see if we can discover any

---

[9] Bellamy went to a German university and fell like Marx under the spell of the totalitarianism of Hegel and other German philosophers.

signs of tyranny developing in the older and more firmly founded free states.

Unquestionably some of them are imperiled by internal corruption, class strife, parliamentary *cretinism,* hungry bureaucrats and politicians thinking only of their own welfare. These and other cankerous growths are developing. But it takes a long time for them to destroy a democratic social system. Like bomb-casting planes in modern warfare, they are capable of doing a vast amount of damage but they cannot strike the decisive blow which conquers a nation. Some one must arrive, as Mussolini did, to deliver the *coup de grâce.* He performed that task in his own peculiar way. In other times dictators have used more subtle and beguiling but no less effective methods.

It is advisable, though by no means imperative, for one aspiring to dictatorship in a democracy to take care to be wellborn.[10] An aristocrat by breeding,

---

[10] There have been hundreds of tyrants of whom we know little or nothing. Among those well known are Orthagoras, Cypselus, Thrasybulus, Periander, Pisistratus, Hieron I, Gelon, Dionysius, Agathocles, Cleomenes, Sulla, Caesar. All of them were nobles, aristocrats, patricians or gentlemen of rank. Cleon, "the tanner," was a wealthy man and Lenin came from the middle class, went to a university and later practiced as a lawyer. Albert R. Williams, who was in Russia shortly after the Bolshevists came to power, reported with his usual extravagance that "the present cabinet is the most cultured cabinet probably in the history of the world." A Dictatorship of the Proletariat without a proletarian! Agathocles, Nabis, Stalin and Hitler are among the few despots who have risen from the lower classes, and they have excelled those from the higher classes in cunning, patience, tenacity and cruelty. With only one exception, the tyrants mentioned had some military training and most of

possessed of wealth and culture, who turns against his kind has little difficulty in becoming the idol of the common folk. He should have a charming personality combined with the ability to express in homely words the simple thoughts of his followers. He must begin his career by smiles and let it be known that he wishes only one thing—to be kind and good. He must have a program for dividing up the wealth of the rich and giving it to the poor. For one in his lofty social position to have such humanitarian aims arouses in the multitude a passionate devotion and removes any possible doubt of his sincerity. He must also on all possible occasions denounce the rich and hail them before the courts as enemies of the people. Once this is done he will be worshipped and can easily destroy those who have aided him. After the point has been

---

them became generals. All of them were demogogues who began their political careers as friends of the people and enemies of the rich.

Some of them were black-hearted scoundrels with an unquenchable thirst for the blood of their fellowmen. The purges of Lenin, Trotsky, Mussolini and Hitler are characteristic of the breed. Agathocles, son of a potter, devoted his talents to the army and when he became king of Syracuse he called a mass meeting of the senate and the leading citizens at which time he murdered all the senators and aristocrats. Hieron massacred his mercenaries as soon as they could serve him no longer. Cataline, a nobleman, was supported by Caesar, the patrician, when he led the armed forces of the *populares*—bankrupts, landless peasants, veterans, outlaws and slaves—against the aristocrats of Rome and killed among others both of Caesar's uncles. Sulla commanded the bones of Marius to be broken, his eyes to be pulled out, his hands to be cut off and his body to be torn to pieces with pinchers. Cataline was the executioner. "This was an exhibition of cruelty," says Seneca, "fit only for Marius to suffer, Cataline to execute and Sulla to command."

reached where no possible rival survives, he is forced in affairs of state to depend solely upon his own family and his armed mercenaries.

Fortunately in the great democracies of recent centuries, no man of wealth, culture and refinement has attempted to use such methods to destroy free institutions in order to advance himself and his family. When George Washington refused to accept a third term, an annoying obstacle was placed in the way of those who seek to become despots in the United States. But strange things are happening in the world today. Who could have believed before the war that Huey Long could have so easily become the czar of a great state in the Union. It is well then not to throw up one's hands when reading the following digest of Plato's study in the technique of the tyrant and shout, "It cannot happen here!" Although the tiresome dialogue is eliminated, the argument is presented verbatim, in so far as that is possible in a condensation.

Socrates is supposed to be speaking. Now the democratic State has three classes, the politicians (drones), the well-to-do and the workers. The politicians in a democracy are almost the entire ruling class, and the keener sort speak and act while the rest sit buzzing about the hive and will not suffer a word to be said on the other side. Hence there is hardly anything . . . which is not of their doing.

The second powerful class is composed of the well-to-do. They are the most squeezable persons and yield the largest amount of honey to the drones.

The third class consists of the workingmen who are not politicians and have little to live upon. And this when assembled is the largest and most powerful class in a democracy. But they are seldom willing to meet unless they get a little honey. Therefore their leaders take the estates of the rich and give to the people as much of them as they can, consistently with keeping the greater part for themselves. Consequently those whose property is taken from them are compelled to defend themselves as best they can and, although they may have no desire to change, the others charge them with plotting against the State and being friends of oligarchy. . . . Then come impeachments, judgments and trials of one another.

The people have always some one as a champion whom they nurse into greatness . . . and this is the very root from which a tyrant springs. When the champion first appears above ground he is a protector. . . . He smiles upon everyone and salutes everyone . . . making promises in public and also in private, liberating debtors and distributing land to the people and to his followers and wanting to be kind and good to everyone. But eventually he turns into a wolf because in order to maintain his power he must live upon the blood of others.

Having a mob entirely at his disposal, he is not restrained from shedding blood. By the favorite method of false accusation he brings his enemies into court . . . some he kills, and others he banishes. . . . After this what can be his destiny? Either he must perish at the hands of his enemies or . . . become a wolf, that is, a tyrant.

He then begins to make a party against the rich. . . . If they are unable to drive him out or get him condemned to death by public opinion, they form the design of putting him out of the way secretly. . . . Then comes the famous request of a bodyguard, which is made by all those who have got thus far in their career. This the people readily grant; all their fears are for him—they have no fears for themselves. "Let not the people's friend be lost to them."

The protector, now a tyrant, finds it necessary to be the overthrower of many, and he stands up in the chariot of State with the reins in his hand. However, he must always be stirring up trouble in order that the people may require a leader. Moreover, he has another object which is that they may be impoverished by the payment of taxes, and thus compelled to devote themselves to their daily wants and therefore less likely to plot against him.

This tyrant must then be careful to look all about him and use his eyes to see who is valued, who is high-minded, who is wise, who is wealthy. Happy man, he is the enemy of them all, and must seek occasion against them whether he will or no, until he has made a purgation of the State . . . not the sort of purgation which the physicians make of the body; for they take away the worse and leave the better part, but he does the opposite.

Hereafter he is compelled to dwell only with the many bad, and hated by them. . . . The more detestable he is in his actions the more satellites and the greater devotion in them will he require. But he must pay them, and in order to protect himself he must enroll them in his bodyguard.

Eventually his parents (the people) who gave birth to this protector, now a tyrant, discover what a monster they have been fostering in their bosom, and when they want to drive him out, they find that they are weak and he is strong. He then turns upon the people themselves and beats them. Thus he becomes as it were a parricide, a cruel, unnatural son to trusting and aged parents whom he ought to cherish. And this is the real tyranny about which there is no mistake.

7. Fair Promises

One should trick children with dice but men with promises.
—DIONYSIUS, THE ELDER

Words had to change their ordinary meaning and take that which was now given them.
—THUCYDIDES (in the revolution at Corcyra)

It is a general popular error to suppose the loudest complainers for the public to be the most anxious for its welfare.
—EDMUND BURKE

Promises are an important part of the equipment of all revolutionists. They are juicy baits to attract the hungry. When my now disillusioned friend Raymond Moley employed the words the New Deal and the Forgotten Man, he gave distinct evidence of genius as a master of one of the most profitable forms of revolutionary technique. Like the most astute politicians, the successful revolutionists have been the loudest complainers for the public. It is a notable fact, observable in all ages, that the people who have been their most ardent supporters have also been their chief victims. Huey Long was supreme in the use of the arts of the demagogue and, except possibly Mussolini, all dictators past and present have been masters of this technique. When seeking the support of the masses, oligarchs and generals at the head of armies have been often as prodigal in their promises as the communists. It is noteworthy also that those who have been least ready to make promises have been the

landed aristocrats, the merchants and the industrialists, although they have been in almost all ages the
staunchest promoters and defenders of freedom and
democratic institutions. It is true that these classes
have not been politically ambitious and their main
interest has been to protect themselves but it is also
undeniable that we owe to them our escape from
serfdom and slavery.

On the other hand one of the most oft-repeated
lessons of history is that when a complainer for the
public has captured the State, he has proceeded to
outwit those who have helped him. It has never been
safe to rely upon the pledges, oaths and covenants of
those who seek supreme power. These statements are
not mere assertions. It is difficult if not impossible to
find a single successful revolutionist who did not begin
his career as a demagogue and end it as a despot.
Caesar, the haughty Conqueror, was an astute politician, an habitual complainer for the public and a
professional democrat. He had for many years been
the most ruthless antagonist of the Roman aristocrats.
As the head of a great army, he could probably have
subdued the country without making any promises,
nevertheless he snared the masses by a program which
was almost identical with the one used nearly two
thousand years later by Lenin. Caesar pledged himself to the abolition of debts, the confiscation of the

property of the aristocrats, the allotment of lands to
the soldiers, and the provision of work and bread to
the hungry and unemployed. Lenin, as we know,
promised the masses work, bread, peace, land and the
factories.

Some of the complainers for the public have acquired possession of great States at bargain rates.
Joseph peddled bread to the famished people of Egypt.
Hitler promised work and bread, while Mussolini
offered work and glory. Our own Huey Long was
magnificently lavish in his bribes. Every man was to
become a king with a car, a radio, a farm and $2500
a year. Huey was truly the spiritual descendant of
those natives of Louisiana about whom Montesquieu
wrote some two hundred years ago. When they "wish
to have fruit they cut the tree at the bottom and
gather the fruit." With astonishing insight he added
this profound comment: "That is exactly a despotic
government." In other words a despotic government
cuts off wealth at its source. Had our prodigy of prodi-
gality lived to enter the White House and ordered the
legislators to go home and stay there, or to use his
own words, had he "bought them like sacks of pota-
toes," we might have had in the United States a dictator whose exploits would have surpassed those of
Caligula. Instead of that climax to a spectacular career, we now find the courts revealing to the enthusi-

astic followers of the munificent Huey that what he really meant when he planned to "share the wealth" was to wrench from rich men a few millions for himself and his retainers.

The great dictators have usually proclaimed themselves lovers of freedom and defenders of peace. Caesar marched his legions into Rome to save the Republic. With charity ill-bestowed, Theodor Mommsen writes of Caesar's "good faith in the possibility of his being able to found a free commonwealth, if not by the sword of others, at any rate by his own. We perceive without difficulty that this faith was fallacious, and that no one takes an evil spirit into his service without becoming himself enslaved by it; but the greatest of men are not those who err the least." Napoleon overpowered the Council of Five Hundred to save the Republic. "What we want," he said, "is a republic founded upon true liberty, civil rights, representation of the people and I swear we shall have it." Trotsky dispersed the members of the Constituent Assembly because they were the enemies of the people. Mussolini led his Black Shirts to Rome to give a government to the nation and to rescue the people from the depredations of imbecile and mentally deficient politicians. The wars of Napoleon were in defense of a "liberated France" and like Hitler, the passion of his life was, so he said repeatedly as he fought from Spain to Moscow, to maintain peace in Europe.

Twelve hundred years after Caesar, the haughty Barons in their revolt against the King did not forget the interests of the common people. At least a third of the provisions of the Great Charter was designed to protect the lower classes from despotism and extortion. In 1653, Cromwell became the Protector of the People and of their Commonwealth, which the Levellers, Diggers and other followers would have written common wealth. At the moment he was suppressing a mutiny of radical social reformers in his armies, Cromwell denounced the laws which enabled the rich to defraud the poor. From the first to the last, the leaders of the French Revolution professed to be the enemies of the rich and the friends of the indigent. In Paris from 1793 to 1795 whenever those in power discovered an antagonist, he was condemned as "an enemy of the people." The same indictment has been sufficient to condemn tens of thousands in Russia. "Where there is liberty there is no State," remarked Lenin as soon as he became the supreme lord of Russia—a statement worthy to be bracketed with that of Robespierre, who defended the Reign of Terror as "the despotism of liberty."

Yet with all their prodigious power, it is curious how careful the autocrats have been not to offend certain prejudices of their victims. Caesar took the title of Dictator (not then repugnant to the populace) because he feared that if he were crowned king he would wound the pride of the Romans. Cromwell became the Protector of the people. Napoleon also feared to take the title of king. Lenin did not call himself the czar nor did Hitler become the kaiser. Mussolini remains Il Duce. The Dictator, the Protector, l'Empereur, Der Fuehrer, and Il Duce may exercise more power than kings, kaisers and czars, but they were new titles, while the old ones would have revealed to the populace their real aims and characters. With favorable conditions the autocrat may move speedily as Lenin, Hitler and Mussolini have done, or he may move slowly as Caesar did, or awkwardly and with misgivings after the manner of Cromwell. Or like Napoleon, he may try to conserve or resurrect much of the old regime. He can do very much as he likes providing he is careful to present himself to his people under a new title and his projects under new labels.

All successful revolutionists have been adored by the populace. Their courage, hatreds, promises and sentiments are captivating. And yet no matter what they promise, the poor are always with us. No matter what their programs are, nor what they do, the inequalities and iniquities which afflict humanity outlast them all. Knowing our problems to be what they are and human nature what it is, there is nothing surprising in the failure of even the best of the revolutionists to keep their pledges. Promises of perfect justice, abiding peace, complete liberty, universal equality, fraternity, work, land, and the abundant life are, however, only a part of their technique for acquiring power. In reality these have never been the aims of successful revolutionists. Their real aims have always been as they are now to capture the State. With it firmly in their hands, everything may be made their own—the corn, the cattle, the land, and the bodies and souls of the people.

CHAPTER V

THE STRUCTURE OF SOCIETY CHANGES

The first act of the revolutionary play cannot be understood until the curtain has fallen on the fifth.

—JOHN MORLEY

1. *The Trilogy*

THE previous chapters have been confined mainly to some short periods in history. Insurrections which have caused widespread concern at the time have been suppressed within a few weeks and the world has gone on much as it had before. The revolutions which have been considered here have also been short-lived. As we look back over these developments we find that they have presented themselves in the form of a trilogy. The last act of the series is almost an exact repetition of the first act of the first drama. In a few months or years the people have returned to the point from which they started, although doubtless some

structural social changes have occurred in the course
of events. When this happens, as it has so often, the
cycle is complete. Here are four well-known trilogies:

Charles I	The Commonwealth; civil war; inflation; Cromwell. (Eleven years)	Charles II
Louis XVI	The Republic; inflation; tyranny; class war; Robespierre. (Seven years)	Napoleon I
The Czar	The Republic; inflation; Kerensky. (Eight months)	Lenin
The Kaiser	The Republic; inflataion; class war. (Fifteen years)	Hitler

In the first play we watch the monodrama of the
absolutist proceeding to his destruction. In the second
we see a Cromwell, Robespierre or Kerensky riding
the storm and attempting, according to his lights and
in harmony with his ambitions, to bring order out of
chaos. We often see also in this second drama unbridled liberty, industry paralyzed, inquisitions, trials,
condemnations, class and racial hatreds beyond the
control of any man or group. In the third play we witness the restoration of a former ruling family or see
emerging from the dark shadows of internal war the
dictator—some John the Pannonian, with, as Robert
Browning says, rough-hammered head, great eye,
gross jaw and griped lips. The hero increases in stature and grandeur with each succeeding scene. In the
final act he has become a Colossus; at least that is what
he would like to believe.

The immediate results of the Great War were exactly

what Bebel and Engels had predicted. The socialists were the heirs of the Hohenzollerns, the Hapsburgs and the Romanoffs. The old dynasties were destroyed and capitalism was mutilated. But that was not the end of the story. The inheritance received by the revolutionists from the hands of their former lords and masters was soon squandered and the heroes of the third drama drove the quarrelsome factions from the stage.

There is nothing new in the rapidity with which this series of plays has been enacted. In recent centuries the entire trilogy has been completed, as we have noted, in a few years. In France it was repeated with variations several times over a period of eighty-two years. The first Napoleon arrived upon the stage in 1799 and left it in 1815, but other monarchs and imperialists appeared from time to time until the last of them, Napoleon III, was driven out of France in 1870. In other countries no similar series of violent disturbances occurred, the monarchs remaining in possession of the stage almost continuously during the nineteenth century and indeed until the end of the World War. Since then we have seen these historic trilogies revived and we may be now entering upon a period similar to the sixteen years when Napoleon attempted to dominate Europe.

There are movements in current history which seem

to be merely the repetition of old familiar stories. Are the people even in the republics on the point of revolting against the sons of Samuel *who walked not in his ways, but turned after lucre, and took bribes, and perverted judgment?* When this happened in Israel all the elders gathered themselves together and came to Samuel and said unto him: *Behold, thou art old, and thy sons walk not in thy ways; now make us a king to judge us like all the nations.*

But the thing displeased Samuel, when they said, Give us a king to judge us. And Samuel prayed unto the Lord. And the Lord said unto Samuel, Harken unto the voice of the people in all that they say unto thee . . . and shew them the manner of the king that shall reign over them.

And Samuel told all the words of the Lord unto the people that asked of him a king. And he said, This will be the manner of the king that shall reign over you: He will take your sons, and appoint them for himself, for his chariots, and to be his horsemen; and some shall run before his chariots. And he will appoint him captains over thousands, and captains over fifties; and will set them to ear his ground, and to reap his harvest, and to make his instruments of war, and instruments of his chariots. And he will take your daughters to be confectionaries, and to be cooks, and to be bakers. And he will take your fields, and your vineyards and your oliveyards, even the best of them, and give them to his servants. And he will take the tenth of your seed and of your vineyards, and give to his officers, and to his servants. And he will take your menservants, and your maidservants, and your goodliest young men, and your asses, and put them to work. He will take the tenth of your sheep; and ye shall be his servants. And ye shall cry out in that day because of your king which ye shall have chosen you; and the Lord will not hear you in that day.

Nevertheless the people refused to obey the voice of Samuel; and they said, Nay, but we will have a king over us.

Samuel does not mention how much his sons were extracting from the pockets of the people. Perhaps he would have been greatly shocked had he known. Those who were paying tribute knew and it is probable that they thought ten per cent of their income, if that was what Samuel meant, was a reasonable price to pay for government. It would certainly be a low rate today. More than one of the benevolent tyrants of Greece conducted the affairs of State at a cost to the people of five per cent and adorned their cities with many magnificent buildings. Joseph advised the Pharoah to charge the Egyptians twenty per cent. The cost of government is very high in all countries since the Great War and will be higher in the days to come.

Americans pay federal, state, county, city and other direct taxes and these combined with levies upon sales and indirectly upon nearly all purchases, place a heavy

burden upon their productive powers. There are so
many diverse and hidden taxes that it is almost impossible to estimate the amount paid by the average
American citizen, but it is likely that it would not fall
far short of the amount paid in 1938 by the average
British citizen, if our many budgets were balanced, our
total debt funded on a long-term basis and we were
paying our bills.[1] Some of the estimates of the experts
indicate that the total tax bill in the year 1938
amounted to twenty per cent of our national income.
Those of great wealth pay a penalty of as much as
three-quarters of their annual incomes for the privi-
lege of keeping their funds in active business. Moreover, after death their estates have been in some instances taxed by the Federal and State governments
for more than they have brought when sold in the
market.

A contributor to *The Round Table* estimated in
March, 1938 that Italy was absorbing forty-two per
cent, France, thirty-nine per cent and Germany, thirty
per cent of the total national incomes. Professor D. H.
Macgregor estimated that Great Britain was spending

---

[1] The Treasury estimates that in 1938 the average taxation per head
per day in the U. S. A. amounted to thirty-one cents. The Northwestern
Insurance Company has attempted the difficult task of computing the
hidden or indirect taxes paid by an American family with an income of
$1,800 a year and finds that they amount to $242 or 13.5 per cent of
the annual total.

in 1938, thirty-three per cent of the national income. The expenditures in all countries are increasing so rapidly that these estimates are hardly worth committing to paper and would not be placed here were it not that they indicate a trend of our times which is having profound repercussions upon the economic system. If, as Sir Robert Peel once said, "money will fructify more in the hands of the people than in those of the State," it can be confidently predicted that the future will yield constantly decreasing harvests. The writer in *The Round Table* tells us that private enterprise is languishing in Germany and Italy and is in serious difficulties in France. In Italy he sees the approach of "a bureaucratically ruled proletarian state." The drones—as Plato called them—have made great progress since the days of Samuel in ways and means of exploiting the working bees in the hive.

Samuel also had in mind a condition of servitude and, we are told, it rapidly developed in Israel after the wars of David. Solomon, it is said, placed upon the people the "grievous yoke of slavery." When they cried out in agony, the son of Solomon said: "My little finger is thicker than my father's loins; my father chastised you with whips but I will chastise you with scorpions." The old dramas of revolution are either unknown or unheeded by the people of the present day and again we hear on all sides the cry, Nay, but we will have a king over us.

There is nothing unusual in the love of the Jews for kings. A reading of history for the past three thousand years teaches us that democracies and republics are brief episodes in the life of man. Their hour upon the stage has been so short that there are only two names, President and Prime Minister, for the leading actors in these dramas, while Tyrant, Dictator, Autocrat, Caesar, Kaiser, Czar, Caliph, Khan, Emperor, Monarch and King are only a few of the many titles given to the despots who have ruled mankind without restraint. Recently three more, with much the same meaning, have been added to the list: Der Fuehrer, Il Duce and Vozhd. In the lexicons along with Despotism we may soon find Leninism, Stalinism, Fascism and Hitlerism. We are making history—past history—in these post-war days.

In enormous areas the people are becoming less and less important. A new era seems to be in the making when they must work long hours at low wages, fight to the death, obey every command of their lords, or be shot. While the women plow the fields, harvest the grain and bear children, the men will go forth to war. As the hero of the modern monodrama increases in bulk the masses will sink lower and lower into the earth, until they can barely see the outline of his rough-hammered head. All this takes time. At present he is a communist, a socialist, a protector, "a big umbrella" (Mussolini) or merely "a humble leader" concerned solely with the welfare of his people. All the great actors as they evolved into dictators said something of this sort. The frail and fading flowers, uprooted by the revolutionists, have had their places taken by plants of a vigorous and aggressive type.

"Revolutions are like the most noxious dung-heaps which bring into life the noblest vegetables," said Napoleon. The desire for destruction, Bakunin thought, is at the same time a creative desire. He did not seem to be interested in what type of civilization would appear out of chaos. History clarifies the subject somewhat. Out of the rotting compost of uprooted and decaying life come forth now, as often in the past, cabbages, i.e., absolutists. Emerging from the recent class wars, passionate hatreds and general destruction, we behold a rare assortment of them. Vigorous, vital and overpowering, their huge forms are pushing up out of the heap of common men. That is a fact. If the despots of our day are not granite, as we fear, but only vegetables, like the great realist who was good enough to name them, then it matters little how tough and coarse they may now be. It is some comfort to know they are perishable plants.

Today these heroes of the multitudes—that is what

they seem to be—have their strutting hour, but sooner or later the hero of another play will take possession of the stage. The new drama may be a comedy. That has often happened in the past but there have been times when the despotic State has survived as a political system for many centuries. The son of Charlemagne was Louis le Débonnaire. The son of Solomon, with the mighty little finger, aroused the Ten Tribes to revolt and four years later the King of Egypt captured the city of Jerusalem. The son of the matchless despot Dionysius lost everything his father had won and when asked why this should have happened he imparted this illuminating interpretation of history: "My father embarked upon his venture when democracy was hated, but I at a time when despotism was odious." That is not, however, a completely satisfying explanation.

Perhaps the chief reason for the appearance of dictators after revolutions have exhausted a nation is to be found in the difficulty always experienced when a government tries to alter quickly the habits, customs and characteristics of a people. Mussolini has said, "There is no revolution which can change the nature of man." The rulers in a new republic have usually tried to transform everything and everybody within a few months. The British and the Dutch, who have been more successful than others in ruling all sorts of tribes and races in many parts of the world, realized long ago that they could not change fundamentally the character of either their own or any other people, by laws or by force. The American colonists taught the British a useful lesson, and the Irish, whom they have never understood, gave them another schooling.

We ourvelves remain untutored in this subject, although we are constantly witnessing everywhere in our country the futility of laws which are opposed by the people. Few of us seem to grasp the significance of the fact that we could have prohibition and all we cared to drink at one and the same time. Americans do not require a Supreme Court to throw laws into the wastebasket. They do it themselves, although it must be admitted that often they have to pay the politicians large sums to avoid annoyance. From the point of view of democracy this is very bad, but from that of some politicians it is all to the good and they pass as many obnoxious laws as possible in order to increase the opportunities to levy tribute upon a freedom-loving and often lawless people. In the long run anarchy of this sort obtained by bribery will bring democracy to an end, because, as Plato pointed out, the most aggravated forms of tyranny and slavery arise out of the most extreme form of liberty.

Force may crush and enslave a people but it cannot change their inherent qualities and characteristics.

Several invasions have swept over India which the conquerors have looted ruthlessly again and again. They
have attempted to force upon the people new religions,
social systems and class relationships. Not even Akbar,
one of the greatest and most enlightened of all rulers,
was able to change the inherent qualities, religious
rites, class distinctions and moral attributes of the
natives. After thousands of years, despite these waves
of foreign domination, the great masses remain almost
immutable in their essential qualities.

Much the same resistance to change is observable in
the various tribes of Russia. Peter tried to Europeanize
and Witte to industrialize that vast country. The moderate socialists under Kerensky endeavored to create a
republic there; Lenin sought by decrees and his Red
Army to communize Russia; and Stalin has not only
followed in his path but has also been trying to create
great State industries. How successful his efforts will
be, no one can know but apparently underneath the
surface the whole country has been seething for years
with rebellion against "socialized" property. Recent
visitors to Russia tell us that private property, the
capitalist, the *rentier*, old customs and religions are
coming back. If war and imperialism are to follow,
it is safe to assume that so long as the armies are victorious, the present regime will endure.

The German socialist, Ferdinand Lassalle, once declared that there would never be a revolution in Russia because the masses were content to befuddle themselves with vodka and would never complain if they were only permitted to have enough black bread and sour cabbage soup. He would seem to have been a poor prophet in view of what has happened in recent years. But, however right or wrong he may have been about the character of the Russians, it is evident now that, while there have been widespread disturbances in Russia, there has been no fundamental alteration in the position of the masses.

Let us examine the situation. Before 1917 the masses were ruled by an army and swarms of bureaucrats and police spies under an absolute monarch. Today it is the same. In Lassalle's day and long after, peasants and workers were sometimes driven to labor and their products confiscated. If they rebelled they were exiled, imprisoned or executed. It is the same or worse today. In 1917, although many of the peasants were propertyless, nevertheless, about eighty per cent of the arable land of Russia was owned by peasants. Today they are all propertyless. For those who lost their estates or positions in the court or government, there has undoubtedly been a revolution, but what have the masses gained?

After all the changes, upheavals, bloodshed and agony of these last years, we may well ask: What has revolution accomplished in Russia, Germany and Italy? If we look for the answer only to the short cycle and confine our view to political developments, we may find it in the words of the Macedonian slave, Phaedrus: "In a change of government, the poor seldom change anything except the name of their master," or in the cynicism, too often justified, of the French pessimist: *Plus ça change, plus c'est la même chose.* For the people it has often been worse than that. Marx deceived the proletarians when he said: "You have the world to gain and only your chains to lose." It is probable that they have lost what little they had and more securely enchained themselves. However, the short cycle, the fatal trilogy, is only a small part of a greater drama.

2. *Economics of Revolution*

The right of all to all things and consequently the war of all against all.

—HOBBES

The spoils of revolution are gathered not by those who win the first battles, but by the groups which have ridden the whirlwind and directed the last storm. In the previous chapter we have dealt with the technique of those who have remained in possession of the field at the end of the short cycle. The methods used by Joseph and the Tyrant to transform social institutions should have been placed in this chapter but much essential material which belongs here is either not dealt with at all or only briefly touched upon. All that is required here is to give a few examples of the methods used to undermine the capitalist system of production. How best to cut the fruit trees at the bottom is made clear by the English Marxist, G. D. H. Cole, who states that the main purpose of a socialist government should be "to destroy confidence . . . in the prospect of sustained profits" and to remove "the very foundations on which the opportunities for capitalist profit-making rest." Von Mises, the distinguished Austrian economist, has systematically and thoroughly examined the devastating economic, fiscal and monetary policies of the Marxists.[2] I shall confine myself to a short review

[2] *The Theory of Money and Credit*, New York, 1935 and *Socialism*, London, 1936.

of five which seem to me most likely to interest the general reader: (1) Taxation, (2) The Abolition of Debts, (3) Devaluation, (4) Inflation and (5) Outright Confiscation.

Taxation. In another chapter we have dealt with the revolutions which follow wars. The prime movers in these upheavals are those who are asked to pay the bill. The cost of war is always paid—paid even when all debts are repudiated—and the classes which are victimized are in the forefront of the rebellion. Whenever possible in the good old days the countries defeated in war were forced to pay the entire cost. Cicero says that Paulus Aemilius, as a result of his victories, had all the wealth of Macedonia in his power and brought an "infinite sum into the treasury" at Rome. "The single booty of one general superseded the necessity of all taxes for the future." Loot from the defeated countries poured into the coffers of the conquerors. After the Roman generals and governors had plundered their enemies abroad and stripped clean their own provinces, they turned upon their wealthy neighbors at home. Napoleon lived on the countries subdued by his armies; and the Prussians after the war with France collected as an indemnity not only one billion gold francs but also Alsace and most of Lorraine.

After the World War, the bill was presented to the

Germans, which the Allies expected them to pay. A considerable part of the cost of the war to the United States consisted of loans made to other nations, which we expected them to pay. These expense accounts were forwarded from one capitol to another but only a minute part of them was ever paid by the debtors. The fact is they could not be paid in a world where the goods and services of the debtor nations were not wanted and gold was not available in sufficient quantities. It is hardly conceivable that the ones who drafted the Treaty of Versailles ever expected them to be paid. The only way in which the Allies could have collected the colossal indemnities from the Germans was to have treated them as the conquerors of old times often treated their victims; that is to have taken all their chattels or to have dealt with them as Vespasian did with the Jews.

In other centuries, defeat in war placed a double burden upon the losers: they paid their own costs as well as those of the victors. The result of this has been seditions and rebellions, as we have seen. When the Barons were asked to pay the cost of King John's wars, they revolted. After the wars with America and with Napoleon, the British workmen paid most of the cost. No sentiment of social justice complicated the distressing task of assessing the heavy burden of taxation. Before the imposition of income, inheritance and other

taxes the well-to-do were often doubly blessed finan-
cially during wars and for decades afterwards. During
war immense profits were made in business, farm products and moneylending. After war those who had invested their funds in government issues usually continued to receive not only a high return upon their
loans but also a gratifying increase in their principal.
The Rothschilds, who are said to have bought enormous quantities of 3 per cent British Consols at about
55 when they received the news of the defeat of Napoleon at Waterloo, found that by 1850 their principal
had increased by 80 per cent and for thirty-five years
they had been receiving 5.4 per cent on their money.
Moreover the index of wholesale prices had fallen
from 225 to 120 so that their income enabled them to
purchase nearly twice as much in this world's goods.

The creditor is not always so fortunate. At times
he may receive from the debtor more in terms of goods
than is due, at other times less and at still other times
nothing at all. However, during the period under review, the *rentier* was profiting handsomely while the
entire underworld was, as we have seen, a "universal
powder mine of inflammable mutinous chaotic elements." Sitting in comfort on top of it, not wholly free
of course from anxiety, was a large class of investors
watching no doubt with some satisfaction the value of
their capital and income steadily rising. After 1814 in

Europe the unemployed were left alone to fight their battles and although they often threw themselves against the forces of the government they were invariably defeated. The upper and middle classes had been saved, the working class sacrificed. Only one comforting thought comes to mind when reviewing the sorrows of this tragic era. The capital which was preserved at that time began to flow after 1848 into all parts of the world to finance new enterprises. The seeds which were scattered in all the democratic countries by the capitalists of Europe grew into orchards of fruiting trees. Nearly all the countries producing raw materials, including the United States until 1914, were their debtors.

In Britain, after the World War, all classes except the very poorest have been forced to bear the charges upon the tremendous national debt and these have been apportioned with some attempt at equity according to the incomes received. The strain has been almost unbearable but no revolution has occurred and democracy has thus far survived the ordeal. In the defeated countries, the armed proletarians and peasants and the assaults of the communists so terrified the governments that the middle class was forced to bear the burden and as a result it has been almost extinguished.

Taxation is too often in times of distress only another name for confiscation. It can make and destroy classes. It can bring industry to a standstill. It has ruined many nations. It can bankrupt the farmer, the industrialist, the moneylender and directly or indirectly "wring from the hard hands of peasants their vile trash." But in this age when there are "taxes upon every article which enters the mouth, or covers the back or is placed on foot . . . on everything on earth and on the waters under the earth," it is hardly necessary to discuss at length what has been in almost all ages the most effective weapon in the hands of the State to accomplish its ends whatever they may be.

The Abolition of Debts. After all long wars public and private debts are galling and they become almost intolerable when prices fall as they do when the conflict is over. All debtors, including the State, are sorely tempted to find some method by which they can repudiate all or part of their obligations. Debtors were in acute distress when they placed a halo about the head of Caesar. They were hard pressed when the Barons rebelled against King John; when the States-General was convoked in France in May, 1789; in all countries during the deflation which followed the World War; and again in 1933 when Hitler led his forces to victory in Germany. Perhaps the main secret of social trouble is to be found in the alteration of the position of debtors and creditors and the taxgatherer, as the MacMillan Report suggests. Nevertheless whenever

the creditors have had their savings confiscated by the
debtors, the worst elements in society have displaced
the better. What Keynes calls the euthanasia of the
rentier has in the past closely coincided with the birth
of tyranny. Dionysius of Syracuse, who excelled Lenin
in confiscating the property of his subjects, drove out
the money-changers and permitted no one in his State
to receive interest on his money.

Cicero saw clearly the consequences to society of
relieving debtors of their burdens. His words are
memorable. "As for the project of forgiving debts, I
can see no reason in the world for it, unless it be reason that another should buy land with my money; and
that he should have the land, but I never have my
money . . . nothing so cements and holds together
in union all parts of a society, as faith or credit; which
can never be kept up, unless men are under some force
and necessity of honestly paying what they owe to one
another. This design of having debtors excused from
payment was never attempted with greater eagerness
than whilst I was consul: men of all ranks and degrees
in the state took up arms and formed camps for bringing it about; whose endeavours I resisted with so much
vigour, that the republic was soon delivered from so
pernicious an evil. [Cicero refers to the insurrection led
by Cataline.] There never were known greater debts
in the city, nor ever more easily and faithfully paid;

and pray what was the reason of all this? Why, because when their hopes of defrauding were cut off, they found themselves under a necessity of payment."

Cicero made a valiant effort to save the Republic from destruction but his stand availed nothing and when Caesar marched into Italy with his legions and was proclaimed dictator, his program for the abolition of debts was carried through. The cement—the faith or credit—which had held together "all the parts" of Roman society was decomposed. The warring elements had to be subdued, their positions in the new society altered and their places fixed by the will of despots in control of the armed forces and resources of the State.

Devaluation. During their many wars the Greek states were often in dire financial need and subject to revolutionary upheavals but they did not use paper money or resort to devaluation except on one occasion toward the end of the Peloponnesian Wars. Was this one of the reasons why democracy in Athens was able so often to resist the attacks of enemies from within and from without?

Debasement of the coinage was first undertaken by the Romans to ease the financial strain of the Punic Wars. Having discovered that to clip, adulterate or devalue the coinage was one of the least suspected and most readily available forms of taxation, the practice became habitual with the emperors and in all times of stress the State resorted to some method by which every ounce of silver and gold in the treasury would pay an increasing quantity of debt and buy an increasing quantity of goods and services. A coin worth twenty cents in the time of Augustus was, a century later, worth only half a cent. The denarius of Marcus Aurelius contained seventy-five per cent of pure silver. Two generations later it contained only five per cent. While this process of depreciation was gaining momentum the economic system of the Roman Empire was disintegrating. The precious metals disappeared like water through a sieve. Was this withdrawal of active capital from industry, trade and agriculture the main cause of the rapidly increasing impoverishment of the Romans?

As a result of these changes in the value of money, all values began to fluctuate violently, and eventually, as Cunningham has pointed out, men became "unwilling to risk their accumulations in business of any kind, and to use them as capital. The complete uncertainty in regard to prices paralyzed trade, and capitalists were induced to hoard their coins of pure gold and silver for better days which never came. Industry did not offer a tempting field, as the enterprising man of business would often have to face the competition of a manufactory organized by the State and controlled

by officials whom it would be imprudent to offend.
There was even greater disinclination to use capital in
agriculture and apply it to permanent improvements.
Accumulated wealth was hoarded rather than invested,
and general decay ensued; money and circulating capital are not necessary for the maintenance of human
life, but they were necessary for the maintenance of a
civilized society like the Roman Empire.[3]

All historians who have written of the decline of
Rome tell much the same tale. Norman Angell in *The
Story of Money* makes the following statement upon
the growth of the State: "It did not confine itself to
managing the currency but undertook at times, as part
of its type of Imperialism, the management of import
and export of foodstuffs, so that although commerce
was held in contempt by those who ran the State, the
State was often merchant and 'entrepreneur.' Plainly,
in these circumstances, the economic task which it
undertook was larger than it was competent to handle.
. . . The Roman State was, by virtue of its imperialist
exploitation, a great commercial concern run by men
who held finance and commerce in contempt." Draper
has this to say about the Roman demagogues: "As is
the instinct of their kind, they made political capital by
attacking industrial capital. They lowered the rate of

[3] W. Cunningham, *Western Civilization in Its Economic Aspects*,
London, 1924.

interest, prohibited interest, and often attempted the abolition of debts. . . . The accumulation of power and wealth gave rise to a universal depravity. Law ceased to be of any value. A suitor must deposit a bribe before a trial could be had. The social fabric was a festering mass of rottenness."[4]

It has been estimated that at the death of Augustus (A.D. 14) the store of precious metals in Rome amounted to approximately $1,790,000,000. This was an immense treasure. With the help of modern banking practice the British before the war found half that sum sufficient to finance their transactions throughout their wide-flung empire. As soon as the government in Rome began its assaults upon the medium of exchange and the economic independence of the middle classes, the funds available for trade began to diminish with alarming rapidity. Commenting upon the affect of this reluctance to use capital in active business, Keynes asks: "Whether it was a coincidence that the decline and fall of Rome was contemporaneous with the most prolonged and drastic deflation yet recorded."[5] The interesting point in this quotation is not whether a coincidence is contemporaneous, but the assertion that there was for centuries a drastic deflation; and the significant question to be answered is whether the lack

[4] Draper, *The Intellectual Development of Europe.*

[5] J. M. Keynes, *A Treatise on Money,* New York; Harcourt, Brace and Company, 1930, Vol. II, p. 151.

of precious metals or the lack of *the use* of precious metals in productive enterprise was the cause of the deflation.

Failure to use funds productively in industry and commerce is more often due to the antagonistic policies of the State than to a diminishing supply of metal from the mines. Fear of invasion, confiscation and devaluation; alternating periods of inflation and deflation; the inability to employ funds profitably or, if so employed, of preventing voracious taxgatherers and war lords from sucking up the earnings—these and other obvious causes have sent into hiding in all ages enormous quantities of precious metals. Whenever fear for the safety of one's property arises, hoarding becomes a passion. It is not a malicious act: it is simply the outward and visible sign of inward terror. Or one might better say an inward and invisible sign.

Devaluation of the coinage did not end with the dissolution of the Roman Empire. At the time of the Norman Conquest, the pound sterling weighed approximately a pound in pure silver (4995 grains troy). Debasement began in the year 1300. Two hundred and fifty years later "the pound" weighed only 400 grains. It is difficult to determine what effect, if any, the depreciation of the coinage had upon the relative economic position of the classes. The prolonged wars between nations, between the classes and between the families of the aristocrats almost destroyed Europe. Twice it was miraculously saved from Asiatic domination, in the second instance by Hunyady of Hungary and by the sea power of Venice. The intellectual supremacy of Europe passed to Italy and the most powerful kingdom in the Western world arose in Spain. In England, France and elsewhere the kings triumphed over the feudal lords. The influence of the middle classes diminished and the monarchs came into more direct contact, not always pleasant, with the entire mass of their subjects, the third estate, the common people (Horne). Although villeinage had almost vanished, the masses remained in abject poverty denied by law the right to make any attempt to improve their condition. Repeated devaluations of the coinage again coincided with growing despotism. When the pound sterling was depreciating most rapidly, the leading nations of Europe were ruled by despots but little less powerful than King John.

Under Henry VII, the landed aristocracy had been ruined. Fortunately for England, Henry VIII kept his country out of foreign wars and devoted himself for the most part to sensual pleasures. He plundered the churches, enriched his courtiers and beheaded his wives and others who questioned his authority or attempted to frustrate his passions. He brooked no interference. Then Thomas Cromwell, the agent of

Henry, was England's Robespierre and his reign of terror differs from that of the French Revolution in only one detail: he chose his victims with care and struck down only the noblest and the best. English liberty was a thing of the past. The House of Lords and the Commons were filled with Henry's creatures. His courts of justice were infamous and the lives and property of his subjects depended upon the whims of the King. Questions are safer than assumptions when dealing with long and disturbed periods of history and therefore we shall revise the query of Keynes and ask: Whether it was a coincidence that the rapidly repeated devaluation of the pound sterling was contemporaneous with the astounding increase in the power of despotism? We can answer that question in the affirmative without arriving at the conclusion that there was any causal relationship whatsoever.

There are economists who maintain that devaluation has the same effect upon prices as an increase in the supply of precious metals from the mines. Except for short periods it seems to have had no marked effect on the price of wheat from 1300 to 1500 although silver was devalued fifty per cent. In fact the price fluctuated about a mean level of twenty cents a bushel from 1300 to 1527 while the pound sterling was falling in the index from 287 to 138. Henry VIII and his successor, Edward VI, in the space of twenty-four years

(1527-1551) devalued the currency six times with the result that the index number fell from 138 to 23. While these violent debasements were in progress the price of wheat began to leave its lower levels not only in England but in all countries and the trend was not reversed for long until about 1650.

However this rise in prices was the effect of other causes. In the sixteenth century gold and silver in vast quantities were imported from the Americas into Spain and spread from there to other countries. When they began to pour into England they produced the profit inflation which lasted for over one hundred years. From among those who were enriched by these additions to the purchasing power of the nation arose the classes which have become the rulers of the British Empire. By the time of Elizabeth (1558) the pure silver in the pound sterling *had increased* fourfold in weight. According to the "inexorable laws" of Professor Warren, prices should have fallen. On the contrary, prices continued to rise for nearly a century. The tradesmen began to force their way to a position of equality with the nobles. The Reformation and the Renaissance were under way. Religious and civil wars were, as we have seen, intensified but new and powerful classes were born. A new era in the world's history was at hand and political tyranny and the Dark Ages were definitely a thing of the past. Did the increase

in the actual supply of money and its active employment in trade, industry and commerce create the
classes which laid the foundations of democracy?

Although devaluation of the coinage had been resorted to again and again by monarchs in distress, it
seems to have done little or nothing to increase the
level of prices. Monetary tricks have their effect upon
trade, commerce and industry but not the effect which
money managers have taught us to expect. The attitude
of government toward business determines the success and failure of most monetary policies. A revolutionary government rapidly issuing monetary decrees
has a decisive influence upon the economy of a nation,
especially as a direct cause of convulsions and class
conflicts.

During the last few years every nation in the world
has been drawn into the vortex of devaluation. In
1926 Keynes advised the French to devalue. Eventually England was forced to do likewise, carrying with
her the whole sterling area (1931). A little later (1933)
the United States fell into line and after a few years
of painful deflation, caused by our action and that of
the sterling group, Belgium and France were again
driven to devalue. Holland and Switzerland, after
years of valiant effort against the trend, at last gave up
the fight in 1936. On May 5th, 1938, when the French
government again devalued the franc, Premier Dala-

dier made this statement: "Economic life is in a very bad condition; legitimate profit is tending to disappear; partial unemployment is increasing in every branch of industry; our foreign trade balance is impoverishing us; our production figures are a humiliation to all Frenchmen."

"The power of taxation by currency devaluation," to use the words of Keynes, enabled an incompetent government in France to survive but evidently it has not improved the economy of the nation. It is doubtful if it ever has in any nation except for very short periods. It was not the higher price paid for gold but other far more potent factors which saved Great Britain. With the Labor party crushed by the Conservatives, the investors put their funds to work in active industry. They did not convert their pounds into gold and hide it. In France, the enterprising industrialists were penalized by the socialists and communists while the lilies of the field, as we may call them, were given handsome rewards providing they would neither toil nor spin. Repeated devaluations have placed in their soft, white hands enormous profits. For years the socialist politicians of that country have been saying in effect: "Sell your securities, shut down your plants, dismiss your workmen, place all your available funds in gold or precious jewels, take a long and carefree holiday and we will enrich you free of all taxation, beyond your most delirious dreams." The following table shows the progressive devaluation of the franc:

PAR VALUE OF THE FRANC

			Milligrams (.900 fine)
"Pre-War" franc	1878 to June 25, '28	....	322.58*
"Poincaré" "	June 26, '23 to Oct. 1, '36	....	65.50
"Blum" "	Oct. 2, '36 to July 22, '37	....	49.00
"Bonnet" "	July 23, '37 to May 5, '38	....	43.00
"Daladier" "	May 6, '38	....	27.60†

* The pre-war franc was a silver coin which circulated as a token piece. The figures given here correspond to the gold content named for the Poincaré franc in 1928. The French standard was devalued slightly in 1878, when gold payments were resumed after the Franco-Prussian War.

† Not fixed officially.

Note: At 2.79 cents the "Daladier" franc equals 42.1 per cent of "Poincaré" franc, or 8.55 per cent of the "pre-war" franc. The devaluation since Sept. 26, 1936 has amounted to 57.9 per cent. The appreciation of gold equals 137.6 per cent in current francs as compared with "Poincaré" francs. In terms of old dollars, the "Daladier" franc is worth $0.0165

The amount of gold behind the Daladier franc is only 8.556 per cent of the amount of gold behind the pre-war franc. Therefore, had a thrifty and frightened Frenchman tucked away safely the equivalent of 100,000 francs in gold in 1918, he would now (1939) be a millionaire in francs. His gold would buy 1,168,770 of Daladier's new francs. How many hard-working industrialists who have tried to keep their factories open and their workmen employed have done as well as that?

The Roman Emperors did a fast and thorough job

when they discovered how easy it was to tax their subjects and at the same time "to coin money" by depreciating its value, but the French, in recent years, have left them far behind in the running over the short course. The franc was worth twenty cents in gold during the first World War. It is now (1939) worth only 1.65 cents in gold. That is probably the highest bribe a nation, which should and could have kept its finances in order, has ever offered over so short a period to induce its citizens to sabotage its industries. If, as we believe, rapidly repeated devaluations drive money out of circulation and productive enterprise, much of the misery which afflicted the populace in Rome, and in later days elsewhere, can be readily explained.

Devaluation has been popular among certain groups in every country because in most countries only a small part of the store of precious metals has been in the hands of the State and consequently the money-changers, hoarders and least enterprising have often reaped a golden harvest. As industry, commerce and agriculture languish, unemployment and poverty increase, while those with their hoards who neither toil nor spin are enriched. This is a timid, secretive class without enterprise, energy or purpose except self-preservation, caring nothing for affairs of State or the well-being of society. When capital is idle, labor is idle, and when both are unemployed capitalism and democracy collapse no matter how richly arrayed may be the lilies of the field.

Long before any definite indications of the decay of Rome could be observed, ample warnings were given to all concerned that any funds risked in loans, production or trade were more than likely to be lost or stolen. Similar warnings have come from many capitals in the last decade and since these signals have been given, there has been no considerable extension of private long-term investment. The millions of unemployed in some of the democratic countries are a constant reminder of the fact that in many parts of the world today those who have funds which they would like to invest are living in terror of the predatory and malicious activities of government. A breathing spell graciously bestowed upon business or an occasional soothing fireside chat pleading for business to have no fear does not induce private capital to make the one move which can put idle millions to work—namely, investment in "capital goods." Menace property or prohibit the owners from retaining a reasonable proportion of its earnings, and all the king's horses and all the king's men cannot put private capital to work again. The use of money and credit diminishes and the growth of what Keynes calls "real wealth" ceases.

In many tribes and even in an entire race the fear

of confiscation has so possessed the people that their children imbibe it with their mothers' milk. Again and again through the centuries the only safe place for property has been in hiding. "The history of India at all times," Keynes writes in his *General Theory*, "has provided an example of a country impoverished by a preference for liquidity amounting to so strong a passion that even an enormous and chronic influx of the precious metals has been insufficient to bring down the rate of interest to a level which was compatible with the growth of real wealth." Rich men do not permit their capital to lie idle without good reason, and when the Indians keep an incredible stock of funds constantly unemployed, it is because they do not agree with Keynes in his definition of real wealth. For many generations hoarding has not been profitable in India except possibly for short periods, but from the princes down to the lowliest ryot the old instinctive terror holds sway. The bitter experiences of centuries long past have not been forgotten. Invasions, lootings, devastating wars, ruthless conquerors and inflations have left their scars upon the souls of the Indians.

"Hard money" is the only form of exchange they accept willingly. From Shanghai to Bombay small tradesmen bite and ring coins to test their quality. In Bali, Netherlands Indies, some paper money which I offered as a tip was thrown into the street and spat upon. It is said there were over a hundred species of paper money in Manchuria before the Japanese arrived. War lords forced farmers to take paper for their crops, while all the gold and silver they could lay their hands on was sent abroad or hoarded. Ever since the Great War, especially in those countries where inflation, devaluation or confiscation has been a menace, a great deal of liquid capital has been idle or working short hours much of the time. Socialists and communists speak of this as a strike of capital, but it is in fact a lockout of capital. No man of sense will invest his savings when it becomes clear that they are likely to be lost or will not be permitted to yield the owner a reasonable income.[6]

Rich and poor are alike in their desire to preserve their savings. In fact the communists themselves have not been able to conquer this human passion for security. The case of Bourtzev, the Russian communist, is an interesting example. When he died in Russia a fortune in gold rubles was found concealed in his house. He played the game prudently. Like Ananias, Bourtzev was a devout apostle but he was also discreet and wisely provided himself with adequate in-

[6] India is a land of mysteries and it is no easy task to arrive at any satisfying conclusions as to the causes of the appalling misery one sees there. It is, however, noteworthy that the people in both India and China are inveterate hoarders. When savings are not permitted to "fructify in the hands of the people," the masses must expect to live on the verge of famine.

surance in case events should not come to pass according to the plans of his master, Karl Marx. If communism succeeded he had assured himself of a seat among the mighty. If it failed he would be a rich man.

When a government is hostile to the accumulation of wealth and becomes accustomed to finance its requirements by depreciating the medium of exchange, the thrifty and intelligent hoard all sorts of objects which it is hoped will pass through a period of inflation or devaluation without diminishing in value. Postage stamps, old and rare coins as well as other well-chosen collections may prove to be profitable "investments." Reforested land may become a valuable heritage to one's grandchildren. Imperishable acquisitions which do not require labor for upkeep and are likely to escape with the minimum burden of taxation are especially desirable in a period when the value of a currency is falling. In all perilous times there are many Bourtzevs anxiously occupied in building with precious gems, metals and other rare materials, revolution-inflation-devaluation-proof storm cellars and safety zones for their families. When capital goes into hiding, the workers are the ones who suffer most.

But the mass of people with moderate fortunes are not as wise as the Bourtzevs and when they are impoverished, there is no class left powerful and independent enough to oppose the dictators, who seem usually to select these appropriate moments for their heroic entrance upon the stage. The same monetary policies—deficits, doles, defaults and devaluation—which were employed by the Roman politicians to ruin "the economic royalists" of their time are being widely used in nearly all countries by the rulers of our day. Whatever the future holds in store for us, it is clear that we have been for many years treading upon ground which in the past has proved to be extremely dangerous.

Inflation. When we recall the need for funds which drove the dictators of past centuries to their ruin and the brutal and brazen methods they used to extort money, goods and services from their subjects, we are astonished in this day of promises to pay at the stupidity of medieval royalty. The rulers of the Chinese discovered many centuries before the rulers of the Western world that paper—debts—could wheedle from the populace all that was required to maintain the State.

Along with the heavenly host who attended the birth of democracy there appeared from the depths two sinister figures with an odor of sulphur lingering about them. They were called in their day adventurers and came from Scotland. One of them, William Patterson, bequeathed to all governments in distress Central Banks, National Debts and the necessary machinery for expanding public and private credit. The other, John Law, bestowed upon distressed royalty the doubtful blessing of paper money which, while it often thrust away dark clouds, eventually brought them, as we have seen, to the guillotine. The two Scotchmen may have read the travels of Marco Polo but had not learned that two hundred years before their new era in finance was introduced into Europe the Chinese had abandoned paper money because the most ignorant coolie would not willingly accept promises to pay which he and his ancestors for many generations had so often found to be worthless.

In England, France and elsewhere in Europe the innovations of Patterson and Law were grasped greedily by the impoverished States. Their financial troubles were solved. New vistas of universal plenty opened up before them. Shrewd merchants and traders took a hand in the game. Speculation became a mania and butcher, baker and candlestick maker issued "notes payable upon demand." The great nations of Europe were flooded with "Continentals." The Americans also went into the lucrative business of producing paper money—shinplasters they were called—on a scale worthy of our genius for exaggeration. As most of the worthless issues came from private banks, the governments escaped some of the blame. This was the great era of "baloney," the history of which has often been written for the entertainment of those who are amused by the credulity of less intelligent fellow citizens and also for those who rely upon it for profit.

As the methods of Patterson and Law are admirably designed to obtain goods and services without putting up any hard cash, they offer an irresistible temptation not only to hard-pressed monarchs but also to hungry revolutionists. We remember the harassed leaders of the French Revolution who were bewitched whenever some sorcerer proposed a new plan for getting from the populace something for nothing. "Green cheese" has, for a time, proved to be excellent bait, but it has soon ceased to be tempting when the legislative assemblies have operated their factories day and night. A superfluity has invariably produced a dearth of goods and services and a rebellious populace.

The money cranks of all times have been naïve enough to believe that governments are wise and beneficent and that any party in power can be trusted to manipulate prices and at the same time to restrain its appetite. It is rare to find in history any support for this sanguine expectation. Danger lies ahead of this world of ever-mounting debt, a large proportion of which is irredeemable paper money. If, as Marx once said, every society bears within itself the seeds of its own destruction, the democratic countries may find that their seeds are the promises to pay the fabulous billions which their governments have borrowed. A wag has told us that there can be no revolution in Germany because *es ist verboten*. To refuse to accept paper money at its face value is also forbidden, which makes it possible for the totalitarian states to keep going so long as they can control prices, profits, wages and hours of labor and are not forced by defeat in war to face an armed and irate populace.

Sudden and pronounced changes in the purchasing power of money have been, as we have seen in a previous chapter, one of the most disturbing and destructive factors in social relations. By debauching the currency, one form of cement which had held together the citizens was dissolved after the World War in nearly every nation on the continent of Europe. In the defeated countries, the trade-unions, soviets and councils of armed soldiers and sailors were powerfully organized. The hastily formed governments gave attention only to their demands and other classes and interests had to be sacrificed. As it was desirable that no powerfully organized group should be offended and as it was practically impossible to borrow money, the easiest and most convenient method of financing the requirements of the States was to print as fast as possible promises which would never be

paid, in other words "to confiscate, secretly and unobserved, an important part of the wealth of their citizens."

By a convenient monetary device the State had
before 1923 taken from the middle class about one-half
of its property in England, seven-eighths in France,
eleven-twelfths in Italy and virtually the whole in
Germany, Austria, Hungary, and Russia (Keynes).
When the proletarians, or more properly the Bolshevists, dispersed the members of the Constituent Assembly, final notice was served upon all classes except
the communists that as an influence in Russian affairs
their day was over. In Russia at one stroke rich and
powerful classes lost their possessions and the prospect
of any influence in the political administration of the
country. The communists cherish the thought that
only in Russia was the property of the capitalists
confiscated. As a matter of fact, in all the defeated
countries, the liquid assets—savings, bank deposits,
insurance policies and gilt-edge investments—of the
most thrifty sections of the populace were largely or
entirely wiped out. Many of the landowners and gam-
blers who had managed to profit or survive during
the era of inflation were stricken as soon as deflation
followed. The most intelligent of high and low degree were sacrificed *en masse,* which alone explains

much that has occurred in recent years and indicates what is likely to happen again in the decades ahead.

It was inevitable that appalling disasters should befall European civilization as a result of these irrational monetary policies. They unnerved and devitalized the influential groups which had formerly fought for freedom of enterprise, liberty and democracy. It is a teaching of history, often repeated, that when the middle class has been plundered and demoralized, no barricades have been left to check the movements of those aspiring to dictatorship. Beaten, bankrupt, weary and humiliated, the productive classes since the Great War have turned, in one country after another, with rage and disgust from the demagogic politicians and their black magic of monetary tricks. "The spirit is cowed by that which is unexpected and happens contrary to all calculations," wrote Thucydides during the wars and revolutions which were destroying Greece, and once again in the world's history cowed millions have turned to those whom they believed might bring order—no matter what order—out of dread uncertainty bordering upon chaos.

With the ruin of the middle class came the ruin of the working class; and support for the new brood of Caesars which then arrived upon the scene came mainly from the unemployed and from those who had become half-demented by the loss of their property and their battles with hunger. In Italy Mussolini formed his legions out of this material and in Germany Hitler's Storm Troopers came from the same elements. Most of them wanted revenge and a ruthless cock-of-the-walk powerful enough to destroy "the profiteers," the Bolshevists, the Jews, the clergy, the parliamentarians and whomsoever else they could be led to believe were responsible for their misery. A large majority of the impoverished upper, middle and working classes were sympathetic but many of the more intelligent—they had to be very sane, competent and intelligent—stood dumbly on the side lines not knowing whether to approve or condemn.

Napoleon, Lenin and Hitler arose to power during periods of anarchy of varying degrees and all three had seen the currencies of their countries become worthless. The old upper and middle classes had been impoverished and rendered impotent in Russia, France and Germany. A new class of speculators had arisen in all three countries but they were not interested in government. They were saving themselves in so far as they could. These and other "profiteers" became the object of national hatred and it is never difficult to arouse the populace to strike down those whom it believes to be responsible for a rapidly rising cost of living. Let us repeat: seditions and revolutions are against things, not for things. The people were against those who had led them to war. They were against "the imbecile and mentally deficient politicians" who displaced the monarchs. They were against those who took away their property by inflation, devaluation, default, or confiscation.

Mussolini was the first to recognize the trend of the time and to feel that a reaction was inevitable and he was shrewd enough to rally to his support those who felt that their small properties were menaced. When they won for him his victory he made them, as others had done before him, servants of the State and absorbed for its needs their profits. Hitler is not the only one who has become a national hero by turning hatred of the profiteers into hatred of the Jews and the clergy. The path taken by Il Duce and Der Fuehrer was not new. What is happening or has happened in many countries since 1917 takes us back to the beginning of the Christian era. Those classes from which the cultural reconstruction of Europe was to be expected were reduced to a condition where they could neither help themselves nor their community. As it takes many generations for these classes to accumulate any considerable quantity of savings, it would be illusory to believe that we shall see again in our time in many countries "a government composed of men of moderate fortunes"—the form of democracy admired by Aristotle.

Outright Confiscation. For a government to seize
and make its own all the property of its citizens is a
rare phenomenon in the history of humanity. It is true
that conquerors have often swept over vast areas and
robbed the inhabitants of their chattels but when
they returned from whence they came they could not
take the land with them. Much of this plunder was
often used to enrich the commanders of their armies.
Despots have frequently confiscated the property of
religious orders, moneylenders and rebellious subjects,
but much of this booty was given to their favorites.
Rarely have rulers ventured to confiscate directly the
wealth of all classes of their own countrymen as the
Bolshevists have done. When the latter "nationalized
production" they aroused not only the animosity of an
overwhelming majority of the Russians but also of the
millions who were swept into the fascist states. The
despots of the totalitarian states are following the
example of the Roman emperors who confiscated by
one means or another the wealth of the working
classes; but they are doing their work indirectly, dis-
creetly and gradually. As they capture states one at a
time, beginning with the weakest, so they impoverish
classes.

The history of Rome is like the Bible—a preacher
can find there an apt text for almost any sermon he
cares to deliver. We have torn from its pages those

texts which seemed to us most likely to direct attention
to some of the economic catastrophes which led to
the decline of that great civilization—one of the stages
in the long cycle of revolution. Nowhere else are
these disasters summarized more briefly and effectively
than by Breasted in *Ancient Times.*[7]

The penalty of wealth seemed to be ruin, and there was
no motive for success in business when such prosperity
meant ruinous over-taxation. Many a worthy man secretly
fled from his lands to become a wandering beggar, or even
to take up a life of robbery and violence. The Roman Empire had already lost, and had never been able to restore,
its prosperous *farming class.* It now lost likewise the enterprising and successful *business men* of the middle class.
Diocletian therefore endeavoured to force these classes to
continue their occupations. He enacted laws forbidding
any man to forsake his lands or occupation. The societies,
guilds, and unions in which the men of various occupations had long been organized were now gradually made
obligatory, so that no one could follow any calling or
occupation without belonging to such a society. Once a
member he must always remain in the occupation it im-
plied . . . Even the citizen's wages and the prices of the
goods he bought or sold were as far as possible fixed for
him by the State. The emperor's innumerable officials kept
an eye upon even the humblest citizen. They watched the
grain dealers, butchers, and bakers, and saw to it that they

[7] J. H. Breasted, *Ancient Times,* Revised Edition, Ginn & Company,
Boston.

properly supplied the public and never deserted their occupation . . . In a word, the Roman government now attempted to regulate almost every interest in life, and wherever the citizen turned he felt the control and oppression of the State.

Staggering under his crushing burden of taxes, in a State which was practically bankrupt, the citizen of every class had now become a mere cog in the vast machinery of the government. He had no other function than to toil for the State, which exacted so much of the fruit of his labor that he was fortunate if it proved barely possible for him to survive on what was left.

3. *The Nature of Revolution Changes*

> *The ruling power of the State, like a ball, is snatched from kings by tyrants, from tyrants by aristocrats or the people, and from them again by an oligarchical faction or a tyrant, so that no single form of government ever maintains itself very long.*
>
> —CICERO

When a civilization is progressing, revolutions have often proved to be beneficial; when it is receding, they augment the forces of destruction. Breasted tells us that a century of revolution destroyed the Roman Republic and led to "the triumph of one-man power." Two centuries of peace began with the foundation of the Empire by Augustus and continued into the reign of Marcus Aurelius. During the rule of this emperor a second century of revolution began. The violent disturbances lasted from A.D. 180 to about A.D. 284 and plunged Rome into an oriental despotism. At the end of the first century of upheavals the people had lost their freedom. At the end of the second they had become serfs. In the short cycle progress was arrested by revolution. In the long cycle progress was not only permanently checked but Roman civilization was annihilated. In both cycles the wheels turned backward.

A long cycle, which embraces the rise and decline of a civilization, may be thought of as a revolution—a gradual transfer of power. The rise of a nation coincides with the growing power, freedom, wealth, and influence of the productive classes. When their power is waning, decline sets in. The revolutions which destroyed the middle class in Rome and enhanced the power of the State are similar in character to those which have accomplished the same results in Russia, Germany and Italy in recent years. The revolutions, from 1215 to 1917, which increased the power of the feudal chiefs and later that of the middle and working classes and with each step decreased the authority of the State, have of course an entirely different character. A revolution which enables a ruler to do whatever he likes with the life and property of a subject has nothing in common with one which forces a monarch to place the seal of the Crown upon many such pledges as this: "To no one will we sell, to no one will we refuse or delay, right or justice" (Magna Carta). Needless to say, the revolutions which enable the people or any large groups in a nation, to throw off their fetters differ intrinsically from those which place them under the yoke of serfdom, despotism and the all-powerful State.

Let us turn over once more the pages of history and trace hastily the most recent long cycle and see what justification can be found for the assertions made in the preceding paragraph. Tremendous seismic disturbances had for some years been shaking the foundations of the Roman Republic when Sulla defeated Marius and became dictator. With his armed forces, he slaughtered three thousand senators and knights, the best blood of the aristocracy, and followed this assault with the massacre of tens of thousands of common folk. The Republic had been knocked over as if it had been a house of cards and the people were driven hither and thither like frightened sheep. A few years later there was the uprising of Spartacus and the slaves. Ten years after, Cicero suppressed the armed uprising of the debtors and the indigent led by Cataline. The same year Pompey besieged Jerusalem and subjugated the Jews. Fourteen years later, Caesar crossed the Rubicon.

Catastrophes affecting the history of the world for many centuries after had been crowded together in the space of about forty years. It was said that the former Kaiser possessed a wealth of bitter, sarcastic humor. Evidently he employed it on the occasion of his seventy-ninth birthday when he is reported to have said that he was far more interested in the march of events in Rome about the year 62 B.C. than in the affairs of Europe at the present time. Is it possible that he believes Stalin, Mussolini and Hitler bear any resemblance to Sulla? Perhaps he hopes that after a few decades the people will have had enough of these upstarts and that the old line of Hohenzollerns, Hapsburgs and Bourbons will return. It matters little, after all, what he thinks or what his hopes may be. He at least put his finger on a period of history much like our own—a period which introduced into the world a new era.

For three centuries after the *coup d'état* of Caesar, who was possessed with "such an inclination to villainy, that the bare doing of it was a pleasure to him, without any other invitation" (Cicero), the State was continuously increasing its authority over the populace. The tyrants had arrived and all the wisdom they required was given to Thrasybulus by Periander: Cut off the tallest stalks, in other words, do away with the eminent citizens. The procedure must be continuous, relentless, eternal from father to son and so on, if tyranny is to endure. This was the policy of most of

the Roman emperors and the results have already been
described by Breasted. The State had developed into
a malignant cancer, thrusting out its dense fibrous
stromata which devitalized with their morbid growths
all the healthy tissues of the social system. The car-
cass of Roman civilization was in fact being devoured
by the barbarians when Sidonius stood on the thresh-
old of the Dark Ages, "tranquil amid the swelling
seas of the world."

Roman civilization perished but humanity did not
perish with it. In the long run, Periander's advice
proved to be impractical. As soon as it was possible
and profitable for them, anxious, industrious, little
human ants were scurrying about frantically to repair
the ravages of tyranny and to create for their families
better living conditions. The irresistible multitude was
everlastingly thrusting its young shoots upwards, although it required centuries in dark and dreary misery for the lower social groups to build houses, enclose fields, accumulate capital, defend their rights
and recapture little by little the power which they
could not believe men of their like had ever before
possessed. Eventually resistless creatures appeared as
militant lords and barons with their fortified princi-
palities which emerged like rockbound islands in a
receding ocean of oppression.

No State can de-kulakize its nation forever. Without wars it might be done, but dictators must have wars and they sorely need an abundance of supplies, equipment and livestock, which the indigent cannot supply. Moreover they must have the loyalty and courage of able and intelligent leaders, which slaves do not provide. As war follows war, the autocrat must permit the classes which eventually destroy him to grow stronger and richer. He is forced to let the stalks grow tall. As this feudalism grows, the monarchs, when they require the necessaries of war, are driven to all sorts of humiliating expedients. They must sell crown lands and titles, bestow decorations and grant favors. They must confiscate the chattels of their enemies, rob the moneylenders, tax and extort, invade and pillage, imprison and murder. These acts of tyranny, as well as their benefactions, are in the end the source of their undoing.

Thirteen hundred years after Caesar became dictator of the Roman Republic, there were in England, once a province of the Romans, two million inhabitants, nearly half of whom were slaves classed with the cattle by their owners. The other half were freemen, most of them artisans and "lower orders" living precariously. However the gain had been substantial and King John, owner of all the land in England, faced at Runnymede, rich and powerful Barons with sufficient armed retainers to bring that arrogant monarch to terms.

In the financial distress of kings after defeat in war lies the opportunity of their subjects to free themselves from despotism. King John was forced to grant to his subjects freedom not only from the tyranny of the Crown but also relief from the extortions of his "sponges"—the moneylenders of the time. The sections of the famous charter which were designed to restrain the usurers and to relieve distress, though rarely discussed, are of no less importance than those which guaranteed independence to the Church, the nobility, the merchants, the tenants and the serfs. Nothing but the need for services, supplies and money could have induced the King to have made such mortifying concessions; nothing but extortion and financial distress could have united the Barons and their retainers in rebellions against the Crown.[8]

The people recover from the State powers which they have lost only by armed rebellions. About five hundred more years of civil conflicts and revolutions

[8] Although I am tracing here the rise of democracy in England, my readers should be reminded that in the thirteenth and fourteenth centuries, the power of *all* the monarchs of Western Europe was restricted by constitutional laws and representative assemblies. In Spain, the people of Castile and Aragon had won quite as much freedom as the English. In France, the States-General only could legally levy taxes. Three centuries later, with the single exception of England, the kings of all the countries of Europe had been successful in regaining for themselves supreme power.

had to be endured before the British kings were forced to keep their pledges and democracy got a solid foothold in England. During these centuries the nature of revolution was changing and with each forward thrust the productive classes were increasing their wealth, power and influence. In the year 1689, the State, with its army, courts and treasury, was again in the hands of the commoners. Instead of four or five distinct groups, dominated by the monarch, there were then in England nobles, knights, the landed gentry, the upper and lower middle class, the yeomen, the peasants, and the upper and lower working class. Over sixteen centuries had come and gone since Cicero lamented in Rome, "only the walls of her houses remain standing . . . our republic we have lost forever."

The age of democracy began with the "glorious revolution" of 1688-89. It passed into an aggressive stage when George III forced a republic upon the thirteen American colonies. The carefully designed political machinery of the federation of states was described in writing and those perversions which the designers thought likely to develop, were proscribed. Never before had a democratic constitutional convention been able to do that. Sitting amidst the ruins of a long war, with economic ⬛⬛⬛ and fiscal problems as serious as tho⬛⬛⬛ ⬛-

sian Republic in 1917, the representatives of the nation, nearly all of whom were well-to-do if not affluent,
were able to confer calmly and deliberately about the
problem which had baffled in all ages the best minds
among the political philosophers. Many humane men
had put forward their plans for a beneficent State, but
no two had agreed upon where the enormous authority which every State possesses could be most
safely, permanently and wisely lodged.

It will be recalled by those who have read Plutarch's account—a precious bit of fiction—of the *Dinner of the Seven Wise Men* that this was the main
topic of conversation. Time and again government has
been almost exclusively in the possession of either
tyrants, kings, generals, priests, aristocrats or oligarchs.
In recent times, the votes of the citizens of all classes
have placed the power in the hands of their elected
representatives. On rare occasions, it has been con-
ferred upon the wisest or the best citizens. On occasions no less rare it has been forcibly taken by serfs
and slaves. When the indigent, the debtors and infuriated mobs have taken possession of the State, their
domination has usually been short-lived. It has either
brought the social system abruptly to an end or prepared the way for native or foreign conquerors.

Those who fr...........Constitution of the United
S...............................rned throughout their

many sessions with ways and means for controlling the power of government. Could it be placed where it would not be abused? The men assembled in Philadelphia represented a people which had just laid down its arms after having defeated the armies of the monarch of the foremost State in the world. Naturally, they were determined that nothing like him should be allowed to develop in the United States. The most striking feature in the great document is the attempt to restrict the powers of the Federal government. It is surely unique in history that a body of legislators should deliberately devise methods to limit their own authority and to guarantee, so far as possible, to the citizens and to the several states freedom from the exactions and tyrannies of a central government. Nor were they content to stop there. They also limited the powers of the three branches of the Federal government so that the President could not become an autocrat, the Senators could not acquire the power which they possessed in the Roman Republic and the House could not overthrow the others by some form of mobocracy. A Supreme Court was established to interpret the law of the land and to protect the people against any assaults upon their rights.

No matter what ills may befall the people of the United States as a result of other destructive forces or what perversions, which could not be foreseen, may develop in our form of government, the glory of the Fathers of our Republic will be everlasting. Unfortunately, a constitution is only a scrap of paper and when forces arise which are strong enough to tear it to pieces, it cannot defend itself.

The architects of our political system thought that they could "best promote the improvement of the nation by strictly confining themselves to their own legitimate duties, by leaving capital to find its most lucrative course, commodities their fair price, industry and intelligence their natural reward, idleness and folly their natural punishment, by maintaining peace, by defending property, by diminishing the price of law, and by observing strict economy in every department of the State." This epitome of a truly democratic government was written by Macaulay fifteen years after Napoleon was defeated at Waterloo. His country, as we know, was prostrated by post-war upheavals much like those which afflict the world today and these words stand at the end of a crushing attack upon the fantastic political and financial theories of Robert Southey, a befogged state socialist of that day.

A hundred years ago earnest, clear-thinking and militant liberals with aims like those of Macaulay were able not only to arrest the threatened expansion of the powers of government but also to expand the many blessings of democracy. The Reform Act of

1832, free trade, the abolition of slavery, the establishment of parliaments in most of the countries of Europe, the right of labor to organize for its protection and the extension of the suffrage to women were some of the forward steps made by the forces of democracy in its glorious progress. Suddenly in 1917 this movement was reversed and hundreds of millions of human beings have since been thrust back into an age which resembles that which witnessed the arrival of the emperors in Rome.

In the long cycle which we have just traced we observe in the first stage the State crushing capitalism, democracy and the Republic in Rome; in the second, the populace slowly and painfully regaining the freedom, property and power which had been lost; and in the third, the flowering of capitalism and democracy with the State being curbed and disciplined by the people triumphant. This cycle, beginning with a republic and after passing through dark ages of tyranny emerging as a democracy, was in progress for approximately twenty centuries. Compressed within the small compass of a quarter of a century, Russia and several other nations have passed through a complete revolutionary short cycle, beginning and ending with despotism; a tragic spectacle which we have already described as the last stand of the czars, the revolution triumphant and the return of the czars. At the moment when democracy seemed to be well on the way toward conquering the entire world, the nature of revolution abruptly changed.

An ominous change in trend is also to be observed in the old and well-established democracies. Probably at no time since Cicero was fleeing from Rome has this world seen harnessed together so strange an assortment of discordant elements—communists, fascists and democrats—distrusting each other and yet all of them pulling and pushing forward the Royal Coach of State. The intelligentsia, idealists, social reformers, liberals and industrial unionists, who believe the government alone is capable of showering upon them in particular and mankind in general inexhaustible blessings, are shouting, without a dissenting voice, for the same program. State Planned Economy—*Planwirtschaft*—under the control of some class, group or "leader," is the goal toward which all countries are moving. It matters little under what banner they march. Socialism, State Socialism, State Capitalism, Communism, Collectivism, Bolshevism, Fascism, Nazism, State Planned Economy, The Ever-Normal Granary, Militarism, Managed Money, National Salvation, National Investment, Totalitarianism, Authoritarianism, all lead to the same end—the tyranny of the State. Those who believe that a continuous increase in the power of the State is the only remedy for our prob-

lems are masking their movements when they denounce Stalin, Hitler and Mussolini. They are all
traveling with varying degrees of speed toward the
same goal.

The "forward-looking men" as well as the avowed
revolutionists are now turning to *Planwirtschaft* as
the panacea for our ills. It is the *Zeitgeist*. German
words are used because the modern conception of the
State Supreme was, if we may say it, "made in Germany." Its aim, spirit and form are the products of
Hegel, Marx and Bismarck—each working toward
some particular end he had in mind. National Planning
by a State, guided by a leader, an oligarchy or an extra-
legal Brain Trust, has become the divine idea of our
era. We are told that with competent sheepherders in
charge, the activities of the populace can be so ordered and directed that poverty will be banished. The
idea, the promises and the mechanism have the true
ring of despotism and logically permit us to recall the
visions of the socialists who have labored for ninety
years with the fervor of fanatics to persuade the people
to place their lives under the control, and their productive property into the ownership, of the State.
Once that was done, they believed—many of them
sincerely—that the State would disappear as a compulsory institution; would "die out," as Engels had
predicted. When the revolution triumphant endeav-

ored to put into operation the communist program of the Marxists we found that it did not weaken the State. On the contrary, it strengthened it, not only in the countries where the communists have been in power but also in the countries of their bitterest opponents. Where revolutions and counter-revolutions have been victorious, the power of the State has become absolute. There are no signs which indicate that it is dying out.

Bernard Shaw is not easily deceived and when he said that he was not sure that a Hitler in England would be such a bad thing, he realized that some form of despotism is the logical conclusion at which any intelligent Marxist must arrive. To find the Fabians, who have always been thought of as "reformists," defending the most violently revolutionary section of the socialist movement has mystified many observers. It is easily explained. Their conception of compulsory socialism has a common basis and their alliance is perfectly consistent. This is not a conclusion arrived at since the Bolshevists came to power in Russia, or since Shaw and the Webbs went there to greet the conquerors and to praise their work. Prince Kropotkin, Rosa Luxemburg and H. G. Wells, not to speak of others less widely known, discerned in the first decade of this century the essential harmony between the aims of Lenin and the Fabians.

When Lenin led his forces to victory over the Menshevists in 1903, he had already fully developed, as the reader may recall, his program of action and his conception of a socialist system of production, planned by a bureaucracy of the faithful directed by a single master mind. What is now called the *Fuehrer Prinzip* was revived at that time. Upon the same authoritarian principle, Lenin based his technique of revolution— the organization of compact and thoroughly trained groups of professionals, whose secret activities were to be controlled by *the* leader. Not being a prophet nor greatly impressed by the forlorn Russian exiles assembled in London, the decision of the conference to accept Lenin's program did not seem to me a matter of the slightest significance. I was convinced at the time that storm troopers, secret agents, conspiracies and hierarchies had been safely buried with Blanqui, Bakunin, Nechayeff, *The Revolutionary Catechism* and the ill-fated *Norodnaya Volya.*[9]

My conviction was not shared by the Menshevists who were deeply agitated by the course the Russian socialists had chosen. When I talked with Kropotkin, who was not affiliated with either group, he said with emphasis: "If the workers follow this path, it means

[9] In *Socialists at Work* (New York, 1908), and in *Violence and the Labor Movement* (New York, 1914), I conveyed this impression, although in the second book mentioned I gave an extended account of the technique of these insurrectionists.

the guillotine, despotism and the end of any prospect of democracy in Russia." Rosa Luxemburg was also greatly disturbed by the thought of a secret organization of professionals dominating the movements of the working class. With keen insight she pointed out the essential relationship between the dictatorship proposed by Lenin and the State socialism grafted into the program of the British Labor party by the Webbs. A few years later, H. G. Wells scented danger and wrote *The New Machiavelli*. It is interesting to recall these forecasts now that powerful, despotic, totalitarian States form a line from Gibraltar to Yokohama.

As we see, the concept of a *Fuehrer* Supreme did not originate in the minds of Mussolini and Hitler. It is probably the most ancient of all forms of government. Again and again in the history of the Indo-Europeans, it has expired but invariably it has been born again. At the end of the war when many thought it was dead and buried forever, those who were supposed to be its irreconcilable enemies appeared in the armor and weapons of the corpse. "This horrible resurrection is only temporary," said the liberals and democrats. But that was not true and in fact was not meant to be true. Marx made that clear when he phrased his concept of the Dictatorship of the Proletariat. Others have dramatized this theory of govern-

ment and millions have seen and heard the plays and
operas which have developed the theme.

Whenever I read that Adolf Hitler is reviving his
faith at the Wagnerian Festival at Bayreuth, I recall
an evening in Berlin before the twilight had set in
over the Hohenzollern gods, when I watched with
amusement the Kaiser and the royal family bestowing
their acclamations upon a magnificent performance of
the *Götterdämmerung*. Wagner conceived the Ring
during the German Revolution of 1848, when he was
under the spell of the Russian anarchist, Bakunin. Let
us have Shaw explain the meaning of the operas. In
The Perfect Wagnerite, he says: "Really, of course,
the dwarfs, giants and gods are dramatizations of the
three orders of men: to wit, the instinctive, predatory,
lustful, greedy people; the patient, toiling, stupid, re-
spectful, money-worshipping people; and the intellectual, moral, talented people who devise and ad-
minister States and Churches. History shows us only
one order higher than the highest of these: namely, the
order of Heroes." After a few words in praise of Caesar, Shaw points out that Wagner's hero makes an end
of dwarfs, giants and gods. When the drama of the
Ring was moved from the stage to the street, the
Hohenzollerns were destroyed but other gods and
giants took their place while the dwarfs remained and,

according to the most recent reports, are multiplying more rapidly than ever.

In *Pygmalion*, Shaw dramatized his conception of social management. Here we become acquainted with *Der Fuehrer* and with Shaw's personifications of the classes which are to be recast by the hero, Potter, or whatever we may wish to call him when the revolution has transferred all power into his hands. Recently when I watched the delighted faces of those whom Shaw would call fashionable "Do Littles" at a performance of *Pygmalion*, I recalled the German royal family in their box in Berlin and also the remark of Marie Guimard when, on the eve of the French Revolution, she saw the first performance of the *Mariage de Figaro*: "I should not have believed that it could be so amusing to see oneself hanged in effigy." Shaw has been inciting the hangmen for fifty years and what could arouse in him more hilarity than to see the very ones he is condemning to perdition applauding his work.

Let us look more closely into the true meaning of the characters in *Pygmalion*.

DOOLITTLE. A dustman, lustful and pleasure-loving, with the predatory instincts of a capitalist—as Shaw sees him—merrily engaged in "taking money out of other people's pockets." He is the parent of neglect and misery who eagerly grasps the opportunity to sell his daughter for a five-pound note. As a highly moral Fabian, Shaw believes in compensating the Do Littles for the loss of their property, after which they are graciously permitted to retire to a public house to spend their money in drink. As a Hero would be quite capable of transforming human beings and their institutions in a few weeks, Higgins is quite confident that he could make Doolittle into a Lloyd George or a Welsh clergyman.[10]

PROFESSOR HIGGINS. The composite of a Hero, *Der Fuehrer, Il Duce,* Lenin and Mr. Squeers, the disciplinarian of Dotheboys Hall. He should have been called Professor Potter or simply the Potter. Ill-mannered, self-centered, infallible and tyrannical, he is absorbed in remolding Elisa nearer to *his* heart's desire.

ELISA. The proletariat. A dirty, half-starved, ignorant good creature, capable of acquiring under the management of a Hero, the manners of a Duchess, the dialect of the English gentry and the impudence of a fighting consort. The Hero rescues her from lustful lovers, sniveling half their time over her and the other half giving her black eyes. By means of insults, brutality and terror, she is eventually taught to bring the Hero his slippers.

---

[10] Forty years ago Shaw thought socialism could be got into working order in a fortnight. *Fabian Essays,* London, 1899, p. 186. Rightly enough, *Pygmalion* is the most popular play in Germany.

It is a distressing omen that Shaw should have chosen the name of Elisa for the working class. That was the name of the queen of Carthage, who, when her lover deserted her, thrust a knife into her bosom as she was burning upon her funeral pyre. As the heroes have always deserted their Elisas, the outlook for the proletariat in a Potter's Paradise is not a cheerful one.

In what has just been written, the writer has not strayed from the main thesis of this chapter. When Lenin led his Knights of the Blade to victory over the Menshevists in London in 1903, the first master potter of our time appeared. His technique and his conception of authoritarian socialism were injected into the most comprehensive and aggressive—perhaps too comprehensive and aggressive—democratic movement the world has ever known. The war destroyed the old dynasties and out of the chaos evoked by the revolution triumphant the heroes appeared, and immediately sent their Alberichs and Lokis to drive the dwarfs back into "the mines" from which they had come. Shaw's Order of Heroes had emerged victorious. And now we are all asking the same question which troubled Omar Khayyám nine centuries ago: "Tell me then, who is the Potter, pray?" With certainty we can answer that he is not a celestial such as Omar had in mind but is rudely fashioned out of the common clay from which so many despots have been made. Some of them have been named in this book—beginning with Joseph in Egypt and ending with Joseph in Russia.

Once again in the tortuous history of humanity, the potters—call them heroes, *fuehrers, duces* or czars if you like—have firmly fixed hundreds of millions upon the discs of their revolving wheels. The State has become in the course of recent years once more the absolute master over the lives and property of the populace in a score or more of great nations. It may remain the master, as it has before, for many centuries since what can prevent it doing what it will so long as it controls the army, the police, the law, the treasury, the banks, the press, the radio, the church, the schools, prices, hours of work, wages and what not? Supporting the modern *fuehrers* are three pillars: the army, Red, Black or Brown, the *Gestapo* or Ogpu, and propaganda. Stalin, Mussolini and Hitler have become the Great Leviathans. Naturally, they will impose upon their subjects order, discipline, subordination and maximum productivity. In order to defend themselves and to maintain their armed forces, they must take from the workers all their products except the little required to feed, clothe and shelter them.

We are seeing with our own eyes what a beast the State can become when no group of citizens is strong enough to oppose it. The living death now being inflicted upon the Jews, kulaks, aristocrats, and the once proud and independent middle classes in a score of nations is evidence not to be disputed that the nature of revolution has changed and that the czars have returned. The revolution triumphant was nothing more than a riotous, aimless, destructive interlude to the revival of an old and tragic drama.

The czars, ruling Russia since October 1917, have committed three major crimes, the penalties for which will be paid by the people of many countries even unto the third and fourth generation: (1) they dispersed with their armed troops the elected representatives of all Russia—members of a Constituent Assembly which might have done for their country what the Constitutional Convention did for the United States; (2) they confiscated the property of all the people rich and poor; and (3) they launched a reign of terror, which for its continuity, scope and ferocity has rarely, if ever, been equaled in the Christian world. Much has been written about the extermination of disillusioned comrades, of the Kamenev-Zinoviev conspirators, of the Radek-Piatakov factions and of almost the entire staff of generals in the Red Army but these are minor crimes compared to those above mentioned. From the beginning the Red Army, the *Cheka* and now the Ogpu have been used to suppress the aspirations of the people, to shoot those who protested, and

to rob the peasants of their holdings of grain and livestock.

One of the many afflictions being visited upon
civilization for the sins of the Bolshevists is the formidable ridge of authoritarian States which now ex-
tends from Lisbon to Tokyo. Lenin and Trotsky taught
the white, black and red terrorists of Europe a simple
and effective technique for acquiring supreme power.
Under the pretense of saving their countries from communism and the annihilation of religion, national independence and cherished native customs, Pilsudski,
Mussolini, Hitler, Franco and other soldiers of fortune
became distinguished members of Shaw's Noble Order
of Heroes. The authoritarians of all creeds are now
being drawn into a menacing military phalanx by the
essential unity of their common aims. Casting greedy
eyes upon the vast stores of wealth in the "capitalist"
countries, they seek to crush at home and abroad the
forces of democracy. It can be seen now that their
hatred of each other's ideologies was a feigned frenzy
which has served its purpose. It was a pretext to induce the people to shout their approval of the heroes
who set forth after 1917 to make their fortunes by
civil war. The most fantastic delusion of our age has
been the hope of some of the statesmen in the democratic countries that they could win the support of
these adventurers, who having conquered their native

lands and having been able to retain them by force of arms are now imperialists seeking to prey upon neighboring nations.

Sensing instinctively the perils of freedom at home or abroad and with a passion for regimentation bred in their bones, the magnates of revolution have fought democracy at every step in their careers. Many of them were the product of the terrifying reaction from Bolshevism which fell like a black-out all over Europe in post-war years. That it was coming was clearly foreseen by sincere social democrats who had lived and labored for the commonweal without suspecting that every form of socialism was by nature authoritarian. When they assembled in Berne in 1918, they were already in despair. As they saw the mighty tides turning against them, they warned the Russians—to the amusement of the Bolshevists—that "the slaying of democracy would end in the dictatorship of the reaction." In fact Bolshevism itself was the first sign of the reaction and its first victim was democracy. Of course the socialists in the parliaments of Europe had the problem of votes to contend with and they were already alarmed by the rushing millions who were fleeing from their clutches into the arms of the heroes, but oddly enough both those who attacked private property and those who alleged they were trying to preserve it have endeavored to make the State supreme in the territories which they dominate.

The modern tyrants may not be students of Aristotle but instinctively they are going about their work in a businesslike way and are moving along the path which he knew to be the only safe one. The rules are these: (1) the populace should be kept poor and abjectly submissive; (2) they should have no confidence in each other; and (3) they should be totally without the means of doing anything, for no one undertakes what is impossible for him to perform. The people must have neither mutual confidence, power nor spirit. In such a world there is no place for individual wealth, exceptional intelligence or for self-supporting and independent classes.

The series of battles to diminish the power of the State which began in 1215 ended so it seems in 1917. Lenin's program of action turned back the rising tide of democracy. One of his first acts was to annihilate the diminutive middle class in Russia. Many organized groups are working toward the same goal in other countries. Aristotle was observing the same sort of destruction when he warned the Greeks that only where those of moderate fortunes are strong and prosperous can the rich be spared from pillage, the poor from serfdom and all classes from despotism. The new society which is opening up before us and into which many have already entered is as old as time. In some countries the process of throttling the political and economic independence of the productive classes may take a century or more but when it is completed we shall find something remarkably like that which existed in the reign of Diocletian. There were then left, roughly speaking, four social layers with varying degrees of wealth and influence: (1) the dictator and his aids at court; (2) his military, naval and civil servants; (3) his agents in control of land, trade, transport and industry; (4) the servants of these servants—soldiers, sailors, taxgatherers, middle men, artisans, laborers, serfs and slaves.

It is difficult to discern any material difference between the social system which existed in the time of Diocletian and that which the Bolshevists decreed in Russia, where there were to be only four classes recognized and legalized by the State: (1) the communist bureaucrats in charge of all activities; (2) their defenders, the warriors enlisted in the army and navy; (3) their peasants working the land, and (4) their proletarians working in the industries of the State. Social systems much like this are developing in Mexico, Italy, Germany, Japan and other countries. In Germany Hitler is all-powerful. In Japan, the army is in complete control. Twenty corporations now discipline and organize, under the direction of Mussolini, the whole of Italy's economic life. Three hundred and thirty-two years elapsed between the time when Caesar became Dictator of Rome and the totalitarian State of Diocletian was completed. In one generation, several acts of the drama have been enacted before our eyes in this modern world of speed, but the trend is masked by the use of words which have lost their meaning.

The revolutions of the last twenty years—not only in Russia but in many other countries—have, as we see, been wholly different in character from anything known in the Christian world since the year A.D. 284. The forces which first kindled the flames of revolt were republicans, democrats, trade-unionists, socialists and communists but the widespread confiscation of property by direct and indirect methods, turned the populace throughout a large part of Europe toward the all-powerful, one-man State. With astonishing rapidity, great nations have passed through three stages of revolution and at the moment the masses seem to be content with security, such as it is, and a uniform. If the history of the past is a safe guide, we know what these developments mean. As we look about us, we can decide whether a revolution is destructive or constructive as soon as we know whether it increases or decreases the power of the State and conversely whether it decreases or increases the inde-

pendence, power and wealth of the productive classes.
This observation, dogma, or whatever else one chooses
to call it, is repeated as the sum and substance of this
chapter.

4. *The Collapse of a Civilization*

> *Dicaearchus gathered together all the causes of destruc-*
> *tion—floods, epidemics, famines and the sudden incursion*
> *of wild animals in myriads—and then proceeded to show*
> *by way of comparison how many more men have been*
> *destroyed by the assaults of men—that is, by wars and*
> *revolutions—than by any and all other sorts of calamity.*
> —CICERO

I am now venturing into a field of which little is
known and my readers may think as I progress that
this study of revolution should have ended with the
preceding paragraph. I am tempted however to add a
few lines in view of the recent trend in many nations
and because some years ago I was profoundly moved
by a visit to the famous ruins of Angkor Thom, buried
in the swamps of Cambodia in Indo-China, where the
masses about five centuries ago completely destroyed
the State and all its works. Thus far our study has
been confined to two distinct types of revolution: (1)
those in which the State acquires unlimited power
over a nation and by means of its armed forces or by
measures less direct is able to subjugate the people and
if it chooses to make their property its own; and (2)
those in which the people rebel against the State and

succeed in divesting it of arbitrary power over their lives and property. During the first three or four centuries of the Christian Era, the revolutions in the Western world were of the first variety. Most of the revolutions since the World War also belong in this category. From 1215 to 1917, the revolutions in Europe and America, with a few notable exceptions, belong in the second class.

There is, however, a third variety. In many places scattered over the vast area embraced by the five oceans, the Arctic, Antarctic, Indian, Pacific and Atlantic, there can be found the ruins of many cities which were the seats of government and the centers of rich and powerful communities and of highly developed social systems. Many students have devoted their lives to the study of empires which have perished—the Sumerian, Egyptian, Hittite, Persian, Greek and Roman. During the last two thousand years many civilizations, outside the pale of Christianity, have come and gone. After a period of constructive achievement, followed by an age of splendor, they either became "dust bowls" buried beneath the drifting sands or were repossessed by the jungles. As the dead do not tell tales it is difficult to find any revealing records of how and why these catastrophes occurred.

Civilizations, like all other living things, pass through the three stages of creation, consummation and destruction. This we all know but it should not be forgotten that humanity survives all calamities and the story of mankind never ends. Contemporaneously with the decay of one civilization others were born and the progress of humanity, considered as a whole, has continued. This observation brings us little satisfaction since it is natural for us to be interested in our own immediate outlook. We are deeply concerned with anything which affects us as individuals, with the welfare of our families and the well-being of our nation. Although we know that we are subject to the unalterable laws of birth, life and death, it does not comfort us to be told that, when the end comes, we and the particular civilization of which we are a part may fertilize the earth and enrich the generations of the future. From that point, some other nation or race must carry forward the banner of progress. And yet we know that the great civilizations of the past scaled the heights only to find that they had then to begin the decline and to sink lower and lower into the dark valleys where they were destined to remain for centuries. Some of them, like Angkor, are still there and give no indication of ever attempting another ascent.

If we were to include all Indo-Europeans and chart their progress during the last twenty-five centuries, the line would be a series of waves resembling a sinusoid. The crest of each wave would rise higher than the one which preceded it. If we think of civilization as the progressive elevation of the masses, the line would start in Persia at a low level and end in our time at a very high level. All along the line there would appear troughs to represent the breaking up of empires, the destruction of economic systems and the external and internal conflicts which undermine the well-being of all classes. Only rarely would the waves, whether rising or receding, be continuously upward or downward. Deviations lasting for decades and in some cases for a century or more would frequently intervene and force the line for a time to move in a direction contrary to the long-term trend.

Despite famines, plagues, wars, revolutions and the rise and fall of empires, Western civilization has, with some marked interruptions, moved slowly but surely upwards. Contemporaneously with this Indo-European development there have been uprisings in other parts of the world which have completely destroyed the State, the ruling classes and civilization itself. Almost invariably when one State is destroyed another takes its place, but this does not always happen. In some nations the people have passed immediately and directly from serfdom to unrestrained anarchy—from Hitler's, Stalin's and Mussolini's work and bread to idleness and starvation.

The revolution in Angkor must have been some such

violent movement from the one extreme to the other. There can be no doubt that the State was all-powerful, the rulers arrogant and cruel, the middle class intimidated and the masses hard-pressed beasts of burden. And yet for many centuries the social system apparently functioned with incredible efficiency. No one can doubt that who has once seen the magnificent structures which were built in the terrific heat of the tropical Cambodian jungle. The great State of the Khmers grew richer and richer and seemingly more and more invulnerable until a series of wars made it necessary for the rulers and their professional army to call to their aid the working slaves and to beseech them to defend property which was not theirs and to protect masters whom they hated.

Pictured in stone upon the walls of the ill-fated city of Angkor all but the last scene of the drama is enacted. Not a word is spoken but not a word remains unsaid by the loquacious bas-reliefs which extend along the endless corridors of the palaces and temples. Wherever one goes in the dead city, works of prodigious creative power and evidences of an orgy of destruction meet the eye. The Brahmanic gods who directed this civilization were the Trimurti, the triad or trinity: Brahma, the creator; Vishnu, the preserver; and Siva, the destroyer. As it is impossible to believe that the universe is destined to be annihilated, Siva was also worshiped as the god of fertility and reproduction. Always associated with him is the linga.

Long ago the great city was abandoned, despite all its grandeur, by those who made it. Little is known of its earliest days but from the beginning of the ninth to the end of the thirteenth century the inhabitants were creating magnificent temples, monasteries, dwellings, palaces, bridges and monuments throughout the entire area of this rich and fertile region. Ruled and guided by a powerful monarchy and an extensive priesthood, a highly profitable commercial and agricultural system was developed. A multitude of builders, stone carvers and tillers of the soil—throbbing with creative energy—cleared away the almost impenetrable jungle, terraced the fields, canalized the torrential river and created a rich and luxurious civilization. The spirit of Brahma, active for about five hundred years, had brought forth, at least in material development, what was one of the outstanding accomplishments of all time.

The old city is still surrounded by a great wall from twenty to thirty feet in height which makes an enclosure extending two miles in each direction. No one knows how many people lived in the vicinity of the walled city and while it is believed that most of them were slaves, they must have been well fed and contented during their creative era to have carried out so beautifully the many vast projects. They were a vain people. Their gods, the portraits of their rulers, the movements of their armies, the laborers in their industries, the animals they rode and the sports they enjoyed—polo, fishing, wrestling, etc., were all carved in bas-relief upon the walls of the palaces and temples, which are best described as tapestries in stone. There are miles upon miles of these dramatic pictures, so deftly executed that every figure seems to be in action.

When the era of construction was coming to an end in the thirteenth century, their supplications were directed to Vishnu, the preserver. Creation had almost finished its task and the vast treasures had to be conserved. Youth was gone and late middle age with all its fears for the future had arrived. There were internal and external enemies coveting their treasures and threatening to destroy their glorious civilization. The beautiful temple of Angkor-Vat was built to invoke the favors of the god of conservation. The carvings which covered every foot of its extensive corridors were exquisitely executed in a soft and flowing bas-relief. The bestial power of the earlier rulers was gone. The men of the court have no longer the grim, heavy, and often brutal faces of the mighty overlords whose portraits were sculptured in earlier centuries upon the *Bayon* and the *Terrace du roi Lépreux*. Gone also were the strong-muscled mothers of men; they had become

coy, alluring, ornamental, willowy, graceful, and use-
less.

Some of the stories of the old gods were told again.
Nearly a mile of sculptured wall described the wars
and love of Rama. There was something ominous in
the various subjects represented. Domestic scenes,
sports and handicraft no longer interested the people.
War and legends of war dominated their minds. Even
the Churning of the Ocean of Milk indicated a spirit
of unrest. The vast armies of soldiers were well
equipped and the proud nobles and arrogant war lords
on their elephants and superb horses were gorgeously
attired. Evidently the spiritual power of Vishnu, the
preserver, could no longer be wholly trusted by the
people and Siva, the god of war, with his mighty
weapons, must sustain them.

From their earliest days Siva had been worshipped
by this vigorous, vital and indomitable people. In
their youth they made him appear inscrutable and
contemptuous; as they grew older he became more
menacing, as if they hoped that all who ventured to
look upon him would run away in terror. In every
village, temples and shrines were dedicated by the
Hindus to this "Lord of the Universe," who transforms
life into death and death again into life. He is the
sovereign who rules over these twin mysteries which
have bewildered the world from the beginning of time.

When he appears as the Destroyer, he is terrible as he smears himself with the blood of his victims and hilariously plunges his long, sharp nails into the quivering flesh of the prostrate forms beneath him.

When we first saw the *Bayon* the evening sun was casting timidly its shifting rays of red light upon the legion of Sivas which confronted us at each step on one of the upper terraces. Whichever way we looked among the four-faced towers there appeared a host of leering images. And then came the shadows of a starless night and a thousand ghosts of thought. They came and went as I tossed upon my humid bed in the heat of the tropics. What do these many Sivas mean? The myriad of phantoms gave no answer. Outside my room were the empty palaces of the dead and hidden in the jungle were millions of human beings sleeping in their huts. When I thought of them and the destruction which had been wrought, I recalled the words of Bakunin, the Russian anarchist: "The end of revolution can be no other than the destruction of all powers— religious, monarchical, aristocratic and bourgeois—in Europe. Consequently, the destruction of all now existing States, with all their institutions—political, juridical, bureaucratic and financial."

Bakunin would have adored Siva, I thought in that sweltering night, almost as ardently as he did his favorite Catiline, Satan, whose biography he had often planned to write. Anarchy meant to him "terrible, total, inexorable and universal destruction." Only after that could there be "a complete manifestation of unchained popular life."

Something much like this happened at Angkor, as Henri Marchal indicates in his *Guide Archéologique aux Temples D'Angkor.* His explanation of the precipitous fall of this civilization in Indo-China is the repetition of an old, old story. A crushing defeat in war was followed by an uprising of the populace in which the royal family, their agents, representatives and priests were massacred. The carnage must have been so complete that not one of the masters nor the wife or child of a master escaped. After I had read Marchal and Aymonier, the historian of the Khmers, Siva became to me a trinity of destroyers: the State Supreme, whose greed for the products of labor could never be satisfied; War, whose thirst for blood could never be slaked and lastly, Anarchy, the unruly, ravenous offspring of their union.

Surely few other dead cities in the world could stir one emotionally as much as Angkor. The complete picture is there. The magnificence of the past and the ragged poverty and squalor of the present confronted us at every turn. As we motored through the swamps and dense forests along the fine roads built by the French, we studied the Khmers with lively interest and had it not been for their portraits on the walls of every corridor we could not have believed that they were the descendants of the builders of great cities and of a civilization which was once one of the richest, most productive and powerful in the Far East. Only a few hundred years before, their ancestors had drained this land, canalized their great river and built palaces and temples rivaling those of Athens and Rome. In the rich silt of the irrigated lands enormous quantities of grain had been planted and harvested. On the higher levels great herds of horses, elephants and cattle had grazed. The people are now living in mud huts and under bamboo shelters, ignorant, listless and poverty-stricken. There is little food for them or their scanty supply of livestock. The river has overflowed its banks and inundated the land. The rapacious jungle is relentlessly advancing. In the same century when Spain was becoming a world power and America was discovered, the god of war, revolution and anarchy had finished his gigantic task in *Sroc Khmer* and the long cycle of the rise and fall of this civilization was completed.

INDEX

Adler, Victor, 4
Aemilius, Paulus, 302
Agathocles, 13, 274-275
Agrarian revolts, 38, 92
Agriculture, 45
  mechanized, 221
Akbar, 298
Albert, 59
Alexander II, Czar, 142
Alexis, Czar, 136
Alfonso, King of Spain, 83
Alsace-Lorraine, 70, 143, 302
America. *See* United States
American Revolution, xiii, 297, 303, 341 ff.
American Socialist party, 148
Anarchists, 6, 72, 183, 209, 218
Anarchy, 58, 121, 129, 245 ff., 298, 365, 371
Angell, Norman, 310
Angkor Thom, ruins, 362, 364 ff.
Annuities, 108 ff.
Anseele, Edouard, 5
Anti-Semitism, 85 (*See also* Jews)
Antonov-Ovseënko, 231
Arago, 59
Aristotle, 1, 42-43, 53, 82, 85, 150, 195, 205, 213, 245, 249, 265, 267, 271 ff., 331, 359
Armada, Spanish, 93, 98
Ashley, Lord, 57, 65
Assembly, freedom of, 66, 68
Assignats, 112 ff.
Athens, 29, 271 ff., 308
Augustus, 309 ff., 334
Australia, 84

Austria, 4, 85, 125, 131, 153, 161,
  revolution (1848), 57-58, 67-68
Authoritarianism, 175

Babeuf, 209-210
Bakunin, 32, 136-137, 198, 209 ff., 214, 220, 246, 262, 295, 351, 370
Balabanoff, Angelica, 7, 18 ff., 24-25, 196 ff., 254
Ball, John, 32, 38, 209
Barons, English, revolt, xiv, 37, 336, 340
Bastille, fall of, 110
Bebel, August, 4-5, 7, 31 ff., 80, 141-142, 147, 149, 197, 203, 211, 245
Bela Kun, 79, 203, 216
Belgium, 2, 4-5, 86, 149, 316
Bellamy, Edward, 272-273
Berlin, 57, 66 ff., 141 ff.
Bernstein, Eduard, 7, 98
Bethmann Hollweg, Chancellor, 143 ff.
Bismarck, Otto von, 5, 198, 347
Black Death, 38
Black Shirts, xi, 240 ff., 283
Blacklist, 56
Blanc, Louis, 59 ff., 211
Blanqui, 32, 72, 75, 209 ff.
Blum, Léon, 193, 246
Bolshevists, 13, 19 ff., 151, 162, 213 ff., 223 ff., 248, 255, 332, 358
  Central Committee, 227 ff.
  revolution, 40, 202
  technique, 206-207, 239, 242

373